NOT BEING

The Art of
Self-Transformation

Steven D'Souza | Khuyen Bui

PRAISE FOR *NOT BEING*

"The considerable individual independence that each of us is enjoying today was bought at a high price. Countless men and women throughout history had to struggle heroically, or even die, so that we can enjoy the personal freedom we tend to take for granted. But we have pushed independence to the point of isolation and alienation. Rediscovering interdependence is the most urgent task before us. Steven D'Souza and Khuyen Bui tackle this task head-on. This makes *Not Being* a must-read. Their skillful teaching through delightful stories, quotations and poems makes it a book you won't be able to put down."
Brother David Steindl-Rast, Network for Grateful Living

"Part extended prose-poem, which weaves together stories, experiences, philosophy, business theory and insight, *Not Being* unfolds like a song. It is a siren call pulling us to acknowledge our truth as human beings. Our fact and fate is that we are connected to each other and our planet. This is a truth that, if we can acknowledge and embrace it, brings us the joy, wisdom, fulfillment, meaning, significance and sense of belonging we crave. It lays the foundations for a new moral and political economy, as well as new rules for our life together on Earth."
Nicola Reindorp, CEO, Crisis Action

"*Not Being* by Steven D'Souza and Khuyen Bui is a call-to-arms, an elegiac reminder that how we deal with disruption defines us. We've all been upended in every part of our lives. Use their book to reset. To not be who you are, but whom you want to be. Disrupt yourself."
Whitney Johnson, author of *Build an A Team*, *Disrupt Yourself* and *Dare, Dream, Do*

"*Not Being* has come into my life at the right time to help as a guide for me to explore new territories, beyond my tried and tested methods which no longer serve me. *Not Being* is full of wisdom through stories, not overly complicated theories. Rather, it's more a gentle encouragement to see different perspectives and let what comes come, without prescribing."
Jamie Davies, Head of Planning and Reporting, British Petroleum

"*Not Being* is a compelling guide to a sustainable model of leadership. D'Souza and Bui provoke us to go beyond narrow identity interests to embrace ecosystem leadership."
Megan Reitz, Professor of Leadership and Dialogue, Ashridge Hult Executive Education, and author of *Speak Up* and *Mind Time*

"A thought-provoking read as we emerge from the seismic shock of the pandemic into the so-called 'new-reality,' and as we have the opportunity (and obligation) to reassess and reset ourselves as leaders and human beings. Through anecdotes, stories and provocations, D'Souza and Bui offer a route to a different and more resilient relationship with the volatile and uncertain world we find ourselves in."
Sue Bonney, Vice Chair and Head of Environmental, Social and Corporate Governance, KPMG UK

"*Not Being* invites us to see our lives and our practice of leadership as an inquiry, challenging us to move from advocacy to curiosity, and from self-centeredness to the recognition of our fundamental interdependence. This is a go-to book for leaders driving a connected and sustainable world."
Sarah Barron, SVP, Global Talent Management, Vestas Wind Systems A/S

"By exploring our oneness with nature, and revealing how self is inseparable from otherness, this timely book opens the door to being and at the same time makes you ready, willing and able to embrace your own becoming."
Joseph Pistrui, co-founder, Kinetic Thinking, and Professor of Entrepreneurship & Innovation, IE University

"The self is a process, a construction — it is neither an unchanging essence, nor an identity to be preserved at all costs. *Not Being* takes these insights, which are rooted both in ancient philosophy and in modern brain science, and applies them to the challenge of working and living well. The lesson, as D'Souza and Bui persuasively explain, is that by recognizing that change is at the heart of who we are, we can be more effective in what we do."
Anil Seth, Professor of Cognitive and Computational Neuroscience, University of Sussex, and author of *Being You: A New Science of Consciousness*

Published by
LID Publishing
An imprint of LID Business Media Ltd.
The Record Hall, Studio 304,
16-16a Baldwins Gardens,
London EC1N 7RJ, UK

info@lidpublishing.com
www.lidpublishing.com

A member of:

BPR ✸

businesspublishersroundtable.com

Printed by Severn, Gloucester
ISBN: 978-1-912555-90-1
ISBN: 978-1-911671-28-2 (ebook)

Cover design: Maria Helena Toscano
Page design: Caroline Li

NOT BEING

The Art of
Self-Transformation

Steven D'Souza | Khuyen Bui

MADRID | MEXICO CITY | LONDON
NEW YORK | BUENOS AIRES
BOGOTA | SHANGHAI | NEW DELHI

To Uncle Teo (18 February 1947 – 20 February 2019)
You taught me by example the meaning of the word
Resurrection — to give one's life away to your community.
And so you live on, in our hearts.
Steven

To all my friends and teachers who lovingly mirror who I am,
and to the ancient mentor whom I once thought I had
forever lost. You are still here.
Khuyen

CONTENTS

FOREWORD

Toward the end of the last millennium, I lost my mind, my body and everything else that gave me a sense of separation from others.

Having suffered a couple of bitter disappointments, I traveled with a friend to my first Burning Man event in the Nevada desert — an annual utopian happening that gives one a glimpse of what life would be like if artists ruled the world. While my pilgrimage was more about repairing my heart and ego, I experienced a kind of 'collective effervescence.' Over the course of a few days, my sense of guarded separation evaporated, replaced by a communal joy that overcame me. During the following years, I've noticed the ever-presence of this feeling in my daily life and in the workshops I facilitate for others.

The epigraph to E.M. Forster's *Howard's End* comprises just two exclamatory words: "Only connect..." That is what I felt at Burning Man, and it's also what I felt while reading this powerful treatise on what it means to be in community with the world.

With the Covid-19 pandemic still rampant, *Not Being* by Steven D'Souza and Khuyen Bui arrives at the perfect time, promoting the power of reflection and connection when it has become most needed in my lifetime. This book is a deep, profound rumination on expansive liberation. It is an antidote to the disconnection and loneliness many of us have felt in the past year or two. It is like a rich, exquisite box of chocolates. It is something not to be read in a single sitting, but lingered over, allowing your soul to digest its wisdom.

I've spent my life constructing the scaffolding of my ego identity. I grew up a shy kid, with imaginary friends, and was pushed by parents to succeed and be more of an extrovert. My successes in my later adolescence ushered me onto the 'hedonic treadmill,' with a constant desire to one-up my last accomplishment. At 26, as one of America's first boutique hoteliers, I started Joie de Vivre Hospitality, which grew into the world's second-largest boutique hotel company. The fact that we weren't the largest caused me great consternation.

Then, I had my real 'Not Being' experience. While I should have been at home nursing a broken ankle and septic leg from a sporting accident, I was on a book tour and giving a speech in St. Louis, Missouri, to a large audience. I was on a strong antibiotic, and after my speech I lost consciousness while still on stage. My heart stopped multiple times during the next 90 minutes. The paramedics had to shock me back to life.

There I was: 47-years-old, with a collection of people I didn't know, going to 'the other side' and coming back both disoriented and strangely feeling freer than I'd ever felt. The fact that this happened on stage, on crutches, after giving a speech, was enough divine intervention for me to realize that it was time to reinvent myself, but without the scaffolding. Ironically, the first boutique hotel I ever created, in 1987, is called The Phoenix, after the mythical bird rising from the ashes. This mythical bird was my guide to no longer be the person I had been.

This is when I started to notice that my primary operating system of living was moving from my ego to my soul. No one warned me that this shift was coming, but I felt it was time to take down the scaffolding and expose the real me to the world. I'd spent my whole adulthood comparing myself with others, donning a raft of different identities, yet feeling constrained, always in a straitjacket. Now, though, as I embraced the shift, I began to experience the tranquility of being connected to everything.

Pondering the later life stages, developmental psychologist Erik Erikson suggested, "I am what survives me." After I turned 50, this became my mantra. What a joy it was to let go of being the 'sage on the stage' and to embrace being the 'guide on the side.'

As a result, new opportunities arose that allowed me to be of service, less focused on *what's in it for me*. I was asked by the young founders of Airbnb to be their in-house 'modern elder,' mentoring CEO Brian Chesky. This helped me appreciate that servant leadership would now be at the core of my career. After leaving a full-time role at Airbnb, I co-created the world's first midlife wisdom school, the Modern Elder Academy, helping people regenerate themselves in service of others. To be of service gives me the greatest joy I've experienced in my life. I don't think I'm the only leader who's discovered this.

Sociologists tell us that, with the greater longevity of human life and the increasing obsolescence of many careers, midlife now starts around the age of 35 and lasts for around 40 years. Midlife, then, can feel like a marathon bereft of the rituals and rites of passage that help us strip away what no longer serves us, creating openings for something new. For many of us, midlife is a time of exhaustion from the sheer volume of the identities we inhabit, in person or online in the era of social media. If you find that you've been carrying too much baggage, wearing too many masks, then this book is for you.

This may be a moment of great existential importance for you, determining how you want to live your life, what you want to be and, equally vital, what you do not want to be. The poet John O'Donohue once wrote, "Soon you will be home in a new rhythm for your soul senses the world that awaits you." This book is your dancing teacher to find that new rhythm. Enjoy your tango with life!

Chip Conley
Author of *Wisdom at Work* and
Founder of the Modern Elder Academy

THE
ENCOUNTER

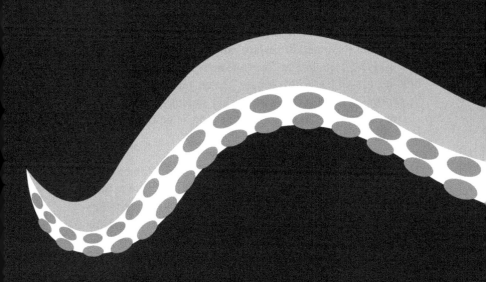

CHAPTER 1

"We are contaminated by our encounters; they change who we are as we make way for others."

Anna Lowenhaupt Tsing, *The Mushroom at the End of the World*

The waves crashed and roared on the rocky shoreline of the Western Cape, sending a mist of spray high into the air. Just beyond the rock pools, among the shadows of a kelp forest that lay beneath the emerald surface, an important meeting was taking place. It would transform one man's life forever. "I must hold my breath just a little longer," he encouraged himself, as he continued to resist the Atlantic chill and his lack of oxygen. He was determined to stretch out, as long as he could, one of the most magical moments of his life.

The octopus's suckers attached one by one, tracing a sinuous path from his palm to his elbow. They gently explored his bare skin, tentatively sensing, feeling through millions of nerve endings the spellbound human in front of her. His camera captured this moment after weeks of careful observation and tracking. She, for her part, had seen that he did not present a danger and had expressed her curiosity. Maintaining a fixed and safe position in her den, she had demonstrated a first sign of trust by extending a tentacle and initiating physical contact. Not wanting to alarm her, but much in need of oxygen, he slowly withdrew his arm and pulled his hand away. He surfaced rapidly, took in a large gulp of air, and then dived down again.

Craig Foster, a wildlife filmmaker and founder of the Sea Change Project in South Africa, captured this moving relationship between human and mollusk in the Academy Award-winning Netflix documentary, *My Octopus Teacher*, directed by Pippa Ehrlich and James Reed. Foster's immersion in the wild was his response to overwork and burnout, which were affecting his mental health and family life. He wanted to return to the natural environment that he so enjoyed in childhood. Foster began to swim regularly without a wetsuit in the cold ocean waters. He found that his thinking became clearer and the endorphins released made him feel more alive.

"I remember the day it all started," he recalls. "I found an area protected by a kelp forest. It was murky and I couldn't see a thing. It was a 200-meter patch that you could dive. An incredible place. I saw a strange shape to my left. Even the fish seemed confused." Suddenly, an octopus emerged from an assembly of rocks and shells that it had used to camouflage and defend itself. Initially, she hid under the algae, but the more he watched her, the more he realized that there was something special about her; that he was being presented with a remarkable opportunity to learn. "I then had this crazy idea. What happens if I went every day?"

My Octopus Teacher captures Foster's daily visits and occasional interactions with the octopus after that first sighting. He witnesses her being attacked by a pajama shark, resulting in the loss and regrowth of one of her tentacles. He learns about her strategic intelligence, refined through a million years of evolution, evidenced by her color changes, camouflage and mimicry of the movement of algae. He watches her skillfully evade a shark by riding on its back, and observes her own hunting methods, becoming complicit himself when she exploits his presence to hem in and capture a crab. He is present when she mates, signaling the end of their physical interaction as she dedicates her remaining days to motherhood. Over the course of the film, we see filmmaker and octopus develop trust, with the human benefitting from the acquisition of knowledge, which feeds his burgeoning appreciation of the natural world.

The moment of first tactile contact is recalled by Foster with a smile in his eyes. "When you have that connection, it is absolutely mind-blowing. There is no greater feeling on earth.

The boundaries between her and I seem to dissolve. Just the pure magnificence of her."

Fascination gives way to obsession, not just in Foster's daily visits, but through his nightly study of scientific papers about the common octopus. He discovers that two-thirds of her cognition comes from the 2,000 suckers on her tentacles, which can all sense independently. A man who, before their first encounter, felt disassociated from life and without a purpose, suddenly finds his own life entangled with that of an octopus, and he is irreversibly transformed.

The boundary between self and environment has become porous. It is for this reason that Foster experiences the shark attack on the octopus so viscerally. He is almost in tears when he describes it on camera. "I felt as if what happened to her happened to me in some way. It felt like I was going through the same dismembering. I started thinking about my own death. My family. She was teaching me to become sensitized to the other, especially wild, creatures." When the tentacle grows back after the shark attack, he finds a personal metaphor in the experience: his own life could be renewed. "In a strange way, our lives were mirroring each other. My relationships were changing." Foster becomes closer to his son, who, fascinated by his father's daily underwater stories, begins to accompany him on some of his visits to the octopus. Their relationship heals.

By returning to the same patch day after day, Foster noticed more patterns and distinctions that would not have been visible if he were simply a tourist. He began to appreciate the interdependence and connection of the wild, how everything was bound together in a complex and intricate web:

> Thousands of threads going off from the octopus to all the other animals, predator or prey, and then this incredible forest just nurturing all of this. And now I know how the helmet shell is connected to the urchin and how the octopus is connected

to the helmet shell, as I draw all these lines, all these stories are just being thrown out. It's almost like the forest mind. I really could feel it. That big creature that was thousands of times more awake and intelligent than I am. It's like a giant underwater brain operating over millions of years that just keeps everything in balance.

As the documentary progresses to day 304, then to day 324, we watch Foster coming to terms with the end of the relationship as the octopus's natural life nears its end. Every moment he spends with her is "so precious and way too short." One of the most moving scenes in the film is the last time he makes physical contact with her. He sees her sweeping her tentacles at a shoal of fish — not hunting, but playing, it seems — and then suddenly she loses interest in them and swims rapidly towards him, attaching herself to his chest in what he experiences as a hug.

In her final days, her body is emaciated, literally used up by giving birth to and nurturing her offspring, which have only a small chance of survival. Foster watches her sacrifice her body so that life can continue. "She made me realize just how precious wild places are. You go into that water, it's extremely liberating. All your worries, problems and life drama just dissolve. You slowly start to care about all the animals, even the tiniest animals. You realize everyone is very important." Yet, the enduring lesson he has taken from their time together, and that he now appreciates in his son, is the value of gentleness.

By observing the vulnerability of sea creatures, Foster came to understand how vulnerable we all are. Having felt atomized and disconnected before starting to swim regularly in the sea, Foster had come alive, appreciating that he was part of the wild, not separate from it. "I fell in love with her, but also the amazing wildness she represented and how that changed me. What she taught me was to feel you are part of this place, not a visitor, and that's a huge difference."

PART I:

FRAG
MEN
TA
TION

Modernity is characterised by

uncertainty, rapidity of change and

kaleidoscopic juxtapositions
of objects, people

and events.

Finding
our uncertain way through

these uncertainties is

a prime task of contemporary existence,

for individuals as well as

for cultures as

a whole.

~ Stephen Frosh, 'Identity Crisis'

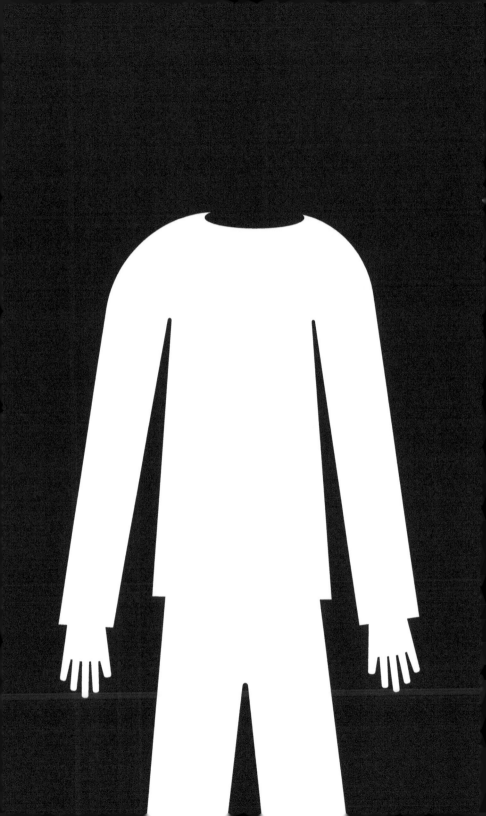

THE DYSFUNCTIONS OF THE SEPARATE SELF

CHAPTER 2

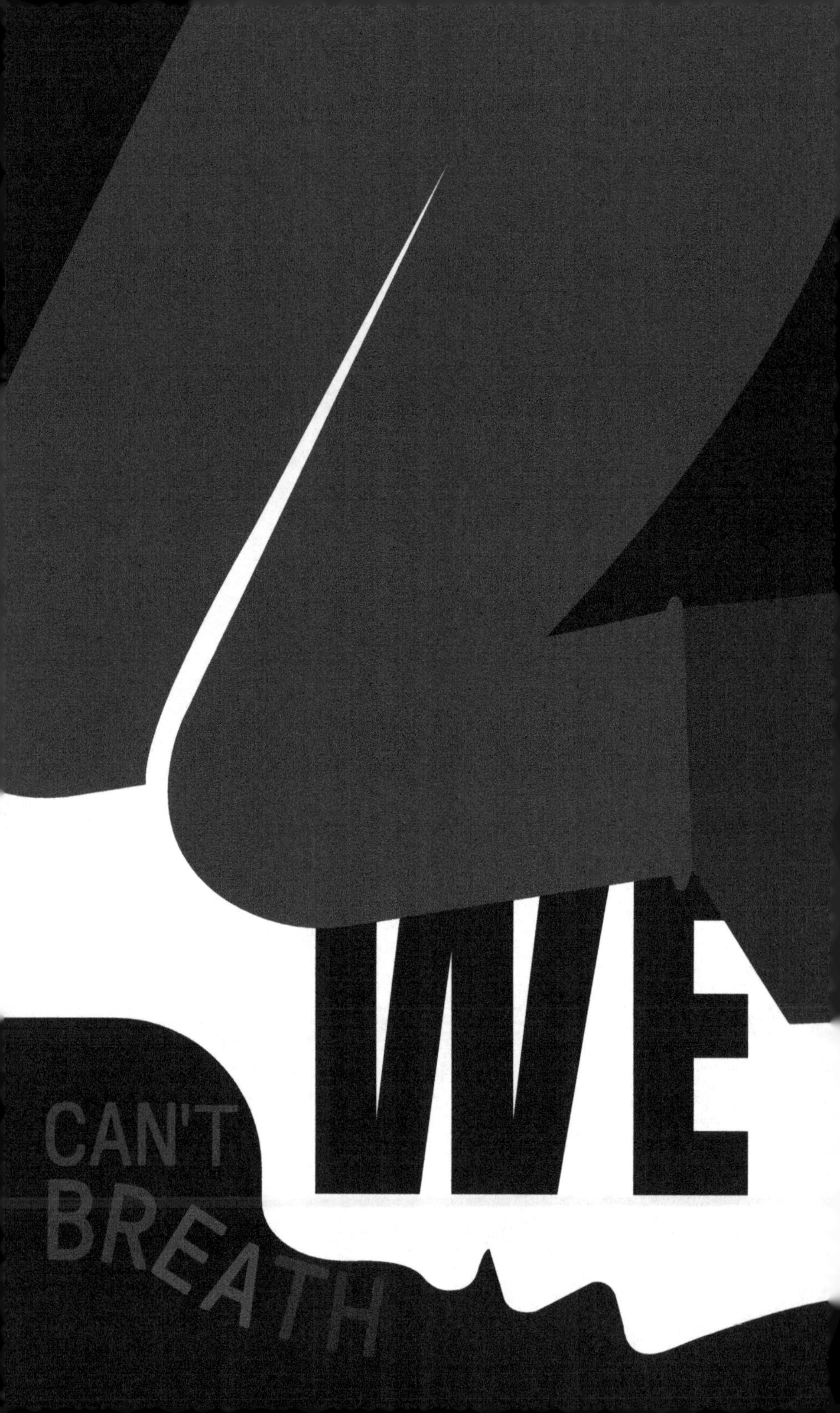
WE
CAN'T
BREATH

"Of all the creatures that live and breathe and creep on earth, we humans are weakest."

Homer, *The Odyssey*

The skyline of the San Francisco Bay Area is tinged ominously red, orange and purple by the ash that hangs in the air. The city smells of burnt dust, black particles floating everywhere as if a meteor had crashed nearby and broken into a million pieces. It is an apocalyptic spectacle for the terrorized citizens who look on from their homes, in shock at what is happening to their city. The dystopian scene is like something lifted straight from one of the *Blade Runner* movies.

California went through several days of hell in August of 2020. More than 12,000 lightning strikes hit the state in a week, igniting over 600 fires, many of which joined together in complex patterns due to the wind and tinder-dry conditions. At times, the days and nights blurred into one, with the blood-red sun and the orange-tinted moon merely exchanging places. The southern part of the state witnessed 130-degree Fahrenheit temperatures, some of the hottest ever recorded in human history, as close to a million acres of land was ravaged by fires.

With more thunderstorms threatening to spark more fires, over 238,000 people either had to evacuate their homes or were put on alert to do so. Others retreated indoors, watching the tragedy unfold on their screens, kept inside by both pandemic quarantine restrictions and the effects of the fires. Neighboring forests rapidly became the graveyards of once vibrant wildlife. According to People for the Ethical Treatment of Animals (PeTA), an "inconceivable number of foxes, rabbits, deer, frogs, mice, coyotes, and other animals were smoked out of their homes and burned alive."

The wildfires affected everyone, although there was a discrepancy between their impact on the rich and the poor. While human fatalities were fewer than those caused by other natural disasters around the globe, there was something portentous about the Californian conflagration, especially in the context of the pandemic and the social unrest triggered by economic hardship and police brutality against African Americans in particular. It felt like there was something irreversible about this particular moment in history. The convergence of multiple crises was choking the lungs, hearts and minds of people across the United States and far beyond its borders.

As the activist Terry Tempest Williams poignantly observes in *The Pall of Our Unrest*:

> We cannot breathe. This is our mantra in America now. We cannot breathe because of the smoke. We cannot breathe because of a virus that has entered our homes. We cannot breathe because of police brutality and too many black bodies dead on the streets. We cannot breathe because we are holding our breath for the people and places we love.

The 2020 fires, both literal and metaphorical, in California, Australia and elsewhere have burned away our notion of a separate self that can seek safe shelter while all around everything collapses. Our very being, our understanding of who we think we are, is under threat, becoming moribund. The excessive pursuit of self-interest has trumped shared purpose, broken communal bonds and destroyed our environment. We wade through the ashes, self-centered, disconnected, unraveled, adrift.

START WITH I

"A blight comes down on him, on his mind and on his country from nowhere. It's irrational. It has no source. It just happens. Like things do, they just suddenly change, and it's to teach us that everything is fragile and that what happiness we think we've got and imagine will be forever ours can be taken away from us in the blink of an eye."

Ali Smith, *Summer*

Beyond the fires, 2020 was a year during which most people experienced upheaval owing to the effects of the coronavirus pandemic that swept the globe. While immediate public health and economic measures were put in place — including quarantine, social distancing, stricter hygiene norms, furlough support, grants and loans — the longer-term impact on mental health, the economy, education, homeworking, privacy, social norms, and the arts and service industries, like hospitality and tourism, may not be fully felt for generations to come. It is likely that anyone reading this book has found that their own lives have not continued as before, and that at least a part of the world with which they were familiar has unraveled.

Of course, we are not short on global challenges, but Covid-19 has served to bring into sharper focus many of them, highlighting

fractures and divisions, fomenting activism and civil unrest. The long-term economic effects of the financial crisis of 2008 have been exacerbated by a new wave of financial crises. Race and class tensions have been heightened by the perception of inequality in the handling of the pandemic and by police brutality, with the death of George Floyd re-energizing the Black Lives Matter movement. And, the brief glimpse of a world without heavy industry and constant traffic during the lockdown period, and the environmental and ecological benefits that arose from it, have given renewed impetus to protests regarding the climate crises, particularly among the young. Crisis is not new. What is new is the speed, intensity, scale and entanglement of a variety of crises that simultaneously impact our lives.

Disruptions and challenges can often appear to be happening 'out there' in the world, away from our personal lives, affecting national politics, institutions and economies. With the pandemic, however, we have been forced to recognize that the disruption is also close to home, affecting our communities, families, routines and mental health. Had the situation endured for only a few weeks, it might have been viewed as a blip, with people rapidly resuming their lives as before the pandemic. But, its duration and nature have meant that this has not been possible. One wave has been followed by another, and there have been few who have evaded their effects, however tangential they may have been. The unknown, the unexpected, continues to linger just beyond the horizon.

Steven: During the early months of the pandemic, it was hard to adjust. My employer's offices were closed, and I had to work in my bedroom, not at a desk but a coffee table. I remember the awkwardness in the streets as people crossed the road to avoid physical contact and the restaurants and venues for meeting others socially were closed. Every day the media shared more stories of how hospitals were overwhelmed, of how the government was rushing to find ventilators and protective equipment, of how conference centers were being converted into makeshift hospitals.

What if you chose this time,
This moment of disruption
And destruction,

Where it is no longer possible to live
the way you were used to?

Not an alarm clock that you can turn off,
snooze, or stop ringing.

Will the endless noise
of the news of death
Drive you crazy, as you toss and turn,
wanting to throw the clock away,

Yet never finding it?

Alarms going off everywhere:
the next room, the neighbor's room,
the foreigner's room.

There isn't a place that isn't ringing.
You stop.

You notice a gap in the ringing.
The alarm isn't outside
But inside you.

What if you chose this time
To awaken?

At this time, it was difficult to capture in prose the emotions that I was experiencing. I began to find succor in both reading and writing poetry, mulling over the kind of disruption that simply cannot be ignored and the wake-up call of the pandemic.

As with any crisis, after the immediate response and rush to action, followed by the relief that the worst may be over, there often comes a period of reflection and sense-making. As different working patterns and behaviors took root, people began to talk of 'the new normal.' Homeworking was no longer an occasional practice but something commonplace among white-collar employees, who benefited from the hours saved by not commuting. Some employers opted to turn off the office lights permanently, foregoing the expense of commercial real estate. With their home-based employees unable to extricate work from home life, many employers also found themselves benefitting from extra hours of discretionary labor. The 9-to-5 routine was over.

For some, these changes were long-anticipated or already familiar. In this sense, the pandemic did not cause workplace changes, but it *accelerated* what was already emergent, enabling a better way to work with others and to get things done. In recent times, many organizations had made a shift to online learning technologies. Enforced quarantine suddenly made these digital classrooms the only place where people could meet and learn together, with broad and diverse participation. Without the time or cost involved in traveling by train or plane, it became possible to join in with colleagues in, say, Mumbai or London or Sydney or Rio. Everyone won: the participants, the employers, the Zoom shareholders, not to mention the planet, which had fewer fossil fuels pumped into its atmosphere. Location was no longer critical to work performance or effectiveness. Talent had been unleashed, and managers were learning to lead remote teams virtually, adding new recruits from diverse locations, as proximity to a specific office building was no longer a determining factor.

Those who experienced these accelerated, arguably 'positive' changes in working life, though, were the lucky ones. There were many others who had any sense of a working identity yanked away from them, finding themselves either placed on furlough or without a job at all. The economic and health impact of the pandemic was rapid and pernicious. Businesses failed, the demand on food banks increased, hospital wards filled up, and people died in their hundreds of thousands. Then it all started over again. Job losses, the death of loved ones, home confinement, travel bans, and the sudden loss of so much we had taken for granted were inevitable sources of existential angst.

The heightened uncertainty of the pandemic punctured the transparency of our lives. It offered us a unique opportunity in the midst of all the disruption and change to reflect on and question very basic assumptions, to journey inwards. *Who am I? How do I want to live my life? What is important to me?* What is my purpose? Only by starting with *I* could we then look more broadly at our organizations and communities, questioning our collective purpose, exploring how we could improve to better serve others. This was not simply a matter of *doing* better but of fundamentally *being* different.

WHO AM I?

BEYOND PURPOSE

"We are neither what we think we are nor entirely what we are about to become, we are neither purely individual nor fully a creature of our community, but an act of becoming that can never be held in place by a false form of nomenclature."

David Whyte, *Consolations*

When author and inspirational speaker Simon Sinek argued that we should *Start with Why*, he shifted workplace conversations. This entailed moving away from a tactical focus on *what* to do and *how* to do it, including the setting of annual objectives and strategic goals. He encouraged us instead to step back and ask more reflective questions about the purpose that informs and shapes our actions and the meaning that is derived from them.

A clear *why* helps us identify what is truly important, enabling us to distinguish between conflicting options and select those that will align best with our deeper purpose. A clear *why* can also act as an anchor, helping us weather the storms and reminding us to stand firm when the going gets tough. As the philosopher Friedrich Nietzsche observed in *Twilight of the Idols*, "If you have your own why for life, then you can get along with almost any how."

In the face of complex interacting challenges, however, a strong *why* is insufficient on its own, while most default approaches to *what* needs to be done are usually found wanting. In a world characterized by polarized narratives regarding what the right thing to do is, it has become increasingly difficult to resolve tensions and establish a delicate balance between multiple stakeholder interests. The waters are further muddied by leaders who misspeak, obfuscate and lie, as well as by the widespread dissemination of so-called 'fake news' and unverified 'facts.' Science, which should be a source of clear objective direction — albeit colored by subjective values and choices — has been politicized, with the advice provided by scientists bent to suit the purposes of those who govern.

Any cursory reading of the history of climate change denial will affirm that facts alone have never proved sufficient enough to change economic policy, hearts or minds. This also has been illustrated by the schisms within the scientific community during the coronavirus pandemic, with those scientists who argued in favor of stricter lockdown and social-distancing measures condemned for advocating policies that would have a prolonged negative economic impact. Others looked elsewhere, pointing to the initial successes enjoyed by countries like Sweden, which placed more emphasis on individual freedom and responsibility, with the hope of earlier economic recovery. Or, they built cases for herd immunity, focusing on data that supported their arguments. Some models are useful, but all models are wrong. At the end of 2020, the Swedish King Carl XVI Gustaf admitted that their coronavirus approach had failed as the country had experienced many more deaths than its Scandinavian neighbors.

When abstracted, models and purpose do not reflect contextual nuance, the conflicting impulses, the competing priorities, the concessions and compromises that arise in the face of complexity. Our actions, the purpose that motivates them, the frameworks that enable them, the temporary alliances that support them, can all add to rather than resolve the confusion. A change in context, a shift of priority, new stakeholder or public demands can rapidly expose the fragility and vulnerability of the situation in which we find ourselves.

As evidenced in Autumn 2020 by the willingness of British Prime Minister Boris Johnson's government to renege on Brexit agreements previously negotiated with the European Union and ratified in the UK Parliament, our *whys* are neither the anchors nor the unassailable motivators we believe them to be. Often, competing *whys* jostle for position, creating a sense of ambivalence and uncertainty. Our *whys* are subject to constant change and require frequent reassessment. Consider, for example, how our lifestyle and health choices in our teen years are markedly different from those as middle-aged parents, with nuanced changes to underlying motivation and purpose occurring throughout the intervening years.

Similarly, our attitudes regarding pollution, the effects of heavy industry, and our use of transportation that is dependent on fossil fuels are likely to be markedly different today, in the third decade of the 21st century, than they were in, say, the 1980s. Of course, there are many who hold opposing views, pointedly illustrated in the US by the policy differences between the Trump and Biden administrations. Generally, however, there is greater awareness of humanity's impact on our environment, and that has affected our collective behavior. It has also brought into play consideration of our legacy and the duty we owe to future generations, the planet they will inhabit, and the other species that will share it with them. This provides us with an understanding of purpose that is greater than ourselves, extending far beyond what is local and the immediacy of our own life experiences.

SCORCHED EARTH

*"I used to think that top environmental
problems were biodiversity loss,
ecosystem collapse and climate change.
I thought that 30 years of good science
could address these problems. But I was
wrong. The top environmental problems
are selfishness, greed and apathy, and
to deal with these we need a spiritual
and cultural transformation. And we
scientists don't know how to do that."*

Attributed to Gus Speth, *former Administrator,*
United Nations Development Programme

Earth Overshoot Day marks the date each year when humanity's
demand for ecological resources and services exceeds what the
planet can regenerate in a calendar year. In 2020, that date fell on
August 22. In 1970, it fell on December 29; in 1995, on October
4. Every year, the research team at The Global Footprint Network
calculates this date based on the amount of carbon emissions,
forest harvest, food demand and other factors that impact global
biocapacity. At our current rate of consumption, we require 1.7
Earths to meet our ever expanding, accelerating demands.

Few of us consciously think that we are renting our lives on Earth.
Yet, not only is this the case, we are also stealing the Earth's future
resources from our descendants in order to operate our economies
in the present. In 2018, Mathis Wackernagel, Chief Executive

and co-founder of the Global Footprint Network, was interviewed by *The Guardian*. "Our current economies are running a Ponzi scheme with our planet," he said. "Like any Ponzi scheme, this works for some time. But as nations, companies, or households dig themselves deeper and deeper into debt, they eventually fall apart."

For centuries — certainly since the advent of industrialization, and in a tragedy of the commons — our actions have been extractive and consumerist. Whatever implicit contract exists between the planet and us appears to have been skewed in favor of our immediate needs, with no regard to sustainability or the interdependent health and well-being of humanity and the world it inhabits. For too long, there has been an assumption that no matter how much we exploit and conquer nature for our own ends, planet Earth will continue to sustain us.

Until it can't.

In fact, 2020 signaled a welcome easing of the trend that had been established over the previous decade. The Overshoot date in 2010 had been August 7, and in 2019 it was July 29. August 22, without diminishing any of the worry about the harm we continue to do, represented a gain. The imposition of travel restrictions during the coronavirus pandemic, with fewer cars on the road or planes in the air, had allowed the planet to breathe again — even as fires burned on different continents and swathes of the Amazon rainforest were cut down.

We learned that it was possible to slow the environmental damage inflicted by humans simply by staying at home. What we seemed incapable of, however, was slowing our relentless drive for more. Commerce shifted from the high streets and retail outlets to the internet. There was still a logistical demand and a need to plug new gaps in supply chains created by the pandemic. Some businesses prospered as they responded to home-based consumerism, with Amazon stock, for example, trading up by more than 74% by October 2020 compared with the previous year.

In thrall to the capitalist notion that happiness can be found in consumption, people bought into the lie that they could purchase solace and fulfillment. Advertising assures us that through the materialistic accumulation of products and experiences, we can improve our image, status and prospects for a happy future. The paradox is that even though many people in industrialized and wealthy countries buy many more things than they did 50 years ago, surveys show they are less happy. As the author Gregg Easterbrook explores in his book, *The Progress Paradox*, by almost all objective standards, quality of life has improved in the United States and Europe. Yet, surveys of satisfaction and happiness indicate little change there since the 1950s. Tim Kasser, a professor at Knox College who has been researching this link between consumption and happiness for almost 30 years, explains that the more we believe we can buy our way out of sadness and into a good life, the more likely it is that we will suffer from depression and anxiety.

The separate self is consumptive, egocentric, narcissistic and largely disconnected both from community and from the natural world. The separate self makes manifest the increasing separation between the material values of money, status and image, and the intrinsic values of growth, relationships and community. The phrase *we are all in this together* does not resonate with them. In a 2019 TED Talk, journalist Johann Hari reflected on a conversation he had with Kasser about the discrepancy between knowing what is meaningful in life and the antithetical behavior characteristic of the separate self. Kasser argued that our culture, at times, seems like a machine designed to persuade us to ignore what is important, focusing instead on the banal and the self-celebratory.

One aspect of this machinery that is common in deregulated countries like the United States and the United Kingdom is a highly competitive form of consumer capitalism primarily concerned with growth and corporate profit. For this system to function smoothly, it needs citizens, businesspeople and

government officials to focus on consumption and productivity. People need to work efficiently for longer hours, and then they need to be persuaded to spend what they have earned. They fuel the very machine that enslaves them.

The separate self learns to appreciate their value through their own productivity and acquisition of things. Yet, the separate self fails to comprehend their own instrumentalization, whereby they are treated and function as a component in the machine. They are a part of a whole but continue to perceive themselves as distinct from, rather than interrelated to and entangled with, the other components. The separate self fails to see the parallels between their own depression and economic depression. The mental health and well-being of the separate self becomes intertwined with the health of the economy.

The primary experience of a separate self is tainted by a dissatisfaction with reality, by a sense that there is something missing. Whether that is security, comfort, control, recognition, fun, love or connection, there is rarely a feeling of true contentment. This is not a bug, but a feature of being human. Once the separate self has taken hold, there will always be a sense of lack. These two aspects are, as the scholar David Loy observes, "Like the matter and anti-matter particles of quantum physics, they arise together, opposing each other; and they disappear together by collapsing back into each other."

There is nothing inherently bad about seeking fulfillment or wanting material possessions that we use, that bring us value, or that provide what lifestyle personality Marie Kondo refers to as 'spark joy.' However, it's when we start to believe that material attainment can serve as a proxy for inner fulfillment that problems arise. When we try to meet psychological needs through acquisition, it invariably proves to be a poor substitution for what we truly desire. From this perspective, we can understand greed not as a vice to be condemned. Rather, it is an attempt by the separate self to expand, filling the void; an awkward compensation for the lost connections of what Buddhist monk and mindfulness teacher Thich Nhat Hanh refers to as *interbeing*. We can never have enough of what we don't really need, which is why greed is never satisfied. The greedy are transformed into 'hungry ghosts,' roaming the aisles but feeling permanently empty.

The mainstream advertising industry understands this well and plays on our endless desires with attractive substitutions. It's not about the fancy suit, it's the manliness it implies. It's not the latest gadget, it's the prestigious social status for those who possess it. It's not the computer game, it's the sense of adventure and the spirit of social connection. Perhaps the most successful and least suspected example comes in the shape of diamonds and their promise of endless romance, love and companionship, expertly exploited by the N.W. Ayer advertising agency on behalf of the De Beers conglomerate over 70 years ago.

Advertising diverts us from seeing the consequences of our actions, touching our hearts but keeping conscious knowledge from our heads. As such, we don't see the invisible impact and accumulated effect of our repeated transgressions. Every time we fly, drive, use electricity, eat factory-farmed meat or order the latest gadget, there is a cost to the environment and to other people. We enjoy the benefit of convenience even as elsewhere, as a consequence of what we have desired, more non-replaceable materials are extracted from the earth, more pollutants are pumped into the atmosphere, more time is shaved off a child laborer's lifespan. Alienated from our environment and our fellow planetary beings, we fail to appreciate how every decision we make, every action we take, carries the potential to do harm.

The environmental activist Joanna Macy refers to this situation as the 'Business as Usual' story. It is informed by an underlying assumption that everything will be fine, that humans can continue to pursue their agenda of growth, making more, consuming more, continuing to measure their progress with gross domestic product (GDP) metrics. In such a scenario, few people speak for the land, the trees, the rivers and the animals, or consider the mutual well-being of people and the environments they inhabit. There are, however, some encouraging signs and first steps, with specific rivers in New Zealand and India granted the same legal rights as humans, for example, or Bhutan's focus on gross national happiness (GNH), or the adoption of budgeting policies that focus more on well-being than on economic growth in New Zealand, Iceland and Scotland.

Generally, however, most of us don't see, know or feel the state of the planet, but keep on prioritizing our personal security, our comfort, our material acquisition. In such a vicious cycle, the sense of separation is further reinforced as we don't see ourselves as essentially reliant on nature, our environment, or the ecosystems that sustain it. Unlike Craig Foster, the wildlife filmmaker who learned so much from his encounters with an octopus, we neglect the fact that we are both *in* and *of* nature. Instead, we view the natural world as a commodity to be exploited for minerals, crops and energy, or simply as a view to be photographed. With this blinkered mindset, ecological and environmental collapse is vaguely understood as a possibility, but of low priority, to be addressed at some indeterminate future date.

In *The Uninhabitable Earth*, journalist David Wallace-Wells spells out in a series of short essays a frightening scenario that our children's children are likely to face, encompassing dying oceans, unbreathable air, plagues and storms. Wallace-Wells compares the devastating impact of rising sea levels to that of an extended nuclear war. Yet, so many of us remain nonchalant about the systemic effects of our actions on the climate, the environment, wildlife, our own lives and those of our descendants, convinced that, over time, we will adapt to the changes.

The statistics tell a bleaker story. For every flight from London to New York, the Artic loses three-square-meters of ice, which contributes to rising sea levels and accelerates the release of long-trapped gases into the atmosphere. For every half-degree rise in average temperature, there is a 10–20% increase in the likelihood of armed conflict, owing to the impact on our ability to grow and secure our own food or to access clean water and other resources. At current production rates, by 2050, there will be more plastic than fish in the planet's oceans, with 8 million metric tons of plastic waste added each year to the 250,000 tons that already float on the ocean surfaces and the 14 million tons that sit on the ocean floors.

Despite growing awareness of the negative impact of climate change, the competing arguments of activists and deniers have resulted in limited action and policy at a local, national and international level. As a consequence, there has been an acceleration of emissions, with China accounting for 27% of global CO_2 emissions in 2017, the United States 15%, and the European Union (including the United Kingdom) 9.8%. Expressions of climate grief have increased, too, and not just from the vantage point of Western privilege.

Meanwhile, there are an increasing number of major incidents arising from the climate crisis, including hurricanes in the Philippines and the Caribbean, life-threating temperature spikes in Europe, and the aforementioned Australian and Californian wildfires. Suffering has been normalized while our voracious consumption and lifestyle demands continue to destroy the planet's ecosystems. The natural disasters and the global coronavirus pandemic are timely reminders of just how forceful nature can be, and how dangerous it is to think of ourselves as separate from it.

ADRIFT

*"Connection balances numbness.
Connection is the first step towards
any act of acknowledgement,
accountability or responsibility."*

Kae Tempest, *On Connection*

There's an old Hasidic tale about a famous rabbi who visited a village where the inhabitants were quite interested in his ideas. The villagers were so curious that they prepared many questions to ask him, eager to learn from his renowned wisdom. As he arrived at the village hall, excitement filled the air. The rabbi, who had remained silent until this point, suddenly began to hum a tune. Slowly, others joined in. The rabbi started to move around the hall, dancing with each person in turn. Soon, the room was filled with energy and delight as the whole community danced wildly together. Each person experienced transformation, a sense of healing made possible by deep connection and joy. At the end of the evening, the rabbi slowly stopped dancing and the music ended. He looked his hosts in the eye and said kindly, "I trust that I have answered all of your questions."

There are many indigenous stories and traditions that mirror the Hasidic tale's celebration of the power of connection. The late cultural anthropologist Angeles Arriens recounted how she visited an indigenous community to learn about its way of life. Remarking on the happiness of the people she met, she was informed by an elder that whenever someone in the community is feeling depressed, angry or sad, they are asked four questions:

When did you stop dancing?
When did you stop singing?
When did you stop being enchanted by stories?
When did you stop finding comfort in the sweet territory
of silence?

This revelation led Arriens to identify dancing, singing, storytelling and silence as 'the four universal healing salves.' Notably, these are all activities that involve some form of deep connection, with silence creating both the time and space to pause and listen closely to our inner voices and to other people.

In modern society, it is more likely that medication will be prescribed to those who are depressed rather than any of Arriens' healing salves. Exercise or talk therapies may also be recommended. In January 2020, the World Health Organization (WHO) estimated that there are more than 264 million people of all ages around the globe who suffer from depression, with more women affected than men. According to WHO, depression is a leading cause of disability and, in a number of cases, can result in suicide. The findings of a survey of medical practitioners conducted by the physicians' social media network Sermo suggest that depression is a universal phenomenon that manifests itself differently depending on the local culture. It cannot simply be viewed as an epidemic that is a byproduct of the Western way of life, despite there being fewer reported incidences of clinical depression in many Asian and African nations than in, say, the United States.

While chemical imbalances and inflammation of the brain can be causes of depression, another can be disconnection from others, as has been documented by journalist Johann Hari in his book *Lost Connections*. This disconnection is what cultural critic Olivia Laing has described in *The Lonely City* as "an absence or paucity of connection, closeness, kinship," which can create a sense of isolation and loneliness, ultimately leading to depression and other conditions. Vivek Murthy, who was Surgeon General of the United States from 2014–17, has tackled many public health issues, including obesity, alcohol addiction, and the opioid crisis. His first book, 2020's *Together*, explores the "healing power of connection in a sometimes lonely world." Murthy relates how he suffered from an acute sense of loneliness during his childhood, equating this experience with the feeling of being unworthy of love.

Loneliness, he discovered, has a profound impact on well-being, and can reduce an individual's lifespan in the same way that smoking 15 cigarettes a day can. During an appearance on the *CBS This Morning* show in 2017, Murthy observed:

> We evolve to be social creatures, and thousands of years ago, if you were connected to other people, you were more likely to have a stable food supply and to be protected from predators. So, when you're disconnected, you're in a stress state. When that happens chronically, it can have a profound impact on your health.

Loneliness, in fact, can increase the likelihood of developing heart disease, hypertension, strokes and dementia, while those who experience it also are more prone to general cognitive decline and, in some cases, suicide.

A number of factors contribute to loneliness. Murthy highlights the increasing number of people who choose to live alone, the rise of individualism and the effects of technology, which too many people rely on as a substitute for in-person connection and interaction. To rely on online connection alone is ultimately harmful, in his view. Social media may have increased the number of people we can communicate with, but these online exchanges are often less meaningful than time spent conversing and doing in physical proximity to other people.

There is a distinction between a network, both physical and digital, and a community, which management theorist Henry Mintzberg outlined succinctly in a 2015 blog post for the Global

Drucker Forum. In a network, he notes, you can be connected to hundreds of 'friends,' all of whom still behave as individuals. In a community, by contrast, you will find a group of people willing to come together and collaborate when you ask them to help you paint your house.

The importance of physical togetherness — the necessity of community to counteract the effects of loneliness and depression — became all the more evident when they were denied us during the coronavirus pandemic quarantines and lockdowns. Meetings, for those who continued to work, and school lessons were moved online, engendering a new dissociative phenomenon: 'Zoom fatigue.' In an April 2020 interview with the BBC, INSEAD Professor Gianpiero Petriglieri explained that video calls require more focus than in-person conversation, but that genuine connection is challenging.

Video chats mean we need to work harder to process non-verbal cues like facial expressions, the tone and pitch of the voice, and body language; paying more attention to these consumes a lot of energy. Our minds are together when our bodies feel we're not. That dissonance, which causes people to have conflicting feelings, is exhausting. You cannot relax into the conversation naturally.

Such dissonance can exacerbate anxiety and other symptoms associated with depression. In June 2020, three months into the first UK lockdown, the Office for National Statistics reported that the number of people who reported that they were experiencing some form of depression had doubled over a 12-month period.

The research for *Lost Connections*, Hari's study of depression, involved a 40,000-mile journey around the world interviewing leading experts on the topic. The lost connections he learned about accounted for many incidences of depression, but they materialized in several different ways, including disconnection from meaningful work, from other people, from nature, from values, from status and respect, from hope. Trauma relating to childhood events, or disasters experienced in adulthood, were also significant factors. Among many other cases, Hari relates the story of a Cambodian man who lost a leg and his former way of life to a landmine. He managed to overcome his depression through the kindness of neighbors who helped him address his pain as attentive listeners, and then enabled him to start over as a dairy farmer with the donation of a cow. This was community rather than chemicals serving as an antidepressant, as an antidote to disconnection.

For too long, there has been a tendency to view conditions like depression as personal ailments to be remedied rather than indicators of societal malaise. An unfortunate consequence of 19th century industrialization was that people began to be viewed less for their distinct and unique qualities and more as interchangeable, replaceable parts. They were components in a machine that occasionally needed fixing. Brains might need rewiring; bodies were supplied with the lubricant of medication. Somewhere along the way, we lost sight of our collective humanity, of our innate ability to listen and act in service of one another. Studies like Hari's highlight how "we need to stop trying to muffle or silence or pathologize the pain."

The SällBo multigenerational co-living project in Helsingborg, Sweden, is an attempt to put this into practice. Despite the Nordic countries usually placing highly in international happiness indices, reports from the Nordic Council of Ministers in 2018 and WSP Global in 2019 suggest that many people suffer from loneliness in Sweden, and that a significant proportion of young people feel unhappy. Since November 2019, 72 Helsingborg residents of mixed ages and backgrounds have been housed in a repurposed apartment block, with access to shared kitchens, a gym, a yoga room, an arts-and-crafts studio, a vegetable garden and several recreation areas, to enable social mixing with the mutual benefit of company, shared wisdom and conversation spanning the generations. Residents are encouraged to participate in group activities for at least a few hours a week. There are 31 two-room apartments in the block that are occupied by retired people. Another 20 apartments are intended for people between the ages of 18 and 25, half of which are reserved for people who came to Sweden as unaccompanied child refugees and asylum-seekers.

As a World Economic Forum article suggests, loneliness and the conditions it gives rise to have the potential to be "the real Nordic noir." The SällBo project illustrates the power of connection and how it can prevent people from feeling adrift in the modern world. It is a safe harbor from other contemporary ills, such as populism and inequity, inflated egos and victimization.

THE EGO TRAP

"When we are stuck in ego, we never stop to contemplate and to ask ourselves if we really have seen and noticed all that there is to see in our field of vision. Our ego can act as blinkers on a horse. This is particularly true when we look at how we see other people. Have we really seen the people around us as they truly are?"

Simon Robinson & **Maria Moraes Robinson**, *Holonomics*

In 1961, the world witnessed the trial of Adolf Eichmann, the Nazi responsible for the logistics of the Holocaust, whereby millions of Jews were removed from their homes and transported to ghettos and extermination camps. In her 1963 book, *Eichmann in Jerusalem*, Hannah Arendt, who reported on the trial for *The New Yorker*, introduced the phrase "the banality of evil." While the Israeli prosecutors insisted on describing Eichmann as "a monster," what Arendt found before her was an ordinary bureaucrat who was "neither perverted nor sadistic" but "terrifyingly normal." She described him as a thoughtless person, motivated only to please his superiors.

> What he said was always the same, expressed in the same words. The longer one listened to him, the more obvious it became that his inability to speak was closely connected with an inability to think, namely, to think from the standpoint of somebody else.

While this is an extreme example of separation of the self from other people, it remains highly relevant today, especially with the global rise of right-wing populism. Arendt's description of Eichmann's character traits finds eerie echoes in several contemporary political leaders. It is little surprise, then, that there was a huge upsurge of interest in Arendt's book on the trial and her 1951 publication, *The Origins of Totalitarianism*, in the wake of the 2016 US presidential election.

Arendt identified major social problems and dysfunctions that resonate with our notion of the separate self. These included rootlessness, loneliness and homelessness, in the sense of lacking a place or community where people felt that they belonged. With economic uncertainty and widespread unemployment, these conditions gave rise to totalitarianism, with populist leaders exploiting people's sense of disconnection, often uniting them around a simple message founded upon fear of otherness. By mobilizing people *en masse* through a singular ideology, the populists constructed political systems that granted the state absolute power, separating the believers from the non-believers and establishing deep societal divisions. It is a pattern that we see repeating itself with Brexit in the United Kingdom and the two US election cycles of 2016 and 2020, as well as in recent protest demonstrations and their often-violent policing in Hong Kong, Poland, Brazil, Thailand, Belarus and Nigeria.

The 'othering' of people who are unlike us is hardly a new phenomenon. As journalist Ryszard Kapuściński notes in *The Other*, "Conquer, colonise, master, make dependent — this reaction to Others recurs constantly throughout the history of the world." It is a position often adopted to justify monstrous acts of government supposedly carried out on behalf of the people who have given political leaders a mandate to exercise power. But the polarizing effects, the divisiveness, the associated rhetoric, then tend to permeate society and culture, poisoning public discourse, visible in parliament, public fora, the board-room, even at the family dinner table. The question remains as pertinent as ever: what causes populism and division? From our perspective, this returns us to matters relating to identity, to the sense of self, to how the experience of either inflated ego or deflated ego can result in perceived separation from the people and world around us.

In *Fear Less*, sports psychologist and psychotherapist Pippa Grange argues that behind all of our struggles to achieve our best, there is a deep fear of not being good enough, of being found out, of being rejected and abandoned. This is underpinned by the belief that we are separate from others and disconnected. Having worked with many elite athletes and business executives, Granger has discovered that, to overcome this fear, we devise compensatory behaviors that we believe will keep us safe, including hiding from others information that would reveal who we really are. She cites the example of a sportsman who withheld the fact that he was gay from both family and teammates, at immense personal emotional cost. When he did finally reveal this aspect of his identity, he was surprised to find himself accepted, to learn that it was his own fears that had separated him from others, prompting him to lead a double life for so long.

One of the symptoms of separation is the constant need to compare and base our sense of self-worth on others. The foundations for this tendency are laid in childhood, where we repeatedly find ourselves in competitive environments, in the classroom and on the sports field, with rewards granted to high achievers, and the desire to stand out fomented by both parents and teachers. It is a situation poignantly highlighted in the 1999 film *American Beauty*, when Angela (Mena Suvari) exclaims, "I don't think that there's anything worse than being ordinary." Such a mindset encourages constant status anxiety, with our own sense of identity warped by how we compare ourselves to others and by how we believe we are perceived by others. Indeed, as the organizational psychologist Adam Grant observed in a tweet posted in October 2020:

The root of insecurity is craving the approval of others. It gives them the power to inflate or deflate our self-esteem. A stable sense of self-worth stems from putting identity above image: worrying less about what others think of us than what we think of ourselves.

Narcissism is one means by which an inflated ego is made visible. It can involve an individual always putting themselves ahead of others, belittling other people, or imposing their will on them, denying them any possibility of two-way communication. The narcissist is convinced of their own stance, always believing that they are right and that anyone who holds a contrary view is wrong. They show a reluctance to change their opinion, to view things from another's perspective, or to receive feedback from other people. They demand constant attention, showing off in ways both subtle and overt.

The workplace narcissist is in thrall to the frantic drive for high performance, seeking recognition and even taking credit for the work of others. In fact, in *The Psychopath Test*, journalist Jon Ronson identifies the extreme of narcissism as sociopathy; that is, as a total lack of empathy for other people. Ronson's research suggests that CEOs are four times more likely to be sociopaths than the population in general, which speaks volumes about the unfortunate effects of a culture that values exceptionalism, competition, celebrity and quantified wealth over collectivism and collaboration. This is how someone like Donald Trump can end up as the temporary occupant of the White House.

In *The Fear of Insignificance*, psychologist and philosopher Carlo Strenger highlights the modern-day tendency to glorify celebrity. We are fascinated, he argues, by the re-enactment of the mythic transformation of ordinary people to demi-god status, through either their victory on reality-television shows like the *X-Factor*, *American Idol* and *The Apprentice*, or their popularity on social media platforms like Facebook, Instagram, TikTok and YouTube. Strenger cautions against this pursuit of 'significance,' arguing that striving after the *extraordinary* may lead to denigration of the *ordinary*, damaging our self-esteem. Professions such as teaching, nursing and accounting are intrinsically valuable, as often becomes evident during times of crises. However, they can be perceived as mundane in comparison with the sudden media celebrity of the participants on *Big Brother*, whose stars shine briefly and brightly, suddenly famous for being famous, but are then soon forgotten.

Steven: In 2011, I was invited to give my first TEDx Talk in Romania. I followed onto the stage a man who had parachuted down a mountain and ridden a horse with a broken hand to win a race. There were many other incredible speakers like him in the lineup. The theme of my talk, though, was 'In Praise of the Ordinary,' and I began by polling members of the audience to learn whether they considered the other speakers they had heard more extraordinary than themselves. Nearly every hand went up when I posed the question, a response that struck me as both positive and potentially damaging. It was an example of 'the denigration of the ordinary.'

Several years ago, I directed a leadership program for a charity that worked with young people. I heard the persistent complaint that there was a lack of positive role models for people from Black and minority ethnic communities. Yet, I knew many inspirational people from these communities. It was just that their stories had not been widely told, that they were not considered famous.

When I gave a talk to children who had been excluded from mainstream education, I asked whom they most admired. The responses were mostly the names of well-known rappers like Snoop Dogg and Tupac. When I then enquired who had had the biggest impact on their lives, their answer shifted to the people closest to them, such as family members and friends. This, too, illuminated the chasm between the allure of the extraordinary and the reality of what truly influences and inspires us. The real 'heroes' are closer to home than we think.

I decided to tell the stories of the inspirational people I had met from diverse cultural communities, including a comedienne, a hatmaker, an architect, a baroness, the CEO of a beer company, the parents of a child with leukemia, the owner of a delivery company and a health service manager. I was drawn to many of these people for their ordinariness, even those of them who had achieved significant career or creative accomplishments. There was something in the way they showed up that I could relate to, a degree of egalitarianism that appealed to me, especially how they revealed themselves more fully, 'warts and all.'

What I gradually realized, though, was that I found it much easier to share the stories and success of others than to talk about myself. In effect, I had made myself disappear because I did not believe that I had achieved anything extraordinary, that I did not have anything to say of value. I, too, had been blinkered by the culture of exceptionalism. Acknowledging this has enabled me to be more deliberate in honoring what is important and close to me in my life, recognizing that there is much that is special and remarkable in the apparently 'ordinary.'

When comparing ourselves with other people, in what subtle ways do we diminish ourselves? What is your story? Do you tell it and honor it? Who has had the greatest impact on your life? The celebrities, or the ordinary heroes that many other people may never have heard of? While the need for differentiation is universal, it carries the danger that we end up hiding behind our accomplishments, encouraging others to relate to us either through what we have already achieved, or what we say we are going to do, or the selected highlights we choose to share on social media. Such grandiosity is usually a form of performance, a cloak for mediocrity and self-hatred. We obscure who we really are. In most cases, that is a perfectly imperfect, complex human being, who is worthy of dignity and respect regardless of their foibles. Each of us is a biological miracle of inherent value, and to be ourselves we do not need to imitate the accomplishments of celebrities, nor become devotees of self-help literature, nor cult-like disciples of the latest business leader to tell all in a ghostwritten hagiography.

"You're one in a million," announced some graffiti Steven saw in Germany. "Just like everyone else," it concluded, getting to the heart of the matter. We are individuals who are part of a collective. As the network analyst Valdis Krebs puts it, we connect on our similarities but benefit from our differences. We are simultaneously ordinary and extraordinary, navigating the spectrum between the extremes and the excesses of the self-inflated narcissist, superhero and celebrity, through the pride-infected manipulations of the humble bragger, to the self-deflation of the follower and victim. If the former weave a fiction of their successes to bedazzle others, presenting themselves as modern-day superheroes, then the latter betray their fear of taking responsibility for their own lives and actions. Eichmann exemplified this trait when he stated at his trial:

> I sensed I would have to live a leaderless and difficult individual life, I would receive no directives from anybody, no orders and commands would any longer be issued to me, no pertinent ordinances would be there to consult — in brief, a life never known before lay ahead of me.

How many of us do not occasionally wish that life could be simpler? That someone could tell us what to do? That they would show us how to live, tell us who we are? Those with a deflated ego want answers rather than questions. They believe themselves to be wronged, persecuted, disadvantaged, powerless. They are too ready to blame others or their circumstances for their misfortune, yet they remain unwilling to acknowledge the consequences of their own actions.

The research of Michael Hogg on uncertainty and Gianpiero Petriglieri on organizational behavior highlights how we often look to our leaders and 'heroes' for clarity and certainty, for answers that will help us understand who we are, where we belong, what we believe, even more so in times of heightened uncertainty. Unfortunately, however, our eagerness for answers can have an adverse effect. We become too easily led, susceptible to untruths, blinkered by ideological constraint.

Where the inflated ego feels entitled to exercise control, to be at the center of everything, and to command love and respect, the deflated ego insists on its own helplessness, while still demanding special treatment and attention. In his study of adulthood, the psychologist David Richo refers to these two interconnected aspects of the dysfunctional ego as the "King Baby." In elaborating his ideas in *Human Becoming*, Richo argues that "the ego was never meant to be annihilated, only dismantled and rebuilt to make it more constructive." A healthy ego, a more developed sense of self, is essential to navigate these uncertain times.

New Zealand Prime Minister Jacinda Ardern's actions in March 2019, following an attack on a mosque and the Muslim community in Christchurch, epitomize Richo's thesis. In a *Guardian* article, journalist Nesrine Malik reflects on how Ardern's non-divisive response was comforting because of its humanity, sincerity and lack of self-consciousness. Ardern visited and engaged with the affected community, demonstrating both compassion and respect, wearing the hijab and refusing to utter the culprit by name. Her government was also quick to act, implementing new gun legislation. Ardern's ease and human warmth when interacting with the Muslim community contrasted sharply with the anti-Islamic sentiment and xenophobia that has been so prevalent in Western public discourse so far this century. The leadership she role modeled demonstrates what a healthy ego sense of self can accomplish.

THE SELF-IMPROVEMENT FALLACY

*"So often we need a whole lifetime
in order to change our life, we think
a great deal, weigh things up and
vacillate, then we go back to the
beginning, we think and think, we
dislodge ourselves on the tracks of time
with a circular movement, like those
clouds of dust, dead leaves, debris, that
have no strength for anything more,
better by far that we should live in
a land of hurricanes."*

José Saramago, *The Stone Raft*

The personal-development and self-improvement industry is estimated to be worth over $11 billion, with over $500 million spent annually on holistic therapies, products from motivational and spiritual teachers, personal coaching, and other products and services advertised online and on TV. Websites and bookstores are full of literature relating to mental performance, emotional intelligence, productivity, public speaking, body shape and physical fitness, fostering a false imperative for 'improvement' and 'growth' or running the risk of being left behind. There are even people who have started to recruit life coaches for their toddlers, assembling the scaffolding for future 'Super People,' so prevalent have the notions of personal development and self improvement become.

By the end of the 20th century, the dominant ideology affecting global political and economic systems was neoliberalism. Its emphasis on the dismantlement of the state, the free market, individualism and entrepreneurship continues to distort how we view ourselves today. It informs our separation from community and nature, our pursuit of growth and globalization, our competitiveness, our often-misplaced trust in market efficiency, our rampant consumerism, and the personal, economic and political choices we make.

The narcissistic glory of the separate self was an inevitable neoliberal product. In modern society, this separate self feels compelled to seek continuous improvement. For, if they do not move forward, they will go backwards; if they do not continue to grow, they will die. Economic crashes and pandemic-induced recessions simply feed the need to stand out, to compete, to urgently reinvent themselves and maintain some sense of relevance. Under neoliberalism, the self has become a commodity to be continuously developed, invested in and maximized. As the sociologist Nikolas Rose argues in *Inventing Our Selves*, "The enterprising self will make an enterprise of its life, seek to maximize its own human capital, project itself a future, and seek to shape itself in order to become that which it wishes to be."

As the language suggests, this commodified self is dehumanized, disassembled, abstracted. Anthropologist Ilana Gershon argues that it comprises skills, assets, experiences, relationships and, above all, qualities. While qualities should remain unchanged and are considered an indicator of authenticity, each of the other aspects can be worked on, improved, finessed, calibrated, and then repackaged as part of a personal brand. In this sense, the self is a machine, a product, to be taken to market.

The enterprising self becomes an entrepreneur of *oneself*, promising flexibility in adapting to the complexity of context but exhibiting stability in its high level of performance and productivity. Below the surface, though, there is an undercurrent of dissatisfaction — the feeling that there is something wrong with the self, requiring constant attention and fixing in order to remain competitive. This goes beyond the usual curiosity and iteration that enables us to learn how to cook, drive, write or play a sport. There is something compulsive about it, a striving for attention and reward, rather than pleasure taken in the acquisition and application of new knowledge.

Steven: If there were a Personal Development Anonymous group for self-help junkies, I would have been at every meeting. From childhood, I remember this insatiable desire I had to improve myself and to develop. At school, I read every book and did additional study during break time in order to stay ahead of the rest of the class. I was reading personal-development classics, books by Jung, and books on advanced psychology while still in my early teens. I would write down my goals, visualizing them, amazed at the idea that I could create my own reality if only I could harness my powerful subconscious mind.

While a university student, I qualified as a Neuro Linguistic Programming Master Practitioner and certified in Hypnotherapy, and then progressed to Large Group Awareness Training. By my 30s, the focus on personal growth had led me to qualify as an Ontological Coach and to undertake three years of training as a therapist. My intention was to 'grow in my spirituality, by growing in my humanity,' even though I had no desire to pursue a career as a therapist. During this extended journey, I must have spent thousands of pounds on books, courses and webinars.

Eventually, I realized that this self-development impulse was in all likelihood driven by a deeper insecurity. I feared my own insufficiency and was trying to protect myself from rejection by improving myself, by being smarter, more loving, more spiritual. Part of this behavior was culturally rooted, as I had grown up in a minority community on a council estate. I had seen cleverness as a way to avoid bullying and racism, as a way to somehow be considered 'special.'

While this impulse has helped me have a varied and intellectually stimulating career, there is, nevertheless, significant regret that, in my youth, I never permitted myself to accept myself for who I was and just enjoy life. I remember my uncle, a professor, saying to me as an 11-year-old, "Steven, this is the time to be a child now. No need to be so serious. You'll have enough time to do that as an adult." How much did I miss out on by investing so much time in developing myself? What opportunities for interaction and friendship, for community and shared experiences, passed me by that had nothing to do with improvement? What could I have done that would have brought me and other people joy?

Today, while I still enjoy learning, this is more about feeding personal curiosity than in the pursuit of life goals. Certainly, I'm far less concerned with my personal brand or with developing a 'bulletproof' veneer. Now, I find more truth in poetry than in prose, in nature than in classrooms. I've come to the point where I'm tired of the narrative of development and exhausted by the imperative for self-improvement. I'm ending the search. I want to enjoy life on the other side of the personal development project.

Steven has, in effect, chosen to abstain from what psychologist Robert Holden refers to as Destination Addiction. This is centered on the obsessive belief that whatever we are looking for — success, happiness, peace — can only be found elsewhere. As such, we cannot settle. We cannot accept our current circumstance or who we are. We have to move on, in pursuit of more, in search of improvement, on the trail of better, of an idealized sense of self. Yet, when the next thing is attained, the dissatisfaction, the lack, is not assuaged, and we continue on the merry-go-round. It is the unfulfilled search that the self-development project reinforces. The pursuit of happiness is what causes the suffering. In *The Silence of Animals*, philosopher John Gray argues, "The idea of self-realization is one of the most destructive of modern fictions. It suggests you can flourish in only one sort of life, or a small number of similar lives, when in fact everybody can thrive in a large variety of ways."

This takes its toll. Ultimately, if the separate self is treated as a machine, constantly tweaked, pushed to go further and faster, entropy will eventually set in. A 2020 Gallup survey revealed that 76% of employees declared that they had experienced burnout on the job at least some of the time, and 28% stated that they were burned out 'very often' or 'always' at work. Performance pressures — created by expectations, workload and time limitations — keep on mounting until something breaks. Failure, then, becomes an inevitability rather than an exception, but the self-improvement culture prevents us from making peace with this fact. Instead, instrumentalized as we are, our workplace identity becomes coupled with the metrics we are meant to achieve. We are our performance, defined by our successes and failures, driven to chase futilely after the myth of perfection.

Khuyen: As an overseas student from Vietnam studying at a US college, I began to feel acutely the pressure for perfection during my sophomore year. I was determined to make the most of my experience abroad, but the demands for time efficiency and constantly high productivity came as something of a culture shock.

My initial attempts at time management involved pen and paper, but this proved to be a tedious, manual routine. I sought a technological alternative to enable my self-improvement, downloading an app for my phone called a TimeLogger. With three simple steps, I could log the duration of my every action, then review a graph of my time usage at the end of each week. I was on the road to quantification, measuring what could be managed.

At first, I tracked in 30-minute chunks, but soon I got greedy. What if I could get more granular, measuring to the minute? This was a recipe for insanity, my life rendered a computer log file. I became obsessed with the data, looking to save time on socializing and eating, so that I could spend more time researching and being productive. I had become a slave to the machine. Worse,

I had become the machine. There was no sense of satisfaction, just the ruthless pursuit of efficiency.

It took a frustrating, all-night session in the computer science lab to break me out of this self-imprisoning cycle. Unable to fix a problem and at the point of exhaustion, I simply gave up and went to bed. Barely awake in class the following morning, I began to cry, completely overwhelmed. Instinctively, I pulled my phone out of my pocket and deleted the app and all its data. Then I returned home, before wandering for hours without my phone anywhere near me. At last, I was free.

According to social researcher Brené Brown, perfectionism "is a self-destructive and addictive belief system" that encourages people to aspire to perfection in how they look and what they do as a defense mechanism against "the painful feelings of blame, judgement, and shame." This is not so much about behavior as about the way people think of and relate to themselves. Yet, perfectionism, for all its addictive qualities, remains 'an unattainable goal.' In fact, counterintuitively, perfectionism often leads to those very painful feelings we try to avoid. Having failed to conquer its summit, we dwell on our shortcomings, further harming our self-esteem.

In a distortion of the concept of empathy, how we think others think of us, how they see us, and what they expect of us in the various roles and responsibilities inform our own sense of value and social worth. This is linked to the idea of social perfectionism. Failure to meet what we think is expected of us — as a student, as a colleague, as a friend, as a sibling, as a partner, as a parent — diminishes us. The social perfectionist believes that they can only achieve success by working hard to please others. If other people perceive what we do as perfect, then we may too. Yet, the psychological and social cost of such striving for, and failing to achieve, perfection should not be underestimated. This is clearly evident in the number of people who suffer from depression, with an increasing number of young people, for example, claiming to be depressed about their body image. More pointedly, it is highly visible in the rate of successful and attempted suicides.

As social psychologist Roy Baumeister argues in *Escaping the Self*, suicidal people often are trying to escape exceptionally painful thoughts and feelings about themselves and their lives. The process starts, he suggested, when the events in a person's life begin to "fall severely short of standards and expectations." Self-blame for failure then prompts a loss of faith in the individual's capacity to change. If this pattern is repeated enough times, it leads to a chronic feeling of being stuck. This entrapment undermines the ego's sense of being in control. Perfectionism is the quest for the ego's ideal, and failure to accomplish it shatters the ego's self-image. With each failed cycle, the ego loses a little more control. As matters seem increasingly bleak, it results in the ultimate separation of the self from the world around it.

Striving for development, self-improvement and perfection, then, creates a fundamental confusion regarding what the self is. The separate self is already insecure, concerned about an independent existence, unable to lose the sense of insecurity by being, doing or having more. That is When Things Fall Apart.

CHAPTER 3

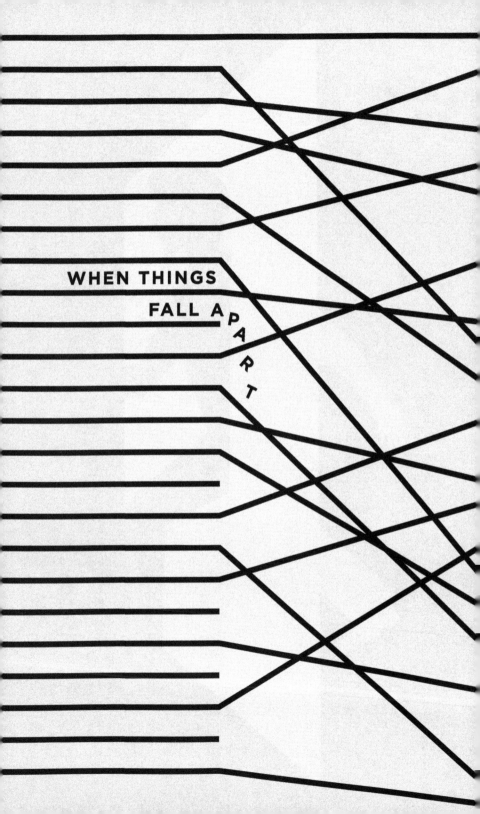

WHEN THINGS

FALL APART

"We are often surprised by change that seems to arrive out of nowhere. [...] Like spring secretly at work within the heart of winter, below the surface of our lives huge changes are in fermentation. We never suspect a thing. Then when the grip of some long-enduring winter mentality begins to loosen, we find ourselves vulnerable to a flourish of possibility and we are suddenly negotiating the challenge of a threshold."

John O'Donohue, *Thresholds*

Clayton Christensen, a Harvard Business School academic until his untimely death in 2020, was celebrated for developing the theory of disruptive innovation. On his office door, there used to be a sign that read, "Anomaly wanted." This was a reference to the most important fuel for his work, the unusual that cannot be explained by existing theories. A theory is statement of causality: 'If this, then that.' It is an algorithm that has been rigorously and continuously tested. It is granted a certain predictive power, enabling us to anticipate what will happen, and what likely outcome will ensue. Those who develop a theory strive to be precise in proscribing the boundaries of what it can and cannot explain. Christensen believed that anomalies were not something to be ignored. They provided significant signals that could point to valuable opportunities for transformation.

Many of us live our lives in the hope of seamless continuity rather than seeking out and welcoming anomalies. When the latter occur, they are often an unintended consequence of other actions, defying predictions, expectations and, more often than not, desires. Anomalies come to us without invitation, forcing us into consciousness. They expose what is broken, and this can be frightening because it demands change. What once was unthinkingly habitual is now noticed as if for the first time. Illness, for example, makes us aware of our previous good health. New choices have to be made. Preserving the status quo can be fatal.

This was well illustrated during the first wave of lockdowns and social distancing measures in the early months of the coronavirus pandemic. What had long been taken for granted — physical contact, freedom of movement, and activities involving large numbers of people in bars, restaurants, cafés, cinemas, theaters, sports arenas and concert venues — was suddenly denied us. Absence and restriction made visible what previously had been hidden in plain sight.

As the pandemic has illustrated, our lives are far from linear and their supposed transparency is frequently punctured by the anomalous. Road closures force us onto different routes, Wi-Fi failures lead us to alternative activities, injury and illness require changes of routine, grief progresses from irreplaceable loss to existential crisis. Each disruption is often unexpected, triggering transformation in what we do and how we see ourselves. This applies equally to those events with a positive outcome: a new job, a surprise promotion, the birth of a grandchild, a marriage proposal, a lottery win. Life always has the capacity to disrupt and surprise us, challenging any illusion of control we may have.

Life, in fact, can never be presented as a straight line, but must be seen as one with many ups, downs, loops and diversions. Sometimes the singular or accumulated effect of our encounters with anomalies is that we feel like we are falling apart. That experience can be sudden, the instantaneous shedding of an identity, as when an actor announces out of the blue that they will no longer perform on stage. Or, it can be more gradual, passing almost unnoticed, as in the 'Ship of Theseus' thought experiment, when the parts of an object are replaced over time until none of the original item remains.

We often tell the story of disruption in hindsight; the narrative of an event in which we make sense of significant changes to ourselves and others. Yet, in reality, transformation is experienced more as *process* than *event*. It occurs over time and is contextually complex. For example, quitting a job can be related, after the fact, as a dramatic event, compressed into that moment when we impulsively handed in our notice and ventured into the uncharted waters of the freelance life. Often, though, this is but a fragment of a larger narrative, omitting the months of frustration and dissatisfaction, the overwhelming desire to do something that better aligned with our personal purpose.

It's also important to note that we don't fall apart just once. We do it over and over. Life is punctuated with anomalies, a continuous call and response, as challenges are thrown our way and we work out how to respond to them. In this respect, both *falling apart* and *coming together* are continuous processes. We breathe in and out, we fragment and reassemble, falling and arising in a continuous movement of exchange.

As we have seen, many personal and societal crises result from the notion that we are separate, atomized individuals, disconnected from others. Rather than seeing ourselves as living organisms that are *a part of* life, we see the world around us as segmented, with ourselves functioning *apart from* life. Within this context, we tend to develop a theory of self, consciously or not, that includes beliefs, roles, perceptions about ourselves and others, that all shape our sense of a coherent identity with a past, present and future. We have a story we tell ourselves about who we are and our own free will. This sits alongside, rather than becoming fully entangled with, the stories other people tell about themselves.

It is our theory of a separate self that is challenged when we face disruption. As with the apocryphal fish that only becomes aware of what water is once it is deprived of it, we can only understand the limits of our current theory of self once it's no longer working. "Things fall apart; The centre cannot hold," wrote the poet W. B. Yeats in *The Second Coming.* "Mere anarchy is loosed upon the world." Disruption, then, is not only experienced personally, but communally and societally as well. It is community and wider society that serves as the waters we swim in, and disruption can make us realize just how interconnected we are with those around us.

In *Things Fall Apart,* Nigerian novelist Chinua Achebe tells the story of Okonkwo, the leader of an Igbo tribal community, who is banished for seven years after having accidentally killed one of his clansmen. The novel explores the events leading up to the fatal incident and his subsequent return from exile. At the same time, it examines the intrusive impact on Africa, and on the Igbo community in particular, of white missionaries and colonial government. Okonkwo's psychological disintegration is paralleled by the social disintegration of his village. Setting his novel at a time of imperial expansion, but writing after the collapse of the British Empire, Achebe knew only too well that 'the centre cannot hold,' that anarchy and chaos arise when the system collapses. Achebe warns that such collapse can lead to cultural, economic and societal loss.

This is a pattern repeated over and again among indigenous peoples who have been subjected to colonization by outsiders. It is also evident in the conflicts that follow the fall of dictatorships, as different factions compete to fill the void that has been created. On occasion, though, there is a more orderly transition following the collapse of the old system, as was the case with post-Apartheid South Africa and its self-identification as the Rainbow Nation, or with the fall of the Berlin Wall and the reunification of Germany.

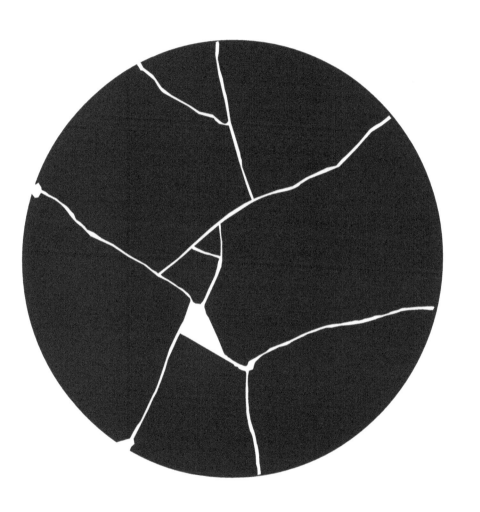

Disruption that arises from persistent anomalies or systemic collapses not only changes behavior, but can cause a shift in identity, in who we think we are, in our relationship to others and the world, in our very Being. It challenges our story of separation and offers us the possibility of something new. What we thought of as an integrated and self-contained self is revealed to be a construction, a perception created by the ego to preserve and protect itself. As neuroscientist Anil Seth argues, "We can all have better lives and be better people if we cling less onto maintaining a specific identity that has to be preserved at all costs. We should allow ourselves to change and to be impermanent."

This notion of fragility, fragmentation and impermanence is reflected beautifully in the Japanese practice of *kintsugi*, in which broken shards of pottery are joined together with a lacquer mixed with precious metals, such as gold or silver. What was fractured is made into a new whole, with its faults made a visible feature, part of the identity, of what is now on display. The shock of collapse has been transformed into the pleasure of renewal. Falling apart has catalyzed creation, with breakage and repair incorporated into the history of the object, into our understanding of what it is.

DESERT

"'What makes the desert so beautiful,' said the little prince, 'is that it hides a well, somewhere...'"

Antoine de Saint-Exupéry, *The Little Prince*

The desert is simultaneously a place of beauty, with its vast waves of shifting sand captivating the eye, and life-threatening danger. Its aridity, its lack of protection from wind and sun, its scorching temperatures by day and sub-zero temperatures by night, its poisonous inhabitants, including scorpions and snakes, all put the survival of the uninitiated humans who stray into its vast expanses at risk.

The physical extremes of the desert are also matched by its psychological challenges. With no traffic, conurbation or marketplace, the desert is stripped of the signs and noises of human activity, marked by the profound silence of an anechoic chamber, carrying only the ambient sounds of the natural world, especially those that come from our own bodies. In such solitude, it is possible to travel great distances in the desert and see or hear very few other creatures, let alone another human. Surrounded by apparent emptiness, with none of the distractions that typify the modern, urban world, we are left with our own thoughts, forced to confront ourselves.

Spending time in the desert has played an important role in many religious traditions. In Judaism, Yahweh appeared to Moses in the desert, and the Israelites spent decades roaming the desert before entering the 'promised land' of Canaan. In Christianity, Jesus retreated to the desert after he was baptized, where he faced and overcame temptations. Islam emerged in one of the hottest and driest regions on earth and the Koran contains many verses inspired by this sacred land and geography.

In many cultures, the desert symbolizes a space where profound internal transformation takes place. We use the metaphor of the desert in everyday speech to convey the feelings of being lost, perhaps abandoned or even cast out. Before we can reach the promised land, we are stripped of all that is familiar, navigating our inner landscape and the detritus that we have previously evaded. We have to contend with our empty mirages, our fantasies and false idols. The desert at its most visceral and testing becomes a transition space of purification. It allows us to form new insights that were not available to us before, while we dealt with the noisy demands and distractions of daily life. It gives us the space to reflect and to rethink who we are by stripping away all that is unessential.

The desert can be a space where we feel lost, alone, wandering aimlessly. But it also shows us that life finds a way to survive and thrive regardless of the severity of the environment. If we only pause to look, in the desert can be found dozens of plants, insects, reptiles and birds that have made this seemingly inhospitable landscape their home. Deserts are not devoid of life but places where life continues to flourish. If we can only adapt our own behavior, there is much that we can learn from it. This is what Anna Chaloupka, a consultant cardiologist at a busy hospital in the university town of Brno in the Czech Republic, determined to do when she first ventured into the desert in Namibia. The vast space gave her a sense of perspective and a feeling of unity with her surroundings.

> I am sitting on a soft, warm dune, the dry wind lifting a veil of sand grains off the surface and into the afternoon's golden air. The feminine curve of the dune is changing, almost unnoticeably, with every silent gust of wind. I put my face close to the sand, squinting, and marvel at how every single shiny grain

is different. The Namib, where I'm sitting, is the oldest desert in the world, having endured for millions of years. The silence here is deafening. I can hear my own heartbeat and sand grinding in between my teeth. I look at the single line of footprints I made as I was walking up the dune and it feels as if I am the only human on Earth. It's both a crushing and liberating thought. In a few moments, the footprints start to disappear.

I am suddenly overwhelmed by the scale of this place, unable to move, tears burning as they run down my sunburnt cheeks. My ego bows in front of this pervasive, timeless space. From this perspective, my existence is a small, temporary thing. For this ancient desert, human life is just a blink of an eye, and my problems seem pretty unimpressive. Whatever happens to me, whatever I do, is of no consequence on this scale. My status is nothing, possessions do not matter, that argument with my boss seems mercifully irrelevant. Deserts offer us this humbling sense of our littleness and, with it, immense freedom. However much we mess up, the world will go on.

As her day-to-day tribulations faded away, Anna began to experience a deeper sense of connection. She no longer felt separated from the world around her.

For a split second, my awareness opens, and I discover that my small, often scared 'self' has been substituted by something much larger. I become one with the desert, with every single grain of sand, the horizon, with every plant that defies the odds and survives in these harsh conditions. Unity. These moments when we are freed from the custom of being at the center of things enable us to see reality with less self-distortion. They open our lives to new worlds and possibilities. Many places and moments can awaken this sense. The desert is definitely one of those places.

The solitude gave Anna an opportunity for both physical and psychological care, offering a small oasis of time away from her demanding career. It allowed her to reflect on who she was in relation to the natural environment and to be more curious about who she was to other people. Anna realized that she did not have to be fixed in the role of consultant or expert, but that there were many other possibilities that were open to her. In the desert, she had no role to perform, no patients to attend to. She could experience who she was in a less defined and more fluid way.

> It's so hard to locate ourselves because we are continually changing. I find it agonizing that there are always so many exciting and viable versions of oneself, and yet very few of these will get enacted in the course of our lifetime. Our respectable self-image — which we create, and society reinforces — is putting even more constraints on us. We are all much more anxious, playful, tender, mean and compulsive than we would ever admit. Only when we learn to accept our own inevitable ridiculousness, are we freed to be who we are.

What Anna noticed as she reflected on her various identities was that in all of them, there was a relationship present.

> We all possess a deeply rooted need for connection with others and a feeling that we are accepted. Relationships with others are at the center of our lives. Have you noticed that pretty much all books, films and conversations are, in one way or another, about relationships? Why, then, is it so hard to create deep, meaningful, intimate relationships and communities? I think that one of the main reasons is because, for most of the time, we forget that others are as fragile and strange as ourselves. We feel so shy and self-conscious opening up to others because we are scared of being judged. Taking a leap of faith that the other person is as ridiculous, angry, self-conscious, loving and confused as we are is quite hard.

Anna's ongoing curiosity regarding her multiplicity of possible identities — her desire to explore them, to give expression to them without being judged — was behind her decision to attend the 2014 Burning Man festival in Nevada's Black Rock Desert. This is an annual event intended to meet the profoundly human need to participate in a meaningful community.

Her first Burning Man is something Anna will never forget. She arrived at the makeshift Black Rock City, the temporary site of the festival, on a chilly desert night. She was all by herself, scared and tired, after traveling half-way around the globe. She walked the dusty streets, hunched over under the weight of her backpack, which contained everything she thought she might need for a week in a desert.

The cold air was filled with a cacophony of electronic music and white dust, quickly covering my inappropriately clean clothes, skin and hair. People often ask me how it is possible to survive in the desert for a full week, covered in dust, without a proper shower. I believe it is an essential part of the experience. Wearing dust at Burning Man is like wearing a school uniform. The class, economic and social barriers vanish under that soft white layer.

As she walked past elaborately decorated, LED-illuminated camps, Anna watched people laughing and dancing. A young couple was having a heartfelt conversation on a pink furry couch hanging from a construction three meters above the ground. A group of friends wearing headlamps were erecting a huge dome that would provide shade during the hot desert days. She quickly noticed that there was a deep sense of unity and purpose in building the community. While you were part of it, you could shed the baggage, however briefly, of your everyday roles and responsibilities, and be whoever you wanted to be.

Similar to being alone in the timeless space of the Namib Desert, in this intricate human beehive, no one cares about my achievements, my status. I am not bound by my past or my hopes for the future. All that matters is what kind of human I am right now.

Anna was struck by the spirit of generosity within the community. What she witnessed was made more forceful by the scarcity of the desert, challenging her own preconceived judgements about giving and receiving. As she walked in the dark, searching for her camp, a stranger stopped her. "Hey, you can't walk here like this with no light, you may get hit by an art car. Here you go, take my fairy lights," he said, handing them over before disappearing into the night. Walking past another camp, she was called over and invited to have a drink. An art car, shaped like a pirate ship, then transported her to her own camp.

I'd heard about the gifting economy at Burning Man, but this first experience was compelling. You realize how commerce and marketing influence the ways we interact with others. In our daily lives, when someone approaches you unexpectedly, you immediately are suspicious that they are trying to sell you something. When someone offers you something for free, you know they will expect something back. It is a skill we have to relearn. To give and not expect anything in return. To receive fully, without feeling ashamed. And to trust that people are interacting with you because that is what they want to do. Can I meet the other person in honesty, expressing my truth, and, at the same time, make them feel accepted and seen, free of judgement?

Personal transformation is painful because at some level it involves loss, deep questioning, and the stripping away of things we are attached to. These can include beliefs about who we are. Even when we desperately want to change, most of us feel we cannot because we are stuck with fixed mental images of ourselves, with identities and roles — daughter, son, parent, spouse, doctor, manager — that are so familiar that it is hard to think of who we are beyond them. If our self-image is rigid, it becomes easy to ignore anything that contradicts it. Yet, it is essential that we reconcile and accept these contradictions.

In Anna's case, she needed both the experience of isolation and human insignificance amid the vast expanse of the desert, and the experience of community and human generosity, in order to explore her identity and come to a better understanding of who she is. Anna was willing to experiment, to try new things, and learn how they felt. She could discover different facets of her personality and examine the disjuncture between long-held beliefs and new actions. She learned that she was in the process of constant becoming, rather than a fixed entity. An individual of frequent contradiction and possibility, as are we all.

COCOON

*"I'm rightly tired of the pain I hear
and feel, boss. I'm tired of bein on the
road, lonely as a robin in the rain. Not
never havin no buddy to go on with or
tell me where we's comin from or goin to
or why. I'm tired of people bein ugly to
each other. It feels like pieces of glass in
my head. I'm tired of all the times I've
wanted to help and couldn't. I'm tired
of bein in the dark. Mostly it's the pain.
There's too much. If I could end it,
I would. But I can't."*

Stephen King, *The Green Mile*

If there is one thing most religions agree on, it is that life involves suffering. We are motivated by both the pursuit of pleasure and the avoidance of pain. Solving the problem of suffering takes a significant toll. We pop pills, avoid difficult conversations, run from conflict, turn up the central heating, bite our tongue — in effect, do anything to avoid or reduce the experience of discomfort or suffering. Too often, our culture encourages us to focus on the positive, on happiness, rather than confront and embrace our suffering. If we acknowledge the latter, it is to diminish it, making it less real by shrouding it in metaphor.

In her essay, *Illness as a Metaphor*, the writer Susan Sontag warns that, in addressing illness and disease, we should focus on the physical symptoms and treatment, resisting the temptation of the metaphorical, the conflation of bodily suffering with a psychological condition. Tuberculosis is not, as some Romantics believed, a signifier of repressed passion. Depression is not the harbinger of cancer's onset. There is a need to be wary of simplification and reduction.

With the right care, though, metaphor can be a powerful means through which we make sense of our lived experience. In *Metaphors We Live By*, the cognitive linguists George Lakoff and Mark Johnson argue that metaphors serve to structure our most basic understanding of what we experience. They shape our perceptions and actions at an almost subliminal level, woven into our everyday speech, conveying ideas that are received by others seemingly without pause for interpretation. To state that 'argument is war' or that 'time is money' is to convey a notion that another will easily understand without taking your words literally.

The evolutionary, metamorphic process via which a caterpillar becomes a butterfly is a well-known metaphor for personal transformation and the acquisition of a new sense of self. During the pupa stage, which occurs between the life of the caterpillar and that of the butterfly, the chrysalis is encased in a protective cocoon. This is the scene of much hidden work. Compared to the majesty and freedom of the creature that eventually emerges from the confines of the cocoon, the interim chrysalis stage is a dark and grim desolation. There is no movement, no rest, no hibernation. Instead, what once was a caterpillar sets about consuming itself in this self-imposed quarantine, producing an enzyme to decompose its own body as it becomes a mushy goo. Everything but the truly essential disappears, with a new form gradually emerging from the cells known as 'imaginal discs,' which feed on the protein of the former caterpillar. This is how a butterfly emerges: from dissolution, to new growth, to rebirth. Creative destruction is essential to a butterfly's life, just as it is to the seasons' cycles, evidenced by the repeated stripping away of old foliage in the fall and the budding of new leaves, flowers and fruit in the spring.

Similarly, for humans, When Things Fall Apart, we experience disintegration and collapse. The destruction of what we knew causes pain and can trigger a crisis of identity. It is perhaps no coincidence that the formal Greek word for butterfly is *psyche*, which also means *soul*. The transformation of our psyche, our way of operating in the world, begins with a disintegration, an undoing of what is no longer essential. The most common way that all of us experience this disintegration is through illness and death. Neuroscience professor Anil Seth, however, also draws parallels with the experience of general anesthesia:

You are basically dead for a bit, and it's so different than sleep. You're gone and then you're back again, and there's no sense of being at all. It's not just the post-anesthetic amnesia. You're not there. You can look at the brain and take a scan and see there's no electrical activity going on at all.

The patient, the mourner, journeys to a dark place and, if they return, they do so as a different person.

Ryan Pereira is a senior executive at a leading energy consulting firm. A confident and positive person, Ryan is no stranger to the effects of illness and grief. He has witnessed the rapid demise and death of both his brother Aron, the victim of an undiagnosed illness affecting his lungs in his early 30s, and his father, who succumbed to motor neurone disease (MND) shortly before his 70th birthday. Ryan has absorbed painful lessons: "While we are all born to die it is also true that every day we are dying. One minute we think we have it all, the next, we feel like we have nothing at all, at least for a period of time." He's all too familiar with how the death of a loved one can envelop you. "Grief," writes Daisy Johnson in her novel, *Sisters*, "is a house with no windows or doors and no way of telling the time."

Aron was ten years older than Ryan, a gentle giant that he looked up to, whose company he enjoyed, and whose advice he tended to follow. Aron was often the one there to lend a helping hand and to praise achievements as Ryan navigated his way through his teens before going on to university. Succumbing to illness, Aron's first symptom was breathlessness, the persistence of which resulted in his hospitalization and eventual transfer to a specialist respiratory unit.

As Aron declined, still the severity of the problem did not really hit us. It was upsetting seeing him sitting in hospital, but I always thought he would be out soon. One day, the medical staff advised us that he was going to be sedated. There were issues with his lungs that meant sedation would be the best course of action. I remember the last time I spoke to him. His advice was to go back to university, not to stay around the hospital, and to make sure that as soon as the exams finished, I partied hard until the end of the final term.

Once sedated, it was like Aron was in his own cocoon. Although not in a coma, and apparently aware of his family's presence, all conversation was now one-way, with Aron unresponsive. Ryan returned to university, heeding his brother's guidance by completing his exams and celebrating with friends. An early morning call from his father, though, summoned him back to the hospital.

Around the bed were more than 20 family members and close friends. We spent those last couple of hours there with him. My mum was stroking Aron's face like he was a baby, and repeatedly saying, "You were born a Prince, now you are a King." Until the minute that he breathed his last, we never lost hope, we kept the faith, but then, all of a sudden, we felt we lost it all. Numb. Pained. Gutted. Stunned. Devastated. Shocked.

People often console you by saying that "time is a healer." I never found this to be the case. However, I think time allows each of us to find ways to cope with how things have changed, and how things will never be the same again. In that sense, significant milestones that followed such as university graduation, success at work, getting married, buying a house, interactions and experiences with people more generally in life, always had that sense of pride, but also partial emptiness.

In the aftermath of Aron's death, and the overwhelming grief he and his family continued to experience, Ryan felt that his role was to stay strong. Nothing could take away the pain of loss. Nevertheless, Ryan found that grief was helping change his way of being, his perspective and values. "The archaeology of grief," states naturalist and research scholar Helen Macdonald in *H is for Hawk*, "is not ordered. It is more like earth under a spade, turning up things you had forgotten. Surprising things come to light: not simply memories, but states of mind, emotions, older ways of seeing the world." What in other circumstances might have seemed significant challenges and rites of passage for Ryan — leaving home, academic attainment, a first job — lacked significance in comparison with the enormity of a lost life.

It was not until six months into my first job that I finally started to put more effort in and then started to excel. My manager at the time asked me what I had changed. I gave him the honest answer: "When I started, given what had happened, work did not mean much to me." However, throughout life, I had always worked hard, and that soon came back. Yet, even today, almost seventeen years later, I am still able to maintain that perspective even in the most high-pressure scenarios.

Aron's death also impacted who Ryan had to be for others, including his younger sister Danielle. Whereas Aron had been patient and understanding with her, Ryan was often the opposite. He could never replace Aron, but eventually Ryan realized he didn't need to, he could just be himself and strive to be as good an older brother as possible. This applied to his role as a son too, especially after his father was diagnosed with MND. Gradually, his father lost weight, strength and the ability to fully function on his own. But, he continued to live life as fully as he could, spurred on by Ryan's mother, and reveling in the company of their wide community of friends, even attending a soccer match at Old Trafford shortly before his death.

When people used to ask about my dad's health, I told them the full truth. When I mentioned MND, the response of many was along the lines of "that is one of the cruelest diseases." I often reflected on this. While I agree that it is so hard to watch a strong father figure deteriorate, I can't help thinking of all those people who suffer from cancer, or malnutrition, or homelessness, or any of the other ways that fellow humans are put into situations of decline and ultimately death. Is it better to go quickly? Is it more difficult to go slowly? Who exactly are the ones who benefit if a person with an illness is actually able to live longer? We can't ignore the self-centeredness of the ones who will be left behind.

As we get older, it is natural that we see further declines among our friends and families and many more deaths. However, I always remind people that we live in a world with a massively growing population, and every loss of life is more than offset by the creation of a new, wonderful life.

After his father's death, Ryan's role subtly shifted again, as he sought to comfort his mother through her grief and give her the strength to carry on. He endeavored to serve as the foundations upon which family life could be rebuilt — for his mother and sister, as well as for his wife and their child, who was born prematurely three years later.

A good friend of mine once beautifully described life as a rental vehicle. Our bodies are like a rental vehicle made from the earth to return to the earth. The same is true for our loved ones.

Both my dad and brother cherished the journey that they had in their rental vehicles, over the inclines and the declines, and eventually in facing death. Since then, our journey through life as a family has had to follow new paths but continue to move forward day by day. I count myself lucky that I had a father and brother who were the drivers of my rental vehicle early in my life, steering me on the right path.

For me, life is about making memories, which are part of a greater journey. When your journey has been as fulfilled, as was the case for my dad and brother, then many stories can be told. These stories make up what my mum refers to as "that little dash," that hyphen between the date of your birth and the date of your final falling asleep. It is the precious time in between that is the most important.

Ryan's story shows us that illness and death, even though painful, can help create significant changes in who we are, in how we think about ourselves and our relationship to others, in our worldview, and in what we value. The deaths that Ryan grieved presented closures but also opportunities for new beginnings, a notion that became intimately entwined for him with the start of another story that commenced with the birth of his daughter. Ultimately, the collapse that had occurred within the cocoon of his family blossomed into something new and beautiful.

MOTHERHOOD

"In a sane society no woman would be left to struggle on her own with the huge transformation that is motherhood, when a single individual finds herself joined by an invisible umbilical cord to another person from whom she will never be separated, even by death."

Germaine Greer, *The Whole Woman*

Transformation comes in many forms and does not have to involve high drama, illness or near-death experiences. One of the most recurrent means of transformation we and many other species encounter is that of parenthood, especially motherhood. This manifests itself in the physical changes to the body, in the side effects of pregnancy, from morning sickness to weight gain to constant fatigue, and in the supply of nutrients, blood and oxygen to another human being. With parenthood — for both mothers and fathers — comes a momentous and generational shift in identity and responsibility, a new layering that now connects you to both your ancestors and your descendants, and with it a duty of care that you owe to both.

Maria Garcia Tejon is a psychologist and psychotherapist from the southern Spanish region of Andalucía, who now lives in Canterbury, England. Maria became a mother in December 2018 when her daughter Lucia was born. Maria found that the nine-month gestation of her child without any conscious effort on her part was the most surreal of bodily experiences.

Yet, what she had not prepared herself for was the fact that the transformation of her own body was only the first in many changes she would undergo as she adapted to motherhood.

Given her career ambitions, Maria believed that there was an enormous risk in stopping work while having a child. This had less to do with material insecurity and lack of income than with the notion of losing control of and power over her own life. Having moved to the UK in her 20s, Maria had spent several years studying intensely for her demanding profession, and had established a flourishing clinical practice both in London and Canterbury, with regular clients. She took immense pride in the fact that, having moved to a new country, she was her own boss, had a secure income, found her work fulfilling, and was able to help others. For Maria, although there was something joyful about becoming a mother, she feared the painful loss of her professional identity.

> I started feeling like I was melting away. There were parts of me were that were vanishing, and I was left in an unknown limbo, figuring out how I felt and who I was without my profession and my financial independence. These were two massive security blankets that I worked hard to consolidate.

On the day of Lucia's birth, within a matter of hours, Maria felt like she had become a different person. It's one thing to rationally imagine having a baby; it's a whole new world to discover that in your arms there now lies a human being who is completely dependent on you for survival. Maria recalls how she was struck by this profound realization: "I felt terrified. I froze. I was paralyzed by the overwhelming experience of it. I became a mother and just like that I ceased to exist as the person I was."

The foundations on which her sense of self had been built were suddenly snatched away. Maria felt that her career, social life, hobbies, everything, was now on hold. Looking in the mirror, she saw a stranger. She was no longer herself.

I remember stripping off in the bathroom, aching physically and emotionally, crying while having a shower. It was as if my body and my soul had been ripped apart. I felt so alien. For weeks, I could not look at my naked body in the mirror nor touch my episiotomy.

Not only did Maria feel cut off from her previous identity, but she also found it difficult to relate to her husband. She felt too exhausted and overwhelmed by her new identity and responsibilities as a mother.

I was unable to connect with him, mainly because I couldn't connect with myself. In less than a day we drifted apart, our configuration changed, we were different people, but we didn't know it at the time. We had to find ourselves again in order to reconnect with each other, which is still a trial-and-error process. The tension, misunderstandings and disagreements between us can be continuous.

This distancing and externalizing of oneself is a signature of When Things Fall Apart. Our understanding of self has to change, has to broaden and evolve, so that a new identity can emerge.

Meanwhile, Maria became completely immersed in her newborn child. Carrying her daughter in her arms was for her an experience of profuse love and vulnerability. What had been within her, a part of her for nine months, was now outside her own body. In some sense, this new life was no longer hers, yet it still demanded her devotion and protection.

I was getting to know her, and vice versa. Like a snake, I felt I had just shed my skin. I felt see-through, skinless; like my organs were on show, like wearing my heart on a necklace outside of my body.

In Western cultures, each person tends to think of themself as an independent entity in which self-determination and autonomy are highly valued. Now, though, Maria found the hardest part of her mothering journey was the forceful surrender of control.

The accomplishment of basic tasks, and the sense of self-worth that came with them — like housework, cooking and shopping — felt beyond Maria as she adapted to caring for the needs of her newborn baby. She became increasingly discomforted by her own reliance on her partner, entrusting more and more things to him that she now felt unable to do, however willing she may have been. A visit from members of her Spanish family was a source of both emotional comfort and valuable practical help.

Three weeks after Lucia's birth, Maria's husband had to return to work and her family also departed for Spain. Maria pushed herself to go out with the baby but continued to struggle. Getting both herself and the baby ready to leave the house took so long that she found she couldn't make it anywhere on time. She felt saddened by her own inadequacy, and almost invisible when meeting others who displayed their excitement about seeing the baby but failed to ask how she was.

> My independence, the freedom before becoming a mother was over. I grieved my old carefree life.
>
> Not only was I lost in myself, but the world around me confirmed it. My social circle changed drastically. Most of my friends don't have children. Some of them are still around and make an effort to stay in touch. Many of them I don't see anymore. There were many plans for social activities where I could not join in with a baby. So, I had to find new friends, fellow mums with children of similar ages.

It took Maria a year to adjust to this new way of being and to assimilate the identity of motherhood. "One year into motherhood I had been adding new layers to my core, slowly finding out who I am, getting to know myself, every so often crashing into this not-being void."

There were days filled with excitement and potentiality. Maria gradually developed a new love for her body, which came as an unexpected blessing as she had always struggled with her body image. She spoke with palpable pride: "I feel like a witch: what my body is capable of is miraculous."

Then there were days that were just crash and burn. When her old competent self seemed so far away from her. Maria coped by creating small pockets of autonomy, with a degree of control over what she as thinking or doing. As she adapted to the bigger identity change that motherhood entailed, she took small steps with little experiments. One of these involved changing her hairstyle, which she did five times over the course of that first year.

What Maria discovered was that she was not alone as a new mother experiencing the loss of self. Talking to other mothers about their conflicting feelings and struggles, she realized that it was a common phenomenon. Eventually, she learned it had a name: *matrescence*, for 'the process of becoming a mother.' This is an essential transitional period that is often compared to adolescence for its transformative effects. Maria was shocked that she and other mothers she met had known nothing about it. They had been given no forewarning of the psychological aspects of the changes to come, which would have helped them prepare, and diminish their feelings of isolation, loneliness and shame.

Maria decided to start a project called Unfiltered Motherhood. Her mission was to normalize matrescence and make it visible, creating a community of women who could talk honestly about motherhood. She organized matrescence workshops for expectant couples, including same-sex couples and single mothers, helping them prepare for and understand their experiences. For Maria, motherhood represented a total transformation of her being, transcending the narrow identity she had before.

I went through a big identity shift, slowly and unexpectedly stripping off layers of myself. What I understood later is that when I birthed my daughter, I also gave birth to myself.

LEADERSHIP

"And where we had thought to find an abomination, we shall find a god; where we had thought to slay another, we shall slay ourselves; where we had thought to travel outward, we shall come to the center of our own existence; where we had thought to be alone, we shall be with all the world."

Joseph Campbell, *The Hero with a Thousand Faces*

Another way people experience an identity shift is when they assume management or leadership responsibilities in the workplace. They are no longer an individual contributor, but now represent something bigger, enabling, facilitating and caring for others. This shift becomes even more significant when they move from leading a team to leading a function to leading an entire organization. This doesn't simply involve a different *style* of leadership, but a transitional shift in how they view themselves and who they are for others.

When it comes to educating and leading teams, Lynne Sedgmore is a true maven. She gets to the heart of organizational ineffectiveness while nurturing and supporting the people she works with. A mother, grandmother and avid practitioner of meditation, Lynne has traveled a great deal through her leadership journey. She has been a base grade lecturer, a college principal responsible for 30,000 higher education students, and the CEO of the Center for Excellence in Leadership (CEL).

CHAPTER 3. WHEN THINGS FALL APART

Throughout her career, Lynne worked hard and usually felt on top of things. She consistently overachieved, surpassing the targets she had been given, co-creating high-performance teams that generated work of the highest quality, regardless of ever-decreasing resources and government funding. Lynne savored every minute of the cut and thrust of her challenges and rose to meet them on every occasion. Nevertheless, she found the transition to the chief executive role at CEL was of another order entirely. The unstoppable force that Lynne was had finally met an immovable object.

This transition was directly tied to Lynne's sense of leadership identity. She knew she had a lot of charisma and leadership skills — visioning, influencing, rallying, empowering people, making things happen. Yet, none of those skills seemed to help her in the new context in which she now found herself. As the former CEO of Girl Scouts of the USA, Frances Hesselbein, once observed:

Leadership is much less about what you do, and much more about who you are. If you view leadership as a bag of manipulative tricks or charismatic behaviors to advance your own personal interest, then people have every right to be cynical.

But if your leadership flows first and foremost from inner character and integrity of ambition, then you can justly ask people to lend themselves to your organization and its mission.

Indeed, what made this transition particularly challenging for Lynne was that it was not about adding *more* to her bag of tricks, but rather the *stripping away* of what was no longer necessary and the discovery of inner character and identity she had not previously been aware of. But how do you discern what to hold on to and what to let go off while taking on challenging new responsibilities? Intuitively, Lynne knew that letting go of her previous way of leading was important, not just for her but for the success of CEL, too.

> I had such close identification with my role as a college leader that to move out of a tight-knit local college into a distributed organization was a hugely disruptive experience, both internally and externally. I desperately missed the deep trust and loyalty that I shared with my previous staff and senior management team.

Lynne found that she had moved from an organizational environment characterized by unity and strong teamwork, with high levels of trust, delegation and performance, to a decentralized organization that was fragmented and disconnected. This required that she shift her leadership style from one founded on 'mothering' to one that entailed stewardship. Lynne would have to undergo a makeover of approach, intensity and, most fundamental of all, identity.

In the beginning, Lynne threw herself into this challenge with everything she had. Usually, such an undertaking would have energized her, but she quickly learned that that was not the case on this occasion. The more she focused on doing, the more she became exhausted and confused. It was as if everything she put in mysteriously disappeared into an organizational black hole.

Lynne sought support, in the shape of senior executive coach Simon Western, as she set aside time to explore and come to terms with the complex process of unraveling that she was experiencing, both as a leader and as a person.

> In the coaching sessions, I began to feel how fearful, protective and defensive I was becoming. My emotional intelligence was low, my self-worth had hit rock bottom, and I had feelings of anger, guilt and blame.

Lynne's inner struggle was a treacherous, maze-like path of self-inquiry, littered with misleading doorways and cul-de-sacs. When you are desperately stuck, any doorway carries the potential of being the gateway to heaven. But, the rush to pass through it can entrap you even further. As you flail around, struggling to get back on the 'right' path, you begin to assign blame, either to yourself or those who are meant to help you. You fall into the trap of activity and busyness, rushing to find and implement solutions to challenges, rather than pausing and reflecting.

The real task for Lynne was to set aside the notion of the leader as a heroic and charismatic figure, the one with a plan, a quick fix, who gets things done. In order to arrive at a solution, she would first have to work with and through the anxiety, confusion and Not Knowing she was experiencing. She could neither repress nor bulldoze her way out of it, but would have to stay within this discomforting state with courage and humility. To do otherwise would exacerbate the fragmentation and disconnection that was affecting CEL.

What made it especially painful for Lynne was that during this stressful time, it seemed like an all-or-nothing situation. For Lynne, despite her previous coaching and meditation experiences, 'letting go' felt like she would be permanently throwing away an essential part of her identity. Her work with Simon necessitated that, like surgeons, they go deep, removing blockages in this monumental, seemingly unified edifice known as a 'self.'

The question was not only a practical one of how to find the best solution to CEL's organizational and leadership problems, but also a deeply personal and metaphysical one about giving life to a new way of being. When it comes to our sense of self, the gap between what is no longer working and what is yet to emerge can seem too vast to fully comprehend.

I felt that I had moved from organizational unity and connectedness to fragmentation and disconnection, mirrored in my inner life by the final stages of a shift from a personalized sacred object to the non-conceptual and the void.

Time seemed to disappear as the experience was *so* deep and visceral. My awareness kept expanding, I felt totally unified, within and without. The boundaries between myself and all around me dissolved and my whole being expanded into spaciousness. I felt fully awake and present, completely here now, without any preconceptions or expectations — just the truth of what is here. Everything I knew about leadership became a construct, an invention in my mind — as did everything I had ever known — all dissolving into a knowing that everything arises out of nothing, I have no self, there is only quietness, stillness, formlessness and emptiness at the core of everything, including me.

I felt liberated, still and peaceful. I also felt full of possibilities, a sense of pure unfolding, emerging out of the stillness — bigger, better and more powerful than anything my conscious mind could imagine. All need for control vanished within the overwhelming sense of trust, which transfused my whole body. I was unlimited and expansive with total acceptance of things as they are, being totally here now, non-attached to things. Everything, absolutely everything, was and would be well.

The inner confusion and Not Knowing that Lynne had initially thought of as obstacles to be overcome ultimately served as catalysts, helping to generate her shift in perspective, informing how she experienced who she was and could be as a leader. In that moment of encountering the void, she experienced a loss of all constructs, a total emptiness. Yet, at the same time, there was fullness, completeness, stillness and deep inner peace.

"While feeling liberated," she reflected, "I was also concerned that if I let go into this sense of emptiness, I would not be able to continue in my professional work." Lynne found herself at the threshold of identity transformation, in a liminal space, where her new identity was not yet knowable. She would need to learn how to adapt to this post-void experience.

GLIMPSE

"The opposite of a glance... is a glimpse: because in a glance, we see only for a second, and in a glimpse, the object shows itself only for a second."

James Elkins, *The Object Stares Back: On the Nature of Seeing*

When Things Fall Apart is not always a frightening experience. But, it can occur instantaneously, unexpectedly, and without any invitation.

Jayaraja has been a meditation and mindfulness teacher and practitioner for nearly 30 years. He is now leading a team renovating Alfoxton Park House, a former residence of the poet William Wordsworth in Somerset, England. Most years, during the Christmas and the New Year period, Jayaraja takes time off for a solitary retreat for several weeks.

My favorite place is a Buddhist retreat center in the mountains above Alicante on the Costa Blanca. It is remote, quiet and beautiful, with four solitary venues spread around the mountain valley. Like each of the huts it is basic: a bed, a wood-burning stove, a small gas cooker, a single cold tap, a few pots and pans, a stock of food, and space for a shrine. It is not so deep in the forest and so has expansive views to the south and west and gets more of the winter sun. Often, I'll meditate out on the roof or do walking meditation. There is plenty of sitting doing nothing but enjoying the sights and sounds and watching my mind.

During his retreats, Jayaraja often found that the temperature would drop sharply at night, but that it could be comfortably warm, even sunny, in the day. As he was coming to the end of one retreat, Jayaraja sat outside in the afternoon sun reflecting on his time, how fortunate he was to have enjoyed such beautiful weather, and how that had contributed to the overall experience. He then recalled the previous year's retreat, which had been in the same venue at around the same time.

It, too, had been a great experience, but the weather had been very different. The mountains had been enveloped by clouds for the entire retreat and he had spent much more time indoors, sitting watching the clouds through the big window or meditating. He remembered also how much he'd enjoyed his time then and, like now, how he had felt blessed by the weather that had contributed so much to his retreat.

The same location, the same pleasure, and yet so different, shaped by the weather. It was during this moment of reflection and remembering the past and present that Jayaraja experienced a glimpse, an unexpected insight. It would change his understanding of who he was.

I was suddenly struck by how much my experience of life is shaped by things that I consider as external to me, and how deeply they impact me. More deeply still, I realized that there is no me, that these events impact but a flow of experience. The experience of me alone in the mountains in a small hut, includes the weather. The weather influences what I might choose to do or not do. The idea of a fixed solid self, a 'me,' that these things happen to, seemed ridiculous and I burst out laughing. There is no me, there is a multitude of relationships, a flow of events and conditions, which the weather is a part of. There is no me that these events happen to. There is an experience which I try and make sense of by having a sense of self. Usually, this takes the form of a story or commentary running in my head to help me make sense of this flow. However, as I sat and looked at the flow of my mind and thoughts it seemed obvious that there was no me just a flow of life of which I am part of but from which I am definitely not separate.

CHAPTER 3. WHEN THINGS FALL APART

Jayaraja returned from the retreat quite euphoric for some weeks, alive to this flow, his mind able to see the empty nature of things and events. Over time, the experience faded, though the ideas still informed his thinking and his desire to practice and live with a sense of connection and sensitivity to all of life.

The Dalai Lama arrived at a similar conclusion 35 years ago. In his book, *How to See Yourself As You Really Are*, he describes reading a passage about how in dim light a coil of rope can resemble a snake. This, though, remains a concept, a construct of the human imagination. At no point does the rope actually metamorphose into a snake; concept and reality only connect in the observer's own mind. The Dalai Lama glimpsed a fundamental truth, realizing that the same line of thought could be applied to the notion of *I*. The idea of separation suggested by the concept of *I* was an illusion.

Suddenly, it was as if lightning moved through my chest. I was so awestruck that, over the next few weeks, whenever I saw people, they seemed like a magician's illusions in that they appeared to inherently exist but I knew that they actually did not.

While, at the time, he did not fully grasp the magnitude of his 'aha moment,' it signaled a burgeoning revelation for him. Emotions, especially destructive emotions, can be stopped simply by challenging the very existence of 'I.'

Momentary glimpses, such as those enjoyed by the Dalai Lama and Jayaraja — almost every day in their mundanity and lack of drama — are probably the most common way that Things Fall Apart for many of us. However temporarily, our sense of separation is forgotten. Immersed in an activity, thoroughly engaged in the moment, in awe of natural phenomena, caught up in creative flow, we lose awareness of ourselves as distinct and separate beings inhabiting time and space.

Steven: Throughout my life, I've had a sense of being separate and often have struggled with loneliness and a feeling of disconnection. It's probably why I began my professional career in the field of diversity and inclusion, allowing me to explore and try to reconcile this tension. Yet, when I reflect back, there have been many moments, many 'glimpses,' in which I have experienced a deep sense of unity and the loss of any sense of separation.

One of these glimpses occurred when I was holidaying with a friend on the Isle of Mull in Scotland. We had gone camping and hiked up a mountain overlooking the white beach and crystal-blue sea. As I sat on a warm rock, feeling the breeze on my face, all sense of separation seemed to drop away. Colors became more vivid. It was if there was only experience but no 'experiencer.' There was a lack of mental chatter, replaced instead by the kind of stillness that is sometimes found on the surface of a lake or pond. The glimpse lasted a few brief moments, but its effects remain with me today, decades later.

Glimpses can cause significant transformations in how people view the world. From a young age, philosopher and conservationist Aldo Leopold was a keen outdoorsman, studying wildlife and hunting with his father and brother. After graduating from Yale, Leopold became an assistant supervisor for the US Forestry Service in Arizona's Apache National Forest, a role that involved protecting livestock from predators, such as bears, wolves and mountain lions. When, in fulfillment of his duties, Leopold shot a wolf and her cubs, it was his glimpse of the "fierce green fire dying in her eyes" that had a profound effect on him.

In *A Sand County Almanac*, Leopold describes how this brief glimpse shifted the path he followed from *ego*-centrism to *eco*-centrism. In the chapter titled 'Think Like a Mountain,' he argues that killing a predator can have a huge impact on an entire ecosystem. By removing one part of a system, there is a devastating impact on the whole. With the demise of the wolves came the rapid expansion of deer and elk herds, which led to overgrazing and the erosion of plant life, producing an arid landscape, starvation and eventual population collapse. These insights prompted Leopold to argue for the preservation of wilderness and open spaces.

The influence of Leopold's work would extend into national regeneration policy. In the mid-1990s, the reintroduction of a small number of grey wolves in Yellowstone National Park was an immediate success story, with a thriving pack helping to restore the park's ecosystem, as well as attracting curious visitors. More widely, Leopold's endeavors to broaden ethical concerns about the natural world, with a greater sensitivity to the non-human, inspired environmental activists around the globe. Leopold encouraged us to go beyond self-interest, developing an ecological conscience that places us within and not separate from a biotic community, calling into question our expedient tendency to extract and exploit.

From one man's glimpse was born a global wilderness conservation movement that, today, continues to challenge notions of separation and humankind's interdependence with its environment.

CHAPTER 4

RESISTING
FALLING
APART

HUNGRY GHOST

"Life is a process of becoming,
a combination of states we have
to go through. Where people
fail is that they wish to elect
a state and remain in it.
This is a kind of death."

Anaïs Nin, *D. H. Lawrence: An Unprofessional Study*

As life involves continual change, it takes extreme effort to remain intact and untouched. In attempting to harden ourselves, occasionally through callousness and insensitivity, we create a barrier that helps protect us from pain, but also prevents us from experiencing joy. Eventually, though, there are experiences and encounters that pierce through this protective armor. As a result, the many layers of who we think we are and what we think is important can begin to fall away.

What is left behind is an emptiness, a disorienting and uncomfortable void. As Aristotle is said to have postulated, "Nature abhors a vacuum." So, we start to replace what was lost, to fill in the space, with other things, with objectives and goals, knowledge, money, self-improvement projects, work, hobbies, artefacts, fame, beauty, authority, relationships. As psychologist Robert Gunn writes in *Journey to Emptiness*:

The experience of not having peace, comfort and pleasure is against every natural impulse of body and mind. Every bit of common sense says it's better to have something good than not to have it, whether that is a relationship, identity, status, power.

Steven: While training as a therapist I had to undergo therapy myself. I discussed with my therapist the feeling of emptiness that I was experiencing. I pictured a black hole, a large void, in the center of my body. While I was not melancholic, I always carried this idea of something missing inside me. No matter what momentary happiness I had in life, it was always there, like a permanent fixture. I described myself as a 'hungry ghost,' walking the streets of London. Hungry because I could never be fulfilled and was always seeking ways to fill the emptiness through personal development, achievement, entertainment and chocolate!

My therapist said something very powerful to me: "Could you learn to live with this emptiness?" This was not about filling the void or removing the constant sensation of emptiness, but about recognizing that it was a part of me. This had a profound impact on me. I would notice that when I felt empty, I didn't need to act to remove the experience but instead I learned to let it be and, over time, to treat it like a traveling companion, an old friend.

Rather than face emptiness, many will settle for the less than satisfactory, for the devil they know. Some will even choose pain over the void, with one series of studies demonstrating how participants would rather self-administer electric shocks than remain in silence with their own thoughts and no other stimuli. There is a fear of the cascading effect of the void, captured by Italo Calvino in his novel, *If on a Winter's Night a Traveler*: "Every void continues in the void, every gap, even a short one, opens in to another gap, every chasm empties into the infinite abyss."

Yet, until we develop a bolder understanding of who we really are, the pursuit of objects and desires takes us down the path of destination addiction, providing little more than minor distractions from the void. As Estragon observes in Samuel Beckett's *Waiting for Godot*, "There's no lack of void." It is necessary to accept and embrace its emptiness before we can develop a true sense of self.

When Things Fall Apart, it is like a shock to our usual pattern of conditioned selfhood. These shocks can wake us up to a different way of being, moving us beyond notions of separation and dysfunction. Too often, however, our response to shocks is to minimize their significance, to brush them aside, to ignore them, passing up the opportunity for change.

In this chapter, we will look at several ways in which we attempt to resist the process of falling apart, attempting to maintain intact our extant sense of self. By becoming aware of them, we have the opportunity to embrace transformation with less resistance, and less suffering.

EMBRACE

EMPTINESS

NOT SEEING

"We can be blind to the obvious, and we are also blind to our blindness."

Daniel Kahneman, *Thinking, Fast and Slow*

Denial, at its core, is a turning away from our immediate experience. It is holding onto a story of how we have always been and how things have always worked, even if that story is contradicted by present evidence or new context. Somatically, it can show up as a rigidness in our body posture. Inflexibility, a fixed or closed stance, signals that we are not open to anything new. Our inability, unwillingness, or denial is captured in the phrases people use to describe this blinkered behavior:

She buried her head in the sand
He had his head in the clouds
They refused to address the situation directly at hand

There are many other expressions we use to suggest the closing off of the mind:

Nothing new
Same old, same old
Keep your head down and play it safe
Business as usual
It has always been that way
He is never on time
You are always like that
That has nothing to do with me
That is not happening

We see only what we want to see, reinforcing our confirmation bias. Data that does not validate our point of view is either not seen, dismissed, brushed over, or explained away. An example of this is what entrepreneur Eli Pariser describes as the "filter bubble." In his book of the same name, Pariser demonstrates how algorithms feed us "news stories" on the web and social media that are determined by our user history — our past online searches. They are automatically curated to resonate with our beliefs and political, religious, economic and other interests. This means that while two different people may enter the same term into a search engine like Google — 'British Petroleum,' for example — one of them will receive results relating to investment opportunities and share prices, while the other will see stories about oil spills and pollution.

The consequences of this filtering are profound: homogenization, stereotyping, ignorance, polarization, *othering*. Our attention is captured by advertisers, lobbyists and other interested parties who have paid for it, as witnessed by the controversies surrounding Facebook data and targeted advertising in the 2016 campaigns for both Brexit and the US presidential election. Over time, we become locked into automated but invisible echo chambers that defend against cognitive dissonance. Our point of view is protected to such an extent that we lose the ability to see the world from multiple perspectives. We become so blinkered that we fail to respond to contextual shifts that require us to engage with other people and our environment in new ways. Difference is denied by the algorithms that influence and ensnare us. As filtering persists, societal division becomes inevitable.

In 2012, Facebook and Cornell University conducted an experiment, manipulating the newsfeeds of nearly 700,000 of the social media platform's users. Over the course of a week, some users were given access to content with a higher-than-average amount of happy and positive stories and words, while others were served material containing sad and negative stories and words. A 2014 analysis of the outcome was published in *Proceedings of the National Academy of Sciences*. It demonstrated that those exposed to positive newsfeeds later went on to post more positive status updates themselves, while the reverse was true of those who were fed negative stories and words, with their own posts and updates tending to be negative, too. Setting aside the ethical furor that surrounded publication of the study, in particular in relation to the issue of informed consent, the key finding concerned the significant issue of 'emotional contagion' and how emotions, feelings and behavior can be influenced without our awareness.

This unwitting withdrawal from other perspectives can also be self-administered. We do not have to depend on third parties to blind us to what does not conform to our worldview. As entrepreneur Margaret Heffernan explores in her book on the phenomenon, *Willful Blindness*, this somewhat counterintuitive concept establishes that you are responsible by law "for something you could have known, and should have known yet instead *strove not to see*." What's unsettling about the idea is that it doesn't matter whether the avoidance of truth is conscious or not. Heffernan argues that this basic mechanism of keeping ourselves in the dark plays out in almost every aspect of life.

> We all want to feel that we have made our own choices, that they weren't predictable, that we aren't so vain as to choose ourselves, and that we are freer spirits, with a broader, more eclectic range of taste... We don't like to feel that we're blind to the allure of those who are not like us; we don't like to see how trapped we are inside our own identity.

The self wants to maintain a coherent worldview, especially the story about itself as this separate entity, and with relatively unchanging traits. It does so because the cognitive and emotional load of trying to hold in mind opposing views of who we think we are seems too much. As such, we pick sides. *Me* and *not-me*, *us* and *not-us*. You can tell how tightly held the story of who we are, and its associated views, really is by how painful it feels when your views are challenged, especially around identity. The more tightly held the story, the more defensive we can be.

As an example, many people think of debate as a wrestling match in which each participant will try to beat down the other person's point of view. The winner's opinion will prevail, while the loser will be forced to change their mind as a result of their opponent's evidence-based logic and reason. In fact, the reverse almost always holds true, for it is rarely about whose facts are more accurate. This is referred to as "the backfire effect" in David McRaney's book, *You Are Now Less Dumb*.

When you start to pull out facts and figures, hyperlinks and quotes, you are actually making the opponent feel even surer of his position than before you started the debate. As he matches your fervor, the same thing happens in your skull.

The backfire effect pushes both sides deeper into their original beliefs. Maybe we start out being too sure of our position, but when forced to defend it we become surer still. Without us being aware, our opinion becomes more rigid, buttressed by ideology and self-image, which makes it even less amenable to change.

Willful blindness, filter bubbles and the tendency to ignore things that don't fit with our worldview aren't fatal flaws. Rather, they reflect a deeply wired human tendency designed to serve a positive purpose. The capacity to quickly and accurately identify if someone is friend or foe has always been essential to survival, as well as to the experience of belonging, affinity and kinship. Our confidence in who we are gives us an 'ego identity' that is able to form attachments, make decisions and navigate relationships in a complex world. Yet, our sense of self, beliefs, opinions and values are not necessarily things we have chosen, but instead have been formed over time, shaped actively by others.

Heffernan uses a metaphor to describe how our sense of self is subject to a pattern of development derived from countless small interactions over time:

Imagine the gradual formation of a riverbed. The initial flow of water might be completely random — there are no preferred routes in the beginning. But once a creek is formed, water is more likely to follow this newly created path of least resistance. As the water continues, the creek deepens and a river develops.

In stable settings, relying on the familiar patterns of self — habits, beliefs, ways of being — is useful. We don't have to spend energy trying to figure out how to act, think or relate, so that they can be channeled to predetermined goals. The world, however, is far from stable. It never has been. As we saw with Lynne's story on leadership in the previous chapter, problems arise not because things inevitably fall apart, but because we attempt to hold onto an old identity, resisting the need to shift our sense of self.

When we really *see* something, when we do not avert our gaze from the uncomfortable and unfamiliar, we are able to engage, to connect, with what is happening rather than with our fantasies, projections or judgements. This gaze, more penetrating than the glimpses we encountered at the end of Chapter 3, can be enough for a deep transformation to occur.

Rather than Not Seeing, it is preferable to actively seek out those who have different opinions than ours. Not necessarily for purposes of validation or consensus, but as a means of engagement, dialogue, curiosity and knowledge exchange. It is a way of acknowledging that that there is an undiscovered universe beyond our own ecosystem. In 'The Crack-up,' a 1936 essay that appeared in *Esquire*, F. Scott Fitzgerald observed, "The test of a first-rate intelligence is the ability to hold two opposed ideas in the mind at the same time, and still retain the ability to function." We can work on developing the capacity to hold conflicting and contradictory opinions within ourselves, and to accept that not everything is clearly black or white, embracing paradox.

Rather than aiming to always be right, we can exercise scientific curiosity about our knowledge and beliefs, allowing the glimmer of doubt, testing out hypotheses, experimenting and assimilating new truths, until they, too, are brought into question. As novelist and essayist Siri Hustvedt argues in *Living, Thinking, Looking*:

> Losing perspective is an intellectual virtue because it requires mourning, confusion, reorientation, and new thoughts. Without it, knowledge slogs along in its various narrow grooves, but there will be no leaps, because the thinner my perspective, the more likely it is for me to accept the preordained codes of a discipline as inviolable truths. A willingness to lose perspective means an openness to *others* who are guided by a set of unfamiliar propositions.

We have to recognize how the context of our culture, upbringing, education, communities and filters shape our convictions, and that the same applies to anyone with whom we interact. In every discussion, each participant carries with them this contextual baggage. In each encounter, the curious, the open-minded, can both challenge and learn, can influence others and, in turn, be infected by their ideas.

Neuroscience has demonstrated how our minds are not fixed, but are plastic and malleable. We all have the ability to *see* if we choose to do so. By opening our minds, looking and questioning, we continue to evolve, to discover new ways of being.

When we dare to face the cruel social and ecological realities we have been accustomed to, courage is born and powers within us are liberated to reimagine and even, perhaps one day, rebuild a world.

Do not look away. Do not avert your gaze. Do not turn aside.

~ ***Joanna Macy***, *'Entering the Bardo'*

NOT FEELING

*"The self is a patchwork of the felt
and the unfelt, of presences and absences,
of navigable channels around the
walled-off numbnesses. "*

Rebecca Solnit, *The Faraway Nearby*

In Aldous Huxley's dystopian novel, *Brave New World*, citizens
can avoid the experience of unpleasant feelings by taking the
drug soma in tablet form. It's something "to give you a holiday
from the facts." Soma is there "to calm your anger, to reconcile
you to your enemies, to make you patient and long-suffering."
In effect, it is an opiate that is administered to constrain citizens
with 'happiness,' preventing rebellion and maintaining the
societal status quo. Dulling our senses, seeking the insensibility
of Pink Floyd's protagonist in their song 'Comfortably Numb,'
has a similar effect. This is life in limbo, in the state of general
anesthesia described by neuroscientist Anil Seth in Chapter 3.
Narcotics, alcohol, comfort-eating, even spirituality, all offer
temporary escapes from or substitutes for feelings.

Where Not Seeing is related to closed minds, self-centeredness,
clinging onto an identity, and failure to appreciate our interconnection with the broader environment, Not Feeling is about
how we close off the heart, avoiding the feelings that arise
When Things Fall Apart.

The psychotherapist and teacher John Prendergast refers to
"The Deep Heart," drawing parallels between our sense of self
and our capacity to feel. The latter can range from numbness
to fine attunement, while our sense of self varies from extreme

constriction and exclusion to infinite expansion and inclusion. When we are caught up in overwhelming emotions, we will endure a sharp split within ourselves, heightened by our separation from others. Prendergast elaborates: "If this state becomes chronic, we will feel that we are lacking or flawed in an uncaring or hostile universe." As we become increasingly alienated and cynical, the feeling of separation deepens the more we withdraw from others and isolate ourselves.

Traditionally, since the advent of industrialization, there was a workplace expectation that the individual would enforce a separation within themselves, between the professional and the private. In the factory and, increasingly, in knowledge work, the emphasis was on logic, reason, rationality and deep specialism in a single function. *Homo economicus* was not permitted to display emotion. This was the preserve of the private domain and, in an era of misogyny and gender stereotyping, of 'women's work.' In recent decades, however, as science journalist Daniel Goleman and others have raised awareness of the importance of emotional intelligence — and as employers have learned that employee engagement is a significant motivator for job satisfaction, employee retention and business performance — feelings have become something to be leveraged rather than excluded from the workplace.

Sadly, as organizations have begun to treat feelings as a form of capital, as a competitive advantage, their employees have become subject to both physical *and* emotional labor, with all the draining effects that entails. All of a sudden, happiness and smiles have been rendered data to be collected, to be evaluated, informing performance and pay in some service industries. Work, therefore, demands artifice, enforcing disconnection from our true feelings. And, when you're required to perform all the time, constantly playing the role of smiling host, burnout is inevitable. In fact, a 2011 study involving over 27,000 participants found that such depersonalizing emotional labor was directly linked to exhaustion and strain.

The separate self protects itself from overwhelming experiences by shutting down feelings and exercising caution about what is shared of ourselves, and with whom. We learn from a young age that if we cry, expressing emotions or discontent, other people will respond in a certain way. We learn that some emotions are welcome, while others are not. As Marc Brackett, the director of the Yale Center for Emotional intelligence and author of *Permission to Feel*, explains, the phrase 'I'm fine' becomes a response of expediency when people ask how you are feeling. It moves the conversation on, at work and in more social interactions, and it hides whatever vulnerabilities we may be experiencing at that moment in time.

As such, even though we may yearn for connection, when it comes to opening up, we are often clumsy, becoming flustered or lost for words. We lack a vocabulary to articulate the complexity of what is happening in our hearts. Rather than express our feelings or our vulnerability, we tend to avoid, deflect, internalize or project. We become disconnected in conversation, allowing our minds to wander from the matter under discussion, waiting to speak rather than listening to what is being said. In so doing, we do not allow for proper engagement, for the togetherness of community. We close down opportunities for the transformative power of genuine contact.

Opening up our hearts almost always has to do with slowing down, pausing, and focusing on what is happening in our own bodies and in our interactions with others. This is a sensing rather than a sense-making process. The experience is as much embodied as it is cognitive, with an emphasis on feelings rather than rationality. When Things Fall Apart, not only are we forced to reconnect with ourselves, but we often establish a more authentic connection with other people. Barriers and masks fall away. As Hustvedt suggests, "We become ourselves through others, and the self is a porous thing, not a sealed container."

While researching his book, *The Righteous Mind*, the psychologist Jonathan Haidt forced himself to watch Fox News, the top TV channel for American conservatives. Haidt was motivated by his increasing concern over the polarization in the political landscape, both in the United States and around the world. By exposing himself to Fox and the political viewpoint that channel espouses, he was confronting his own beliefs, what he stood for as a secular liberal, and his way of being. Not only was this a masochistic experience, but initially Haidt found himself responding viscerally to those who held views so diametrically opposed to his own. What in theory should have been something that could have been resolved through civilized debate in practice triggered an emotive, almost irrational, upwelling of anger. There was something tribal, protective and biologically rooted in how Haidt found himself reacting. It brought to the fore an aspect of his identity — one of "righteous anger" — that had been forged in the 1980s, during the Reagan–Bush era, but kept in check in the intervening years.

Haidt knew that in order to gain greater understanding of the people he was watching and listening to on Fox, he would have to become more open in both heart and mind to their own situations. He could not allow his anger to close down an opportunity for connection. By allowing himself to feel and experience as another person, to approach the world as they did, he gradually began to appreciate the logic of the arguments they made, realizing that, at times, they were attuned to things he had not previously considered. He found himself freed from the psychological shackles that anger had placed on him.

It felt good to be released from partisan anger. And once I was no longer angry, I was no longer committed to reaching the conclusion that righteous anger demands: we are right, they are wrong. I was able to explore new moral matrices, each one supported by its own intellectual traditions. It felt like a kind of awakening.

Haidt could experience that anger fully, but not totally identify with it. He no longer allowed his anger to characterize who he was. By acknowledging it, rather than repressing it, he had come to terms with it, enabling space not only for other aspects of his personality, but for richer engagement and interaction with other people who were not like him.

Opening our hearts enables us to learn the language of our senses again. We can *feel* anger, but not define ourselves as *being* angry. We can embrace the risk of vulnerability, of sitting with our feelings, our emotions, and being able to share them with others. We can listen to and hear the opinions of others, permitting ourselves, however temporarily, to experience the world as they do. We can open ourselves equally to the joys and pains they feel.

One of the most effective methods Haidt developed for exposure to different worldviews was sharing meals with people with whom he instinctively did not agree, because their beliefs contradicted his own biases. He discovered that breaking bread with them, simply being with them, as fellow humans full of life, was a powerful challenge to all his preconceptions. "Sharing food," he observed, "is a very visceral, primal thing. Once you've eaten, shared food with a person, there's a deep psychological system that means 'We are like family.'"

Feelings are invitations, a necessary part of life, that are also signals of When Things Fall Apart. They can lead to a bigger, bolder understanding of who we are, if we are to move beyond fear of their destructive force — if we are able to recognize them, welcome them, nourish them.

This being human is a guest house.
Every morning a new arrival.

A joy, a depression, a meanness,
some momentary awareness comes
As an unexpected visitor.

Welcome and entertain them all!
Even if they're a crowd of sorrows,
who violently sweep your house
empty of its furniture,
still treat each guest honorably.
He may be clearing you out
for some new delight.

The dark thought, the shame, the malice,
meet them at the door laughing and invite them in.

Be grateful for whoever comes,
because each has been sent
as a guide from beyond.

~ ***Jalaluddin Rumi****, 'The Guest House'*
(translated by Coleman Barks)

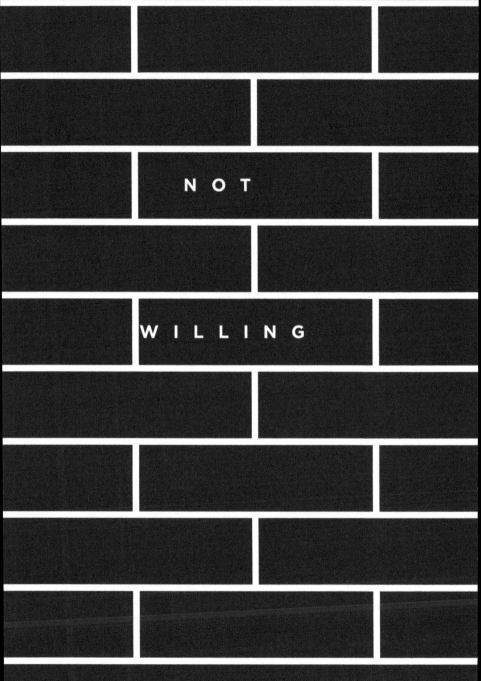

NOT WILLING

"The problem in most situations is not a lack of calling; but a fear of responding to the call. Besides the issue of leaving everything behind there is also the fear of being inadequate and the terror of being overwhelmed. Under the banner of practicality, most of life becomes arranged to obscure and distract us from what called us to come to life in the first place. Most people remain unwilling to be extravagant enough to wander where their soul would lead them, adapting instead to an endless series of short-term goals. People easily misplace their deepest longings and tune themselves to someone else's idea of life."

Michael Meade, *Fate and Destiny*

In *The Hero with a Thousand Faces*, professor Joseph Campbell identifies a monomyth distilled from the study of mythology, religion and literature, which represents a universal narrative revealing profound truths about human nature. At some point in our lives, it is implied, we will all face some great challenge that affects both our inner and outer worlds. If we answer the call to adventure and undertake the hero's journey, we may return from our ordeal transformed, bearing a gift for the greater good of our community.

It is a model that has been repeatedly co-opted, adapted and simplified by the film and television industry, blending fantasy, Jungian theory, Maslow's ideas about self-actualization, our progression from childhood to adulthood, and pedagogical theory. Luke becomes a Jedi, Frodo journeys to Mordor, Alice ventures into Wonderland, Neo reads the Matrix, Harry defeats Voldemort, Indy identifies the Holy Grail, Bond foils Blofeld, Marlin finds Nemo, Lyra journeys through the multiverse...

So often the adventure is catalyzed by disruption. A comfortable life is suddenly thrown out of balance — by a discovery, an invitation, a blunder, an intrusion, a pandemic, a financial catastrophe — and things start falling apart. Action is required. Without transformation, success is impossible to achieve. But what happens when we refuse to answer the call? What happens when we are unwilling to transform? What would have happened if, say, Lynne Sedgemore had refused a national role as CEO of the Center for Excellence in Leadership and instead remained a college principal? Would her identity have been challenged? Would she have developed the gifts she has today as a mentor and coach?

In the essay, 'The Dangers of Refusing to Answer the Call of the Hero's Journey,' psychologist John Breeding argues that often we have to be forced to withdraw from the demands of the external world in order to undertake the intense interior work that transformation requires. He links this to our fear of abandoning the busyness of productivity. In *Not Doing*, Steven and co-author Diana Renner shared how joyless urgency and extreme busyness were worn as badges of honor. Not only did they result in burnout, but in ineffectiveness and in diminished creativity and innovation. Stepping back, disregarding the rules, withdrawing from the tribal beliefs and practices, from the 'madness' of cultural indoctrination, represent necessary first steps if the adventure is to be undertaken, if we are to show willingness to take decisive action. To divest ourselves of this baggage, to strip away our current identity, prepares us for a journey of personal transformation.

To refuse the call, though, to demonstrate that you are Not Willing, is a form of closure. Entropy sets in. The individual, the society, ossifies, maintaining the status quo, resisting change. What was once fertile and bounteous is rendered a barren wilderness. As Campbell observes, "Walled in boredom, hard work, or 'culture,' the subject loses the power of significant affirmative action and becomes a victim to be saved. His flowering world becomes a wasteland of dry stones and his life feels meaningless."

If Not Willing is to be overcome, if we are to move to action after having opened up our minds and hearts, a variety of obstacles must be negotiated in order to achieve renewal.

BUILDING WALLS

"Perhaps the desire to create closed systems and keep time going in a straight line is the reason for the Second Peoples' obsession with creating fences and walls, borders, great divides and great barriers. In reality we do not inhabit closed systems, so why choose the second law of thermodynamics to create your model of time?"

Tyson Yunkaporta, *Sand Talk*

The construction of walls — the Great Wall of China, the crenellated walls of castles, the Berlin Wall, Trump's border with Mexico — is all about protecting what you have and defending against 'the other.' They're an architectural form favored by totalitarians; a sign of intransigence, of refusal to countenance external influence. Ultimately, however, as with the labyrinthine structure built by Daedalus for King Minos, these literal, metaphoric and psychological walls become a method of self-entrapment from which there is no escape without opening our minds and hearts to outside assistance.

While boundaries that provide containment and, at the same time, allow connection, are healthy, wall building can be an attempt to conceal inner lifelessness, or to hide the stagnation of political agendas and business empires, or to cover up corruption and wrongdoing. It is also something of which we are all guilty, hiding our true selves, our intentions and desires. We hide behind so many walls that we come to resemble Matryoshka nesting dolls. By closing ourselves off, we become almost robotic in what we say and do; more machinelike than the devices we increasingly depend on in our work and daily lives.

These personal walls are intended to hide our dysfunctions, failed relationships, regrets, shame, discarded identities. They enclose fragmented shards of what we once were, and possibilities of what we could be, if only we would take the time to sort through the detritus. But by leaving no gaps in these walls, no doors or windows, we stymie the opportunity for action.

Steven: I participated in a feedback session of a learning group that I had been a member of for a period of two years. One of the participants, rather than give behavioral feedback, instead wrote a poem for each group member that served to provide richer metaphors that could be explored further. I was shocked at the metaphor she chose for me. It described me as "in a glass tower, that could not be touched." She was sad that she felt she couldn't really make contact with me or know me because of this invisible, yet firm, boundary. Her poem stayed with me for a long time, as I was aware that I hadn't connected deeply, but the image of a transparent barrier struck me.

Not all boundaries are opaque or external, some are invisible and close to our hearts, but they can be seen or felt by others. In the world of work, there is a common understanding that you only know what the unspoken rules are once you break them. Similarly, while I thought all my personal boundaries were internalized, I learned that others could bump up against them, that they could separate me from genuine contact and interaction.

Over the following months I chose to explore what exactly it was that the glass barrier was protecting, and at what cost. I did not attempt to smash or remove it but simply exercised my curiosity. Over the following year, I experimented more with making the boundary less rigid and disclosing more of myself.

POLARIZATION

*"I hope you will abandon the urge
to simplify everything, to look for
formulas and easy answers, and begin
to think multidimensionally, to glory
in the mystery and paradoxes of life,
not to be dismayed by the multitude
of causes and consequences that are
inherent in each experience —
to appreciate the fact that life
is complex."*

Scott Peck, *Further Along the Road Less Traveled*

Another way that we avoid taking action is through polarization. Every agenda then becomes all-or-nothing. We're either in or out, for or against. Allowed no room for shades of gray, we become stuck and confused, paralyzed by indecision, by the chattering inside our heads, and the stark linguistic constructs that are thrown at us.

> *If you are not moving forward, you are moving backward.*
> *Do or die.*
> *If you don't do this now, it's over.*
> *Succeed at all costs.*
> *If you do nothing for the Earth now, there will be no tomorrow.*

Whenever there is an all-or-nothing quality to a pursuit, it needs to be questioned. Does it sensitize or numb us to the nuances of the situation? When reality is framed as binary, with no possibility of examining the alternatives, a deadening effect ensues. Being open-willed means having the capacity to go beyond either/or thinking and to embrace paradox, ambiguity and complexity. As physician Hans Rösling and his co-authors argue in *Factfulness*, "The fact that extremes exist doesn't tell us much. The majority is to be found in the middle, and it tells a very different story." Understanding this can help us become unstuck, as Alex Schlotterbeck learned on her journey to motherhood.

Alex is in her mid-40s and lives in South London. From a young age, she always knew that she wanted to be a mother, as she had a strong nurturing instinct. As a child, she enjoyed caring for and mothering dolls and she always had a pet. It wasn't until she was in her early 40s that she thought more seriously about how she was going to become a mother.

My dream since childhood was to raise a child in a two-parent family. I vehemently didn't want to be a single mother, as my own mother had been. As a child, I'd always felt like I was missing something because I didn't have a father. I fantasized that with a dad around to share some of the parenting burdens, I would have felt less responsible for and less affected by my mother's stress. As a therapist I observed that often children of single parents felt overly responsible for their lone parent. I did not want to recreate this as single parent. I had longed for a sense of space to feel carefree as a child and I desperately wanted that for my future child.

Although Alex's desire for having a child grew, she was in a relationship at the time that was very argumentative and unstable. It had started with great promise, after a long period of her being single, and she genuinely thought that she'd met "my person."

In retrospect, I stayed longer than I should have, afraid I would never meet anyone more suitable. My inner doubting voice said, "If, in 20 years, you haven't found the right person for you, then it isn't likely to happen." I felt despair and the thought of a childless future loomed like an empty grey horizon. I tried to make my relationship work. I pretty much forced us to go to couple's counseling. Wanting a child became the sticking point. My partner wouldn't commit to having a child in an unstable relationship. With my black-and-white thinking of "either I face a long grey lonely future or I have a child now with this man," I turned a blind eye to the relationship's instability. I brushed aside the reasons why it was not a good idea, trying to force something that just wasn't a fit. We argued, broke up, and got back together on repeat. The hope of us finally working out and the refusal to consider any other options meant I kept hanging on.

Two years went by like this. Eventually, after a miserable Christmas, Alex and her partner broke up for good. It was at this point that Alex saw she had been stuck in polarization: be married and have a child or stay single and remains childless. She had not allowed for the possibility of any middle ground.

I rigidly clung to a negative perspective about being a single mum. With encouragement from friends and family, I reluctantly went ahead and used a sperm donor in combination with IVF and became a mother a year ago. Looking back, I wish that I'd started sooner. I wish that I hadn't fixated so narrowly on trying to create a nuclear family. If I'd started sooner, I would have more time to try for a second child.

Alex loves parenting her son, and it feels like the most important and meaningful thing she will ever do. Being a single mum is hard in many ways, but it is manageable. Rather than having help at hand from a partner, she has created a support network of family, friends and babysitters, trying to ensure that she doesn't repeat the pattern of offloading stress onto her son as her mother did with her. For extra parenting support, Alex also sees a therapist. Rather than focusing on what's missing, she's trying to create a joyful and full life in the here-and-now.

INDIFFERENCE

*"How long ago
did I notice that the light was wrong,
that something inside me was broken?
Standing here, feeling nothing at all.
How long have I been leaving?
I don't know."*

Robin Robertson, *Easter, Liguria*

More often than not, a closed-off will is manifested through indifference and apathy. Many of us give up before we have begun, claiming that there is no point in taking any action — that nothing we can do will make a difference, that we are unable to effect meaningful change. There are many factors that cause this indifference. One is the bystander effect, as we follow the lead of others, looking on, waiting for someone else to do something, like the 'rubberneckers' at road accidents, who slow their own vehicles to observe, but do not stop to provide assistance or call the emergency services.

There is also a self-preservation impulse at play. In the face of overstimulation, many of us shut down mentally and emotionally. In our always-on culture, it is easy to be inundated by stories online and in the media about challenging global issues, from climate change to the refugee crisis. A tsunami of negative information induces in us an overwhelming sense of powerlessness, of despair. We believe ourselves ill-equipped, unable, too insignificant to make a difference. Our only protection against the existential angst this gives rise to is a carapace of indifference.

Such indifference can also be caused by narcissism. As long as our own individual needs are met, it is possible to become indifferent to the needs of others, desensitized to the common good.

Among those who feel the brunt of societal indifference are the homeless, who are often ignored by passersby or are unfairly judged. Indifference pushes to one side personal stories of job losses, relationship breakdowns, mental health issues, escape from war zones, and flight from economic and environmental crises. For the past seven years, Oksana Dovorecka, a 40-year-old, London-based project manager, who emigrated to London from Latvia in the early 1990s, has helped support the homeless during the Christmas period. Any preconceptions or stereotypical ideas she had about homelessness were soon overturned through an encounter with a well-dressed, well-spoken person of her own age, who came from her hometown. No one, she realized, is immune.

> The first thing you notice when you start working with the homeless is that our streets are full of them. They don't appear overnight, they have always been there, but we were all blind or indifferent to them. It is too easy to give our consciousness a populist easy answer to a complex problem: they are all drunks and druggies who choose to exist on the fringes. Which is true in some cases, but only in the way that cancer patients choose to live with cancer.

> Not all people who end up on the streets have pre-existing alcohol, drug or mental problems, but everyone who finds themselves sleeping rough will resort to anything that will dull the sheer terror of having no shelter when you are most vulnerable and asleep.

Many homeless people are too afraid to sleep at night, when their possessions can be stolen, or they can be taken advantage of or attacked. Oksana hears the same stories of misfortune over and again, from countless different homeless people. The indifference they encounter is endemic. It exacerbates their depression and despair, prompting their own resignation and ultimate indifference.

Oksana remembers a female guest at the UK national charity Crisis at Christmas, where she was volunteering. She was brought in from the street by an outreach team, malnourished, unkempt and filthy.

She just did not care about herself and her life and how she felt physically. Her emotional needs were alleviated by whatever alcohol she could find. Her relationship had broken down and her ex-partner and their two grown sons were staying in their family home, while she had been sleeping rough for three months. People she loved stopped caring for her, so she stopped caring for herself too.

It took three medical and two general volunteers an hour and a half to cut her out of her clothes, and a further hour to get her settled in. Two hairdressers spent two and a half hours on Christmas Day combing out her hair, so it did not have to be shaved off. They washed and blow-dried the hair, giving her some waves. Someone brought her a small make-up bag, a comb and a mirror from home. From the pile of emergency donated clothes, an outfit was found. When she smiled for the first time while looking at herself in the mirror, it was all worth it.

There was help out there for her. For her accommodation, for her ongoing care, for her alcohol problems. She just did not know, and she didn't care, because no one else did. Indifference can kill.

When you are a new volunteer, you think of yourself as a Disney princess. You want to help everyone; you think you can help everyone. Reality hits you like a lead balloon after a couple of days. You can't. You feel powerless, you feel frustrated, you feel tired, you feel sad and angry. What you need then is not indifference; you need more caring. You need to go through with it, you need to save all the tears for your friends in the pub. It's tough. Caring is tough. Indifference is easier on the heart.

People don't like to think of themselves as vulnerable. They don't want to believe that they, too, might be one day without a fixed address. If there is a take-away from stories of homelessness, it is that all that separates us from it is three months' rent.

AVOIDANCE

*"It was like I'd just kept turning up,
or I'd kept rolling the dice, and this is
how far along the board I'd gotten.
You see, my life didn't add up. It was
one long fragmented distraction,
or avoidance of truth. Or purpose. "*

Danny Denton, *The Earlie King & The Kid in Yellow*

Acceptance and Commitment Therapy (ACT) practitioners provide a helpful definition of experiential avoidance. It involves "attempts to avoid thoughts, feelings, memories, physical sensations and other internal experiences even when doing so creates harm in the long-run." This avoidance begins with language, which enables the substitution of imaginary events for real events. We learn to avoid not only the *fact* of something (spiders, for example), but the *thought* of it (the fear of spiders) as well. Because of the representational nature of language, we evade our fears, negative thoughts and emotions.

Yet, for all that, we are almost always all under the influence of our thoughts and feelings, which can unconsciously shape our emotions and inform our actions. A colleague's feedback, for example, can stir up feelings of inadequacy within us, prompting us to internalize the criticism, deciding not to put ourselves forward for the promotion that we previously had in mind. Or, we begin to worry about the unpromising quarterly numbers, developing anxiety about job security, becoming irritable about money matters when at home with our partner. There is a paradoxical effect, where language has the capacity to reduce physical threats but also increase our psychological pain.

Usually, When Things Fall Apart, what we suffer from most is this psychological pain, mourning what has been lost as a result of necessary transformation in ourselves or our environment. We fear the dissolution of our own identity, our sense of self, of the stories that tell us who we think we are. To be made redundant, for example, is about more than the loss of a job, of an income and what that enables, such as home ownership. It can also be internalized as the loss of our self-image as someone who is hard-working and dedicated, and it can induce a sense of worthlessness. Yet, the harder we endeavor to avoid such difficult, painful thoughts, the more powerful they become. We feel a lack, and despair becomes a constant companion. Anxiety becomes woven into our very being.

Nic Ellem is a leadership development consultant based in Sydney, Australia. He was invited to speak on the art and practice of leadership to 90 university students drawn from a wide range of disciplines, including architecture, business, health, science, communications, engineering and fashion design. After Nic had led an introductory exercise, he took a chair at the front of the room.

> I sat down and asked the group, "Where do we begin?" There was an unnerving silence. I looked at the people at the front of the room, I looked to the people at the back of the room. There were people smirking, people with puzzled looks on their faces. "So where are we right now?"

Some people asked Nic to reframe the question. He stayed silent. Some people started asking each other where this was going. The frustration and mild chaos continued for about half an hour. Nic then asked the group to "get on the balcony," to look at the situation as if from the perspective of an observer, and to ask themselves what just happened. How did it relate to the theme of the session: exploring the notion of leadership as an activity and authority as a position?

The students started making observations about how they looked to Nic, as a leader, to provide answers and to direct the conversation. They began to see their dependence on an authority figure to provide leadership. When Nic didn't do that, what emerged was an opportunity for them to lead themselves, to mobilize others to learn, and to openly share what they had learned about leading in real time.

Although this group of students had worked with each other for three years on the future of leadership and the practice of adaptive leadership, believing itself to be close-knit, Nic helped point out emergent subgroups within it. Some were vocal, others silent. His reflections and the response of one student in particular, who questioned whether her colleagues even knew who she was, opened up fissures within the group, which began to question its collective identity and sense of unity.

The intactness of the group was being challenged. So, I tried to hold attention of the group to amplify the issue. The group could begin to explore its willingness or otherwise to be mobilized by what was said. What might it do on encountering this news of difference? Some people felt quite shaken, and I noticed the group started to unpack the ideas of its intactness. This unspoken disunity was now in the open for exploration by the group. Vulnerability served to uncover some gaps in the group's level of connection, its intimacy, and the way it worked.

Nic's story shows that avoidance isn't something that is always overt, but that it often lies beneath the surface and carries a cost in terms of participation. By creating a container of psychological safety, Nic was able to help a member of the group raise an issue that had been avoided, and for the group to start to work with it.

NOT BEING

CHAPTER 5

DECONSTRUCTING THE

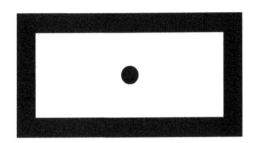

SEPARATE

SELF

*"I no longer want to be anything except
what who I am. Who what am I?
My answer: I am the sum total of
everything that went before me, of all
I have been seen done, of everything
done-to-me. I am everyone everything
whose being-in-the-world affected was
affected by mine. I am anything that
happens after I've gone which would not
have happened if I had not come.
Nor am I particularly exceptional in
this matter; each 'I', every one of the
now-six-hundred-million-plus of us,
contains a similar multitude. I repeat
for the last time: to understand me,
you'll have to swallow a world."*

Salman Rushdie, *Midnight's Children*

On the morning of 10 December 1996, Harvard neuroanatomist Jill Taylor woke up to a pounding pain behind her left eye and total silence, deprived even of the commentary and chatter that usually goes on in our heads. A left-hemisphere stroke had changed her life. Suddenly, for the first time, she could perceive no separation from life.

Because I could not identify the position of my body in space, I felt enormous and expansive, like a genie just liberated from her bottle. And my spirit soared free, like a great whale gliding through the sea of silent euphoria. Nirvana. I found Nirvana.

What Jill went through gives us an inkling of what it is like when the sense of separation dissolves.

To have a better sense of what she glimpsed, try this little experiment. Take a moment to focus on the skin on one of your forearms. Does it feel hot or cold? Notice, not by looking with the eyes but simply sensing through the skin itself, what it feels like to *be in touch* with the air. You might notice how the boundaries between skin and air have become porous, how the border between *you* and *not-you* has blurred. The sense of separation is no longer as distinct as it once was.

This was Jill's experience. Her being felt fluid, as if the boundaries that contained her were dissolving.

THE ILLUSORY SEPARATE SELF

"The problem is, we tend to think we're separate. But it's a delusion."

Ali Smith, *Summer*

Jill's story illustrates that our usual experience of life, filtered through an independent self, is a masterful illusion created by the brain. Our definition of self depends in part on our difference from others. The left hemisphere of the brain has created this illusion of a separate self by noticing a pattern of categorical differences between what pertains to *me* and what pertains to others. *Me*, therefore, is not an absolute concept, and can only be defined in relation to what is *not-me* — and what is *not-me* is usually ignored by the left hemisphere, creating a solipsistic view of the world.

This construction of reality is a process that neuroscientist Anil Seth describes in a TED Talk as "a controlled hallucination." For example, it has been known since Newton that colors are not the properties of objects, but attributes of reflected light. The brain's visual system interprets light wavelengths to determine what color something is. Color, then, is not something that is passively received, but is 'created' by each of us. All perceptions are acts of predictive and informed guesswork processed by the brain when we encounter sensory data.

The brain's predictions are not random constructions. We can still agree that we are both looking at a black dot on a piece of paper. But, they are constrained by our interpretation of sensory data. Importantly, we don't just passively perceive the world as if there is something objectively out there. We actively generate our experience of it. The world we experience is derived as much, if not more so, from the *inside out* as from the *outside in*. This applies to all our perceptions, without exception, including our perceptions of self, body, memory and volition.

Seth elaborates on this idea with reference to the Rubber Hand Illusion. In it, the participant is instructed to observe a fake hand while their own hand lies beside it, but hidden from view. Both hands are stroked simultaneously with a paintbrush. After a short period of time, many people have the uncanny experience that the fake hand has become part of their own body, and that they can feel the sensations from the brush. The observation of touch on the fake hand and the feeling of it on their own hidden hand have been blended by the brain, enabling congruence between the real and the imaginary. "When we agree about our hallucinations," Seth jokes, "we call that reality."

As soon as the fake hand is placed further away from where a person would expect their own hand to be, the sensory effect is lost, and the fake hand is no longer perceived as part of the participant's body. The experiment illuminates how far-reaching the invented nature of our experience is, extending even to the sensory. For Seth, it is a powerful reminder that "the basic background experience of being a unified self is a rather fragile construction of the brain."

THE UNRELIABLE NARRATOR

"The human mind serves evolutionary success, not truth."

John Gray, *Straw Dogs*

If our sense of self is illusory, then there is an unreliable narrator who must be held responsible for its construction. This is the voice in our heads, the one that tells us to accept the job offer, to decline an invitation to meet, to doubt ourselves, to plan for the future, to regret the past. An inner voice that articulates every thought that passes through our conscious minds and serves as the architect of the 'controlled hallucination' of self.

Neuroscientists refer to this voice as the *left-brain interpreter*; an interpretive module that constantly molds and explains sensory input, shaping it into a coherent story, even if that tends more towards fiction than fact. The research that cognitive neuroscientist Michael Gazzaniga conducted with split-brain patients reveals the left-brain interpreter to be a loquacious and convincing storyteller. Not knowing why we feel the things we feel or do the things we do, the left-brain interpreter invents reasons for them.

As Gazzaniga concludes in his book, *Who's In Charge?*, "Listening to people's explanations for their actions is interesting but often a waste of time." These explanations provide a false sense of control over our thoughts, feelings and behaviors. Here, the *I* indulges in effortless self-deception, fabricating perceptions, experiences and identity itself, yet conveying them with certainty.

For many of us, self-awareness permits us to connect, to relate to the world around us, and to make sense of who and what we encounter. People with borderline personality disorders, however, may struggle with identity or a lack of a sense of self. When extreme, this can result in depersonalization, substituting other people's experiences for their own. This can be profoundly disturbing, leading to a form of self-erasure. What Jill's case and the Rubber Hand experiment illustrate, though, is that the vast majority of us can experience ourselves as separate, but we can understand that the separation is illusory. In this sense, having a notion of self is a healthy adaption, which is all the more powerful, affecting how we experience life, when we recognize that that very self is a fiction. We remain porous and entangled beings, however much we might tell ourselves otherwise.

IDENTITY AS DOING AND UNDOING

"Identities seem fixed and solid only when seen, in a flash, from outside. Whatever solidity they might have when contemplated from the inside of one's own biographical experience appears fragile, vulnerable, and constantly torn apart by shearing forces which lay bare its fluidity and by cross-currents which threaten to rend in pieces and carry away any form they might have acquired."

Zygmunt Bauman, *Liquid Modernity*

Neuroscientist Susan Greenfield argues that the experience of *I* consciousness is generated by clusters of "neuronal assemblies," which are rapidly activated in changing patterns. She concludes that identity is not some kind of solid object or property. Instead, it is a type of *subjective* brain state, a feeling that can change from one moment to the next. Identity becomes a moveable feast, a never-ending cycle of doing and undoing, of defining a self, however momentarily, in relation to what it *is not* as much as to what it *is*. Novelist and essayist Siri Hustvedt has grappled with these ideas throughout her career, claiming that the *other* is always hiding in the *I*.

We are born with almost as many neurons as we will ever need. During the first 15 months of our lives, the weight of our brains increases by 30%. The weight gain is not the result of new brain cells but of synapses, the new connections being formed between the neurons. By the age of two, we will have grown more than 100 trillion synapses, which is double that of an adult. For infants, then, life is an overwhelming expansion of the senses as these new connections occur. They can hear the tones in foreign languages that their parents can't, and they can experience synesthesia — the blending of senses, such as tasting colors, hearing visuals or seeing smells. The connectivity within the brain enables it to adapt to a vast array of inputs and potential possibilities. However, such openness does not go on forever.

It is a common misconception to believe that identity formation, the process of becoming someone, is additive. We acquire new skills, new knowledge, new capabilities, in order to do, to be, something else. Yet, the reality is that, as we age, we lose many of those neural connections we had in infancy. Whichever connections are not activated undergo a process known as 'neural pruning.' The expansive receptivity of an infant begins to slow from the age of two, and neural connections begin to die at a rate of up to 100,000 per second. Many scientists have hypothesized that neural pruning is a primary mechanism through which the brain shapes itself to the environment, reinforcing specific responses in a perpetuating pattern. Hustvedt elaborates in her essay, 'Borderlands.'

Every theoretical construct, every system of ideas, every intellectual map created to explain who and what human beings are is vulnerable at the site of incision — the place where we sever one thing from another. Without such dissections, there can be no formal thought, no discrete disciplines, no articulations of human experience. These separations delineate the borders between the inside and outside, me and you, up and down, here and there, true and false.

In this way, a sense of *self* is contrasted, molded and adapted to what is *not-self*. As journalist Will Storr observes in *Selfie*,

"It is what is taken away, not what is added, that really makes us who we are." We tell ourselves stories to bestow an identity, but those stories change as the context changes. Our identities are only ever something of temporal and contextual convenience and are forever in a state of flux; small moments of separation before dissolution into a greater whole.

REIMAGINING DEVELOPMENT

*"And there was a new voice
which you slowly
recognized as your own,
that kept you company
as you strode deeper and deeper
into the world."*

Mary Oliver, *The Journey*

Development in complexity requires a state of constantly becoming. Rather than a separate self, with a fixed and rigid identity, there is a porousness between *self* and *not-self*. Harvard psychologist Robert Kegan argues that, on reaching adulthood, we begin to continuously include elements that previously were considered *other*. His thesis challenges the assumption that development ends at the threshold between adolescence and adulthood.

Kegan's theory is underpinned by two primary concerns. The first is how people construct their identity, making sense of and deriving meaning from their lives. The second is the development and increasing complexity of such construction, from one stage to another, through a person's life. Each stage "transcends and includes" the previous stages. The later stage has a more complex and accurate understanding of self and other, thereby providing people with greater capacity to handle the challenges of life and work. However, each stage cannot be judged as necessarily better or worse than any other.

THE SELF-TRANSFORMING MIND

I hold many identities,
I embrace paradox

THE SELF-AUTHORING MIND

I have an identity,
I make choices

THE SOCIALIZED MIND

I am my relationships,
I follow the rules

ADULTHOOD

Excerpt: Constructive Development
Theory – Robert Kegan *In Over our Heads*

As an example, a junior employee is less likely than a seasoned leader to have the capacity to navigate the political forces inside and outside a large company. Clearly, these abilities are not innate but have to be developed. For Kegan, this involves transformation, a "qualitative change in the structural form of how a person makes sense of the situation." Transformation occurs when someone is able to step back from, reflect on and make decisions about who they were and who they have become. This includes the most entrenched beliefs, roles, perspectives, and their effect on identity.

Kegan's theory proposes a five-stage model of development that starts in infancy. Of particular interest to us are the third, fourth and fifth stages of adulthood, as well as the transitions between them. These are, respectively, the stages of the socialized mind, the self-authoring mind and the self-transforming mind. By the time people have arrived at the third stage, for example, they have internalized one or more systems of meaning, such as family values, a political leaning, a philosophy or a corporate culture. As such, their own immediate impulses and the decisions they make can be subordinated to and shaped by those larger meaning systems.

Internalization, though, carries inherent limitations. Ideology is absorbed by identity, but is rendered invisible to the self, leading to over-identification with specific labels and conflicts founded upon tribal belonging. Kegan's research shows that most of us (about 65% of the general population) never become high-functioning adults, failing to progress beyond the third of the five stages. To borrow from the title of Kegan's 1994 book, we can feel *In Over Our Heads* when life's complexity exceeds our grasp on our current way of being. Continuous attempts to gain understanding and resolve internal conflicts give rise to the fourth stage of development. During this stage, people are able to examine the various opinions, expectations and influences of others, applying an internal set of standards to them that they have constructed from their own reflection and inquiry. They are better able to reconcile the perspectives and feedback of other people with their own point of view, without suffering any trauma where there is divergence.

Only a diversity of experience and sufficient self-reflection can enable the self-authorship of the fourth stage of development. Progression to the fifth stage of the self-transforming mind requires recognition of the limitations of self-authorship, as well as the fact that there can be no complete identification with any system. People at this stage take into consideration not only other opinions and perspectives, but entirely different systems of governance, too. They are less likely to see the world in either/or terms, recognizing the nuanced connections between apparent dichotomies such as good and bad, profit and purpose, doing and being, or even separation and connection. As suggested by F. Scott Fitzgerald, these are people who can hold opposed ideas in mind while continuing to function. In Kegan's view, however, this fifth stage is only attained in midlife and, even then, only by a select few.

Khuyen: One day, I was discussing a presentation with my manager. I had a tendency to focus on getting the thinking straight and the arguments well supported. My visual design skills were poor and, as a result, I was reluctant to exert myself on trying to beautify the slides.

I explained, "I know you think it's important that the slide looks good. It's just not my forte. For me, it's 80% substance, 20% style."

"I can see that," he replied. "For me, it is 100% substance and 100% style."

"That's cheating!" I exclaimed.

His response didn't make sense to my rational mind, which could only think in terms of either/or, right/wrong, better/worse. It was only later in life that I began to understand. My boss had not been speaking about the result of my work, but rather the attentiveness that I could give to the task in front of me.

At the usual level of daily workplace awareness, there will always be strengths and weaknesses. Yet, as I endeavor to pay more attention to each moment, I can learn to do both the unpleasant and the pleasant tasks with equanimity.

THE EXPERIENCE OF TRANSITION SPACE

"A point of liminality where something might exist or might not. Did not yesterday or will not tomorrow. Or becoming briefly visible, surfacing, lifting to the wind, seeds soon covered in dust. But there, briefly, a life. A life at its most honest and complete."

M. W. Bewick and **Ella Johnston**, *The Orphaned Spaces*

In reality, most of our adult life is spent in between stages, with the periods of transition enduring for years or even decades. Jennifer Garvey Berger, a close colleague of Kegan, uses the image of a rainbow to describe the nature of transition space. At each of the numbered stages, there is a single color. In the transitional spaces, the colors merge and blend. "While we can all name the main colors of a rainbow," she says, "part of what gives it its beauty is the way the colors overlap and merge into one another."

Viewed from the outside, maturation — the progression from one stage to another — can seem like a series of gains. Each stage brings with it a greater capacity than the previous one, providing us with more options, allowing us to see more, to do more. However, transition also always involves what Kegan refers to as 'an exquisite loss,' which is experienced subjectively. This can feel like 'the loss of something very precious,' which can involve both pain and grief.

To move beyond the stage of the socialized mind, for example, we risk losing our relationship with and sense of belonging to our tribe. We risk the disapproval or even rejection of those with whom we previously identified. The difficult decisions we make can contradict the default values of family, organization, political party or even nation. Similarly, to move beyond the self-authoring mind, we need to shed our attachment to the psychological and social system with which we currently identify. Sometimes this is forced upon us, as in Jill Taylor's case. Before her stroke, she had a clear idea of who she was and where she was heading. It took Jill eight years to recover from the effects of the stroke, and to develop a new capacity to step back from but still embrace that former identity, contextualizing it in relationship to something bigger than her former conception of self. As she observed, "I am the life-force power of the universe. I am the life-force power of the 50 trillion beautiful molecular geniuses that make up my form, at one with all that is."

INTERCONNECTION

"Listen: you are not yourself, you are crowds of others, you are as leaky a vessel as was ever made, you have spent vast amounts of your life as someone else, as people who died long ago, as people who never lived, as strangers you never met. The usual I we are given has all the tidy containment of the kind of character the realist novel specializes in and none of the porousness of our every waking moment, the loose threads, the strange dreams, the forgettings and misrememberings, the portions of a life lived through others' stories, the incoherence and inconsistency, the pantheon of dei ex machina and the companionability of ghosts. There are other ways of telling."

Rebecca Solnit, *The Faraway Nearby*

The immense number of atoms of which each of us is composed are only ever borrowed, dating back to the universe's inception, and shared through space and time with countless other sentient beings and inanimate objects — humans, animals, plants, vegetables, minerals, ancestors, descendants, aliens, locals. Every time we eat, drink or breathe we absorb new atoms as part of a constant process of exchange that continues with exhalation, excretion and perspiration. This, in turn, is received by the Earth and the atmosphere, carried on the winds. Every day, in one way or another, we exchange approximately 7% of our body weight. Our physical substance changes constantly, even as these fundamental particles that temporarily become us live on forever. We are immortal, even as every moment bears us closer to death.

What we think of as our bodies, moreover, are ecosystems containing trillions of microbes, throwing into question the singular concept of a self or the possibility of separation. "'We' are ecosystems that span boundaries and transgress categories," suggests biologist Merlin Sheldrake in *Entangled Life*. "Our selves emerge from a complex tangle of relationships only now becoming known." Every human is a constellation.

It is the bacteria within, upon and around us that make it possible for us to breathe and digest. Our own constellations are entirely interdependent with the other constellations around us. Without bacteria, the Earth itself would be uninhabitable, plants would be unable to transform the sun's energy via photosynthesis, and there would not be enough oxygen to sustain complex life forms like our own. We are never completely alone or self-sufficient.

The experience of the Covid-19 pandemic — not only through its rapid global transmission, but in the communal responses, both locally and online, to lockdown, grief, and the appreciation of health professionals and caregivers — has reinforced this message. The visceral experience of interconnection, even when facilitated by the internet, social media and videoconferencing, encourages a different way to understand what the self is.

This self is not an object, it is not confined to a single body or a single consciousness, nor is it a single node in a network. Instead, Daniel Siegel, a pioneer in the interdisciplinary field of Interpersonal Neurobiology, suggests that our understanding of self "emerges at the interface of neurobiology and the interpersonal transactions of experience between minds."

Ultimately, our identity is shaped by the integration of top-down concepts and knowledge with bottom-up sensory signals, as well as by our immersion in the web of relatedness to others. Only then can the storytelling mind become more open to the possibility of a new story that sees the self as plural and interconnected, rather than singular and isolated. In this sense, we don't *have* relationships, we *are* relationships, with selves that are subject to continuous and fluid change.

I AM BECAUSE WE ARE

"Whatever happens to the individual happens to the whole group, and whatever happens to the whole group happens to the individual. The individual can only say: 'I am, because we are; and since we are, therefore I am.'"

John Mbiti, *African Religions and Philosophy*

In this integrated and interdependent view, we could say that the self exists not only in one's body or mind but also in the minds of others. When we participate in a video call, for example, even though our voice and image are mediated by technology, there is a version of our selves present in the minds of those with whom we interact, and we carry a version of them within us, too. Even when we die, a version of our selves lives on in the minds of friends and family. This networked, collective understanding of self stands in stark contrast to the notion of separation. To attune to the self in this expansive and inclusive way is to deny the possibility of separation. The other and the self become entwined. *Ubuntu.* I am because we are. You are in me and I am in you. We hold each other in our internal worlds with our inner senses.

People whom we admire and love become part of us, not only metaphorically but physically. We absorb them into our internal model of the world. Our brains rewire themselves around the expectation of these people's presence in our lives. The more they 'live in us' in this way, the more we experience them as an inherent, indispensable part of us. To lose them, as a result of death or the breakdown of a relationship, is so excruciatingly painful partly because it is an aspect of ourselves that is lost. As Kahlil Gibran puts it in *The Prophet*, "And ever has it been that love knows not its own depth until the hour of separation." Loss reveals the very interconnection on which our sense of self depends.

Some cultures implicitly acknowledge the constant shifts in identity and the inherent embeddedness of self in others. For example, in Vietnamese, when a child visits their extended family, they will refer to their grandfather as 'grandson greets grandpa' or to their aunt as 'nephew greets aunt.' This dissolves the separation suggested by *I* and *You* and recognizes nuanced shifts in relationship, dependent on the people involved in any interaction.

There are, then, multiple layers to the self. These reflect both what is unique about us — our embodiment, inclinations, personalities and quirks, shaped by a particular interplay of genetics and upbringing — and what is entangled in our relationships with others and with the broader environment. As cultural psychologist Shelly Harrell observes, paraphrasing psychologist Henry Murray and anthropologist Clyde Kluckhohn, "We are all, at the same time, like all others, like some others, and like no others."

These layers of self cohere into a whole, an integrated self, which Siegel refers to as "MWe." This is a ceaseless unfolding rather than a fixed destination, "a plural verb rather than a singular noun." This self is suggestive of the interconnected relational world in which we are embedded. The transformation from *Me* to *MWe* represents the liberation of the mind; freedom from the dominant cultural narrative of separation.

NOT BEING

"I was the image of what I was not, and that image of not-being overwhelmed me: one of the most powerful states is being negatively. Since I didn't know what I was, 'not being' was the closest I could get to the truth: at least I had the other side: I at least had the 'not,' I had my opposite."

Clarice Lispector, *The Passion According to G.H.*

Not Being is not about angst or absence or limitation or lack of identity. Not Being is the antidote to a narrow view of who we think we are: small, atomized, disconnected individuals who seek meaning in acquisition and action, protecting and preserving ourselves, endlessly seeking fulfillment in development but never finding it. Not Being counters the notions of separation and solipsism, recognizing the complexity and dynamic mystery of who we are, as well as our interconnectedness with one another and our environment. Rather than advocating reductionism, there is an expansive and inclusive quality about Not Being.

Not Being blurs the borders between me and we, dissolving the myth of separation, and positioning our understanding of the self as porous and entangled with others. We are part of something much bigger than any one of us. In this context, our identity includes and transcends any of the labels that are applied to us during our lives. This embraces all the ways in which we self-identify or are grouped and classified according to role, education, gender, ethnicity, faith, nationality or relationships. It encompasses, too, all those occasions when what we know, say or do come to symbolize who we are.

Not Being, the book, is an invitation to exercise curiosity about who we are, to pull back the curtains so we can see what is already, always, here. This is the journey that Craig Foster underwent, under an octopus's tutelage, when he immersed himself in a rich and satisfying relationship with the natural world, overcoming depression, and reconnecting with himself and his family. Foster found wonder in natural beauty and was awestruck by the insights he was offered regarding the interconnectedness and diversity of all of life, in which *every* element plays an essential role. As with Foster's experience, the aim is to open our hearts and minds, to help us appreciate that there is nothing to gain, nothing to lose, nothing to strive for, and nothing to fear. We all belong. Intimately. We *are* life.

What would it mean to live in awareness of this wider sense of being?

What does it take to see that we are so much more than our labels?

What happens when the notion of the separate self falls away?

What would it take to become deep-rooted and lighthearted, holding less tightly to our stories?

What happens if the only way to discover the self is by giving our self away?

In the following portraits we will see how a refugee, a tattoo artist, a martial artist, an activist who works with homeless youth and a bodybuilder can help us to discover more about living a life of Not Being.

PORTRAITS

CHAPTER 6

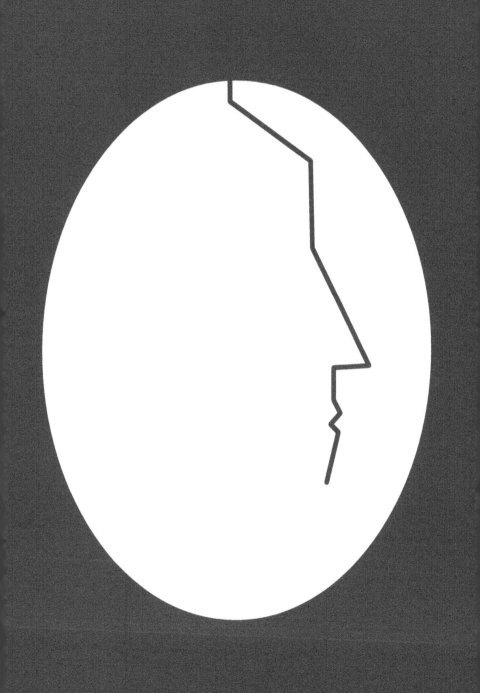

THE REFUGEE: EMBRACING IMPERMANENCE, FINDING HOME

"Each moment is only an impermanence, a kind of purgatory. Is this why we find it so hard to look at the present and at what is directly in front of us, at our feet?"

M. W. Bewick and Ella Johnston, *The Orphaned Spaces*

Not Being is a way of being in the world that recognizes the impermanence of life, and that this disruption cannot always be responded to with a simple change of behavior. Instead, it becomes a crucible, a moment that results in a significant shift in our identity. In parallel to the change in external circumstances, there is an inner shift. Both are intimately entwined. The *I* that we thought we were dies as a new identity emerges, often with a bigger and bolder vision of who we are.

Everything can change, and does change, from one moment to the next. When we know deeply and viscerally that, in every moment, a part of us is already dying and something new is being born, we have the possibility to discover how alive we really are. The one constant in the face of so much impermanence is our awareness of change itself. This is our home.

Hung Nguyen grew up in South Vietnam during the height of the Vietnam War. Among his earliest childhood recollections are those relating to the war. He remembers being carried downstairs and hiding under the staircase because of the bombing. He remembers money flying in the street like trash a few days before the fall of Saigon in April 1975. But he also remembers childish antics.

I just knew that there was a war going on. But children being children, we just knew how to play. So, I remember playing, flying kites on rooftops, and watching helicopters flying around.

A few months after the capture of Saigon by the People's Army of Vietnam and the Viet Cong, Hung's father was placed in a re-education camp because he was a doctor and was seen as a possible ally of the United States. Many endured the same fate, with others tortured and killed. Once freed, Hung's father escaped to the US, fearing more punishment if he stayed in his homeland. Hung, his mother, his twin brother Hiep, and their five siblings, meanwhile, had to survive as best they could.

In Vietnamese, Hung's name means 'a person of bravery.' When he was 13-years-old, that bravery was put to the test when his family was offered a single place on a refugee boat and Hung was told by his mother to take it. The crossings were notoriously unpredictable and life-threatening, and Hung knew that he might never see his family again. Nevertheless, he joined the thousands of people fleeing South Vietnam and embarked on a crossing more treacherous than anything he could have imagined. His boat was lost in the ocean for 19 days, and with no land in sight, no food and low morale among his fellow refugees, he was convinced of his imminent death.

I remember the experience of waking up, looking around and seeing all of these bodies. I didn't know whether they were dead or alive. Then I remember crawling on top of these bodies to the top of the deck and sitting there and looking at the waves coming. I saw these huge waves, and I thought at any moment one of these waves will kill all of us. Then I started praying. I remember praying to Jesus, praying to the Buddha, praying to my grandfather. Then there was a bird that flew by and I prayed to the birds. Suddenly, I saw this huge wave coming and I thought, "Oh, this is the end." So, I do remember very vividly that experience of completely letting go. The anticipation — the anticipation of death — I just completely let go of everything.

I just sat there. I looked at this wave, and then it came, and it went. It came and went. There was this moment of complete surrender and peace.

In that moment of his impending death, Hung experienced peace. His terrified ego ceased to exist. There was no dialogue, no story, only the completeness of the moment. Hung was too young to realize that it was an awakening experience, an awakening to the clear reality of the present moment.

Twenty years later, on the ninth day of a ten-day silent meditation retreat, Hung experienced this familiar awakening once again — the feeling that "there is nothing more or less than this moment." For many, it is the kind of experience denied them by their absorption in life's daily drama; the kind of awakening that can only be triggered by a life-or-death situation or cultivated by deep contemplative practice. What Hung discovered, though, is that the possibility of awakening, of becoming attuned to the moment, is ever-present. All it requires is our own awareness of it.

Hung had survived the tumultuous boat trip, as well as months spent in a refugee camp in Thailand, before he then emigrated to the United States, where he changed his name to Michael. In his early 20s, he had abandoned his accountancy studies and founded a theater company, enjoying success with the play *Laughter from the Children of War*, which offered a Vietnamese perspective on the conflict he had lived through as a child.

Storytelling and theater work became a way for Michael and his peers to address their trauma. By his early 30s, however, he had left the theater company, and was suffering from both insomnia and stomach ulcers. Michael joined the silent retreat led by the Buddhist monk Thich Nhat Hanh in this condition, without really knowing what he was getting himself into.

> I thought I had signed up for a ten-day vacation, because I'd heard that I didn't have to talk to anyone, and that there would be free food and free lodging. Then I got to the hall and realized, "Oh my God, I'm going to be stuck here for ten days doing nothing except sitting and breathing and observing bodily sensations." I literally thought I was going crazy for the first two days.

It turned out to be a pivotal moment in his life. Up to that point, Michael knew how to explore externally in his acting work, but not what was it like to go deeper inside both body and mind. "When you breathe, you are coming home," Thich Nhat Hanh explained. It was a revelation for Michael: he had spent years without feeling any sense of belonging, severed from his Vietnamese roots, assimilated into American culture, stranded between worlds, with a nagging sense of not knowing home. "I had a moment of realization," he recalled. "*This* is home. This breath, this body, this moment is home. I am *always* home, and I can always return home."

In fact, he was so moved by the experience that, after the retreat, he once again changed his name, this time to Home, as a permanent reminder.

THE TATTOO ARTIST: SEEING WHAT IS ALREADY HERE

"The mass of men lead lives of quiet desperation."

Henry David Thoreau, *Walden*

Thoreau's sardonic evaluation of the majority of people's lives may seem harsh, but what is clear is that most of us, if asked if we were truly happy, would not be able to respond positively. We experience life as ebbs and flows, an accumulation of tiny moments that is occasionally disturbed by events of greater significance, by sudden eddies of happiness and insight. Even where all is apparently well, there can be an undercurrent of dissatisfaction that is difficult to explain, a sense that something is missing. It's not often, though, that an inquiry regarding our happiness results not only in changes to the content of our lives, but in a change of identity, of who we think we are.

Ilona Cuinaite is a Lithuanian who moved with her husband to Brighton on the south coast of England in the early 2000s, where she began to work in a local tattoo shop. Ilona enjoyed her work, especially meeting new people from all over the world, and giving them something that they would wear for life.

Some days were great, some not so much, as I was feeling the stress of life. Money was tight. I always wanted something more than I had. Some days I would wake up in a horrible mood, and life looked grim. Some days everything seemed okay.

One rainy fall day, Ilona had an extraordinary experience. Her entire view of reality fell away.

That night my old life died. I remember sitting in the candlelit room on my sofa, eyes wide open, not a thought in my head, just being. It felt so light and free, delicious, peaceful, blissful. I experienced stillness of the thinking mind that I never thought was possible. I don't know how much time passed. It must have been hours. Being in that state felt like home. I was at peace. No worries, no memories, no fantasies, only pure stillness, and the clarity of being present.

Days later, Ilona was left wondering whether it was possible to experience this state again. It had opened an unexpected door, a fresh way of seeing, and she was eager to return to this new home.

At first, there was a lot of anger. I felt deceived. No one had told me that there was more to reality than I had previously thought. But I realized that no one *could* tell me. The only way to taste it was to experience it directly. The anger I felt ignited the search. I wanted to find the truth. And just like Neo in the movie *The Matrix*, I sat by the computer for days, trying to find clues that could lead me home.

Years passed. Ilona was unhappy and ill at ease while she searched for answers, for enlightenment. Although her life, from the outside, seemed completely normal, with the usual moments of happiness and despair, inside she felt a deep longing. She felt trapped, discontented both with herself and with other people. She saw the suffering of others and she suffered too, not knowing how she could help.

After eight years of "aimless wandering" — which included reading, sound healing, crystals — something shifted in the spring of 2010, prompted by a trilogy of books by Jed McKenna that challenged the notion of self.

I remember the intensity of those days. It felt like I was being skinned alive. All I could think was that the truth was nothing but the lies I told myself. At the same time, there was a volcano eruption happening in Iceland and it was nice symbolism for me: being on fire, burning inside for truth.

For a few months, life was very painful for Ilona, lacking in hope. She didn't know what to believe anymore, as she realized that she had been dependent on borrowed beliefs, learned by repetition from others. Pursuing what she had read about the lack of self, Ilona connected with fellow truth-seekers on an internet forum, who informed her, 'There is no you.'

> I remember it was an ordinary morning. I was standing in my bedroom in my bathrobe, looking out of the window, wondering what "there is no you" meant. A question popped into my head: "Is there an Ilona running the show?" That instant, the thinking mind stopped for a few seconds, as if the curtain on the stage was drawn back, the recognition happened and, once again, my old life fell away. I recognized that there is only life, no separate people, no separate shows. It's all one show, a unified movement of totality, manifested through different characters. I discovered that to know experientially one has to face the question fearlessly and look.

Ilona's view of life changed dramatically. It felt like a fresh start, a new book, rather than another chapter in her life. She no longer believed in the idea of a separate self, with free will, choice and control. This gave Ilona "a sense of immense freedom, of joy and mystery. For months, I was high on life, in bliss." Her experience prompted her to create Liberation Unleashed, a blog, forum and website that generated a movement through which other inquiring minds could be guided. Ilona founded it as an act of compassion and selfless service, and it would go on to help others through the delivery of a variety of projects.

Soon after her moment of 'recognition,' Ilona and her husband moved to another town where they set up their own tattoo business. Things were starting to fall into place: new town, new home, new vision. Having her own tattoo shop was much more enjoyable for Ilona. She felt free to work on the designs she liked. It was a small shop above a hairdresser and Ilona and her husband were the only tattoo artists there. Life was simple and rich in inner experiences. By day, Ilona helped people transform their bodies with decorative images in the tattoo shop while, by night, she helped them transform their minds and worldviews through Liberation Unleashed.

It was as if I had discovered an amusement park inside my mind, where new ideas were being born, while the old fell away like autumn leaves. I noticed that many patterns of thinking had changed. Previously, when I thought about the past, I would feel guilt, shame and regret, and I would spend days thinking about what was wrong. Now, though, I don't have those kinds of thoughts. Dreaming about the future has also fallen away. It is so much more interesting to be living in the now, noticing what is happening in the present moment. The mind has stopped looking for drama.

I had found the depth of the ocean, while previously I could only notice the waves. Diving deep into experience and exploring what is, had a flavor of love, love for being alive, love for humanity, for aliveness itself.

THERE IS NO

THERE IS NO SE

THE WISE FOOL: LIGHT-HEARTED, DEEP-ROOTED

"The fool doth think he is wise, but the wise man knows himself to be a fool."

William Shakespeare, *As You Like It*

Not Being requires us to embrace the whole, to include and find nuance between extremes, to transcend polarities. We have to seek out and integrate what lies in between black and white, left and right, us and them. We have to challenge and question the 'rightness' of our own perspective, allowing space for doubt where there is confidence and certainty, acknowledging our own biases, and taking into account alternative points of view.

According to Francis Briers, founder of The Wise Fool School in southern England, who also works as a senior consultant for an employee brand engagement company:

Black-and-white thinking is problematic in all sorts of ways, not least of all in that it is self-reinforcing. The more entrenched I get in my views, the more readily I dismiss and ignore any ideas which might challenge my perspective.

There is a lightness to Not Being, a fluidity and flexibility that does not permit attachment to fixed positions or narrow identities. Yet, despite this, there is, simultaneously, groundedness and depth. By embracing this paradox, we allow something to emerge that is both deep-rooted and light-hearted, as epitomized by the wise fool. Through his school devoted to this figure, Francis has helped to create a community of people from all walks of life who seek wisdom without taking themselves too seriously.

Francis began to explore the wise fool archetype through the study of two quite different disciplines, theater and martial arts, benefiting from the knowledge and experience of celebrated practitioners who happened to live locally. From the age of 12, he participated in a youth music theater company that was under the guidance of a West End theater director and her musical director husband. Then, before starting further education, Francis took a year out, during which he began to learn martial arts with the renowned instructor Steve Rowe.

When he started drama school, Francis was taught the Alexander Technique, which incorporates relaxation and body awareness. Francis quickly perceived the overlaps with what he had learned from martial arts. Both disciplines seemed to be focused on helping the practitioner to find a state in which they could be completely present and grounded in the moment, yet open and ready to respond to whatever happened.

> In theater, this was about an authentic performance on stage. In the dojo, the martial arts training hall, it was about not getting hit! I quickly became fascinated by what my voice teacher, the graceful and magical Trish Baillie, called "the position of readiness." This was not a literal, specific position, but a state, a way of being, a quality of awareness from which you are present to what is emerging and can respond spontaneously, in the moment.

After studying numerous martial art practices and philosophies from around the world, Francis concluded that they all pointed to the same thing: deep principles that lay behind outward physical expression. This related to total awareness while maintaining a fluid relaxation, to readiness without tension.

Francis was drawn to this way of being and continued to study its application in many different domains: performance, martial arts, facilitation, coaching, leadership and, in his view, the most challenging of all, parenting.

It helps to embrace non-attachment. Don't grasp onto anything, but don't throw everything away either. Aim yourself at cultivating this way of being, without trying too hard. It helps to be able to physically root deeply and connect with the ground, so you are powerful, while also being able to move lightly, swiftly and gracefully, and to have this same quality in your mind, emotions and spirit as well. It helps to be totally focused and totally playful.

> For Francis, rootedness enabled him to engage with all of life, to face squarely even the toughest and darkest corners of human experience, but lightness allowed him not to lose his playfulness, open-heartedness and sense of humor.

Dealing with what is really going on, especially in tough times, might seem like heavy stuff, and, in some ways, it is. But what I have found, through exploring the way of the wise fool, is that it is possible to find lightness in the darkness, to be playful in the storm. In the midst of grieving for the loss of our mum, my brother and I could still take the piss out of each other and have a joke. I can be furious with my wife and love her in the same breath. My son can be crazy-making and blessed and beautiful all at once. Life is wonderful and terrible.

> The challenge and gift of the wise fool is to remind us that Not Being is a *whole* being. It is not confined to a narrow and limited perspective of who you are. Rather, it means being present with all of life in all its wonder and horror. The wise fool challenges us to inhabit the poetry of paradox and learn to laugh gently at the part of us that hungers for certainty in a world that has never stopped changing, and never will. We cannot respond to change by either losing our roots or becoming fixed. Instead, we have to be completely engaged in the fluidity of the moment.

To fully meet and deal with reality, to live gracefully through tough times, what we need is to be fully present. We have to soften our edges, embrace humility, open our minds and hearts to new and different perspectives. We blend with the great forces in the world and, where necessary, artfully redirect that which will harm us or those we love.

How do we do that? There is no prescription, only pointers. Instead, Francis draws wisdom from a passage in the ancient Chinese text, the *Tao Te Ching*, which he has translated and paraphrased as follows:

> *The oldest and wisest of Fools were mysterious,*
> *perceptive, poised and totally present.*
> *The depth of their wisdom plumbed the Darkness.*
> *I can't tell you what they knew, but I can*
> *Tell you how they acted:*
>
> *Careful — like a man on thin ice!*
> *Alert — like a child stealing cookies.*
> *Courteous — like a fiancée meeting the in-laws.*
> *Yielding — like chocolate on your tongue.*
> *Simple — like a lump of wood.*
> *Open — like a flower for a bee.*
> *Unknown — like a box of cereal that **might** have a toy in it.*
>
> *Can you wait and finish the cereal to discover the toy?*
> *Can you sit still until the moment is ripe?*

THE SACRED ACTIVIST: GIVING YOUR SELF AWAY

"In sum, we learned that service is the rent we pay for living. It is the very purpose of life and not something you do in your spare time."

Marian Wright Edelman, *The Measure of Our Success: A Letter to My Children & Yours*

As Adam Bucko grew up in Communist Poland, he was inspired by the resistance movement and, in particular, by two Catholic priests who were killed by the government. He recalls the profound impact of watching TV while the tortured body of one of the priests was pulled out of a river. The sham trial that followed strengthened Adam's resolve to fight for justice, while also making him aware of the dangers and consequences of doing so.

As a teen, Adam started to follow his calling, faithful to what he felt had been awakened by the death of the two priests. He assumed an active role in the Solidarity youth movement, which took inspiration from counterculture, punk and reggae. Poets like Benjamin Zephaniah would travel to Poland for recitals

I was swept up and felt part of a movement. It allowed me to revise the values of my life. Unlike many teens, I was not interested in numbing myself with alcohol or getting ahead. Rather, I was interested in building circles of friends where we could support each other to live in a new way that reflected our values.

When he was 17, Adam and his mother moved to New York to join his father, who was already working there. It was a huge culture shock, exacerbated by the sudden loss of social connections and the sense of no longer belonging to a significant Polish movement. No one at his new high school, located on the border between Queens and Brooklyn, shared his interests. Instead, Adam would catch the train to Manhattan and spend time with the Rastafarians there, who at least stood for something and embodied an alternative culture.

Eventually, his increasing sense of dislocation and inner turmoil resulted in a breakdown. In response, Adam began to spend his summers at an ashram, meditating, studying comparative religion, learning about monasticism and dialogue. Ultimately, his experiences prompted him to travel to India, on a journey that would change the direction of his life forever. Indeed, India is one of those countries that you cannot be indifferent to. It's like an assault on the senses, where the whole kaleidoscope of life is visible. Adam was disconcerted by his encounters with the poor and the homeless, as well as with the junkies whom he encountered in the company of a friend from Amsterdam who had established a center to support addicts. He found himself both recoiling at what he saw and responding to the call to help others.

> I was picked up in an old 1920s ambulance. I was freaking out as we drove into the crazy traffic, struggling to understand what was happening. Suddenly we stopped. "There's someone who needs our help," the driver said. He led me to a man who was obviously a junkie, just skin and bones, and invited him to come with us. I could smell his rotting flesh.

> When we got to the clinic, as they took the bandage off the man's foot, parts of it just dropped to the floor. Even the maggots inside it had already died. I left the room in a panic. Everyone at the clinic seemed to be HIV-positive and there was blood everywhere. Every fear I had of getting sick and dying was there right in front of me.

I felt like my identity was cracking. There were kids who were amputees, people sick everywhere, yet I could also see people who were recovering, people who had been nearly skeletal but had now regained enough weight and strength to be able to return home to their families. I shared a room with a very ill patient one night. It felt like his pain was an extension of my own pain, that we were feeling the pain of the world. The part of me that wanted to stay in my cocoon, and be safe, was cracked. I was responding to the wounds of the world as if they were my own wounds.

> When Adam returned to the US, he began to work with a charity for the homeless youth in Florida, initially as a counselor in a shelter, and then doing outreach work, befriending the young homeless in Orlando. He then continued this transformative — and, at times, traumatic — work in New York.

Pimps, drug dealers, the homeless, abused and abuser would all be there, and I would be a container of presence. They could all come and take a break from their identity. They could experience friendliness, kindness, reciprocity and compassion.

> A chance encounter with holistic healer Taz Tagore pushed Adam towards providing practical services, and helping homeless youth discover their vocation and deeper purpose. This resulted in their establishment of the Reciprocity Foundation in 2005, which not only catered to the young but to a variety of other communities as well. While still on the board, however, Adam has now moved away from the day-to-day operation of the organization.

I noticed that I was more called to contemplation as a way of showing up. I decided to train and be ordained as an Episcopalian priest. There was a strong sense of I need to say *yes* to this, or I will miss something important in my life. As (social activist) Parker Palmer says, "There are hundreds of ways of *almost* being yourself." The work with homeless youth had been my life. In the transition, something stopped. It was like sitting in the desert. It took a couple of years to become clear for me what to do next. It was a very painful time, but it led to a more complete *yes*.

In Adam's experience, Not Being entails recognizing that you are intimately connected with others, that life can be lived in service, but that it requires reciprocity. There is a need for dialogue between contemplation and action. "For me," he says, "structure has been important. Something about this way of life now enables me to feel whole. Everything can be in the right relation. A new rhythm of life."

Adam starts each day in silence, listening to his heart and asking himself, "Who do I need to be today?" This informs his day, as, in turn, his day also informs the silence to which he returns during moments of reflection. This dance is the new rhythm of his life, while he provides pastoral care to one of the largest urban communities, in New York. Adam has learned that when our heart breaks open, painful as this may be, we discover our intimate connection with others. This leads to a different way of being in the world that can be deeply engaged and fulfilling.

THE BODYBUILDER: THE PHYSICAL IS THE VEHICLE

"People are much more likely to act their way into a new way of thinking, than think their way into a new way of acting."

Richard Pascale, *Surfing the Edge of Chaos*

Over the past three years, Akash Vaghela and the team at RNT, his online company, have helped transform the bodies of thousands of people from all walks of life and abilities, in more than 20 countries. What is special about what they do is that their work on muscles and physique is only a beginning, a vehicle to a more profound transformation in all areas of their clients' lives.

Akash's father came to the UK as a 12-year-old boy from Zambia, and his mother from Uganda, fleeing the cruel dictatorship of Idi Amin. Akash's father trained as a lawyer, working in the City of London, and there was some expectation that Akash would follow in his footsteps. While Akash did well at grammar school and interned at law firms, he discovered that where he as at his happiest was in the gym.

I caught the bug. It gave me a level of control, confidence and focus. It was my anchor in the day then, just as it is now. I was fascinated by the idea of pushing myself and seeing my body change.

Akash would push himself to the point of failure, where he could lift no more. This would take him into 'the void,' a meditative state in which all sense of separation and the thinking mind disappeared. Eventually, his love of training led him to study sports science at university, to his parents' surprise, as they saw his peers opting for more familiar degrees in law, medicine and finance. Their biggest concern was how he would translate his passion into making a living.

Before he graduated, Akash started training a friend at a distance, foreshadowing what would later develop into his online business. At the same time, he began to train clients in private gyms, achieving good results. He would work long hours and then spend the night researching and reading about fitness.

> I was obsessed. I had low self-confidence, low self-esteem. I was not confident enough to make my own decisions or put my foot down. My dedication to training was my way to transform not just the physical, but all aspects of my life. It was my *why*.

A foundation of RNT's transformation methodology is helping clients identify their *why*. That is, the reason they want to transform: fitness as a means of being a more effective parent, as a coping mechanism for divorce, as a way of tackling type 2 diabetes, and so on. From the start, Akash's own *why* was to use education to transform himself, developing more confidence, and to transform his clients' lives. One of the ways he tested this was to go to the extreme himself — through bodybuilding — so that he could take his clients there too.

Bodybuilding is an intense sport in which the results are fully visible. You can't prep the night before or wing it on the day of. It requires a detailed focus and months of preparation, with nothing less than total commitment. In 2014, Akash won the Junior Edition of the British Body Building Federation, losing 14 kilos and lowering his body fat index to less than 6%. Yet, within seven days of his victory he had put on seven kilos through binge eating, as his body recovered from prolonged starvation. Over the course of the next two years, he learned more about the pitfalls of an endless cycle of famine and feast, vowing never to diet again.

The trigger for Akash to found RNT came from watching one of the other personal trainers on the gym floor. The trainer followed a hellish schedule from early in the morning until late in the evening, his eyes blood-shot from lack of sleep. Although a new father, he rarely had the opportunity to spend time with his child during the week. Akash did not want this to be his life.

He decided that an online transformation company would not only deliver great results for clients but also allow coaches the freedom to follow lifestyles more suited to them as well. It was while on holiday in Thailand, reading communications consultant Michael Hayman's *Mission* — a book about companies with a purpose — that Akash realized his business was concerned with much more than simply personal training. Feedback from his clients reflected that, while they sought RNT out for the physical, they were also gaining courage and confidence, making better decisions regarding their careers and transforming all aspects of their lives.

This led Akash to write a blog post, 'The Physical is the Vehicle.'

If you can master the physical, it's the vehicle to master anything else in your life. We can consider an analogy inspired by the *Bhagavad Gita*: Our body is the chariot that carries our soul. Our mind (mental) is the reins. Our emotions (senses) are the horses. Our way of thinking (education) directs our soul (self) as the driver of the chariot. Only if all pieces of the puzzle are intact can the chariot reach its destination. Now, if the physical is the vehicle, you can only be at your best and perform when it is firing on all cylinders. What is common is that people lose weight but then they put it all back on and then some, because they have not made a shift in their identity. They have not rewired their behavior and mindset to the identity of someone healthy and in-shape. Even if they are now 60 kilos, they may still self-identify as someone of 80 kilos and their behavior will soon reflect that. The aim of transformation is to shift long-term behavior. That means building the structures, systems, and strategies that lead to new behavior that will create a new identity.

Having helped shift the identity of hundreds of clients, Akash warns against any notion of a quick fix. "You can't walk out of the forest in 12 days when it took you 12 years to walk into it." There's a lengthy process required that involves introspection, and then action.

Akash often recommends journaling to his clients, as a way to reflect on their thoughts and notice patterns. "Often the *why* of the client evolves from wanting to impress others to learning to love the journey itself, entailing a shift from the external to the internal."

We live in an age obsessed with the external, yet Akash's story shows how it can be used as a starting point for wider transformation, including a shift in identity. By pushing himself into the void, Akash shows how Not Being is not only a mental state but a fully embodied one.

▲
◀ POINTERS ▶
▼

As you read a book word by word and page by page, you participate in its creation, just as a cellist playing a Bach suite participates, note by note, in the creation, the coming-to-be, the existence, of the music.

And, as you read and re-read, the book of course participates in the **creation of you, your thoughts and feelings, the size and temper of your soul.**

~ Ursula K. Le Guin, 'The Language of the Night'

THOUGHT

S T A Y   W I T H   I T

"Don't think. FEEEEEEEL!
It's like a finger pointing away to
the moon. Do not concentrate
on the finger or you will miss all
of the heavenly glory!"

Bruce Lee, Enter the Dragon

During an early scene in the 1973 film, *Enter the Dragon*, the protagonist played by Bruce Lee chastises his student, encouraging him to remain in the full experience of the present moment rather than becoming stuck in analysis, bogged down by ideas or concepts. The student has to move *beyond* the teacher and the teaching. Instead, he has to see that which is being pointed to. Similarly, our Not Being portraits lead us to insights about the illusion of the separate self, and the need to recognize and embrace our symbiotic existence and interdependent relationship with others. We know ourselves through these relationships in a never-ending process of self-revelation. Through others, we discover ourselves — not as a fixed thing but as something that is always evolving. To relate is to be.

In the previous two books of this trilogy — *Not Knowing* and *Not Doing*, written by Steven D'Souza and Diana Renner — we introduced the notion of Negative Capabilities. This is a concept that the poet John Keats, when corresponding with his brothers, used to describe when people are "capable of being in uncertainties, Mysteries, doubts, without any irritable reaching after fact & reason." As with Fitzgerald's argument for the need to be able to hold two opposing ideas in mind, Negative Capability requires a both/and rather than an either/or outlook. It entails an acceptance of ambiguity, suggesting that the path of subtraction and unlearning has equal validity in relation to additive behavior.

While researching this book, we interviewed many people to discover more about what Not Being meant and how it was experienced. The people who shared their stories with us came from diverse backgrounds and disciplines. What became clear from our conversations with them — including an artist, undertaker and hotelier, among many others — is that we should not fall into the trap of mistaking *being* for *doing*. The generation and pursuit of goals, action plans and strategies as the basis of self-development would be entirely antithetical to our notion of Not Being and the premise of the book.

Instead, we hope that this book serves as a *pointer* towards the state of Not Being, assisting your own exploration and helping you to discover what is already here. As you read, we invite you to focus not only on the text (Lee's 'finger-pointing') but to relax into a space of awareness, taking notice of what is present before and between your thoughts (Lee's 'heavenly constellation'), prompted by what you read, by the white spaces you find on the page, by the illustrations, and by the connections and leaps you make in your mind. Notice when you become lost in thought, when you get caught up in analysis, agreement, disagreement, excitement or aversion. Our invitation is neither to pull away nor to become immersed, but to notice and stay with it, to be aware of what you feel, to be curious. What happens when you go beyond the words? When you read for transformation rather than for information? When you share and discuss your insights with others?

In this second part of the book, we will examine four pointers that can further elucidate the state of Not Being. They are as follows:

Don't Think, But Look

We need to overcome the constraints of the analytical mind, which is often focused on propositional knowledge rather than lived experience. To live with Not Being is to go beyond fixed concepts and definitive answers, leading a life of inquiry, following our curiosity. We will discover how we can widen our experience of being, drawing on the immediacy of our senses, and become attuned to the embodied and relational.

Momento Mori

Not Being requires living with impermanence, with constant evolution. There is no place for fixity. The separate self, the protective carapace, has to die in order to enable a more visceral experience of being. We have to learn to live with loss and grief as well as to appreciate the freshness of each moment, so that we come to see what truly is important to us. We do not evade endings or shun attachments. We learn to hold lightly, letting in and letting go.

Contemplay

With this fusion of contemplation and playfulness, we are asked to recognize how impermanence results in non-attachment and lightness. We develop the ability to engage in life as an infinite game with the energy of the trickster. Here we discover that equanimity is not about bypassing our feelings but about being able to acknowledge and face them. Life becomes more about experimentation, joyfulness and play. We learn how contemplation is not the absence of action, but involves finding our own ways to reflect.

Give Your Self Away

We experience meaning and purpose more fully when we are not concerned with our self but, instead, turn outward to others. We explore what it means to give, the importance of community and belonging, and how we can move from separation to sharing our gifts with the world. We move from an abstract care for the universal to learning to love the particular, the person and the situation before us. The result is that we give our small *self* away, knowing that is how we truly find ourselves: in relationship.

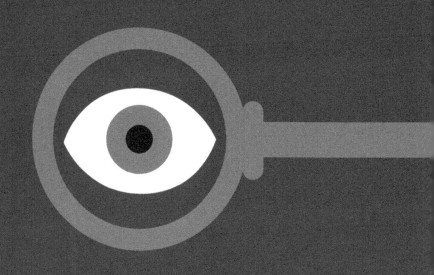

CHAPTER 7

DON'T THINK, BUT LOOK

SEEING

"The act of looking, after all, takes place in the first person. I see the object, but the very act of seeing it breaches the divide between me and it. At that moment aren't subject and object bound together in a unified loop of perception?"

Siri Hustvedt, *Living, Thinking, Looking*

In *Not Knowing*, we explored how, as a society, we tend to privilege knowledge even though the complex challenges that we face require us to be comfortable with not having the answers, with being able to tolerate ambiguity and learn continuously. In the same way, we also privilege thinking as the primary means by which we make sense of the world. In Remark 66 of his *Philosophical Investigations*, however, the Austrian-British philosopher Ludwig Wittgenstein suggests that observation has to come before conclusion. His challenge — "Don't think, but look!" — is an encouragement to look on, to compare and contrast, to detect synergies and overlaps, to map out a network of similarities and relationships. It is, in effect, to engage with the world in a more immediate way, acquiring experiences and data before indulging in any sense-making.

For some, allowing ourselves to look, to see, to experience without thought or judgement, has a profound effect. Hymie Wyse, who practices as a psychotherapist, recounts a childhood story — he refers to it as "The Happening" — that had just such an impact on him.

The year is 1951. The month is August. The place is Connemara in West Ireland. The setting is the Atlantic Ocean. A father and his two sons are out fishing. They have gone out early in the morning. The ocean is calm. With them in the boat is a 13-year-old boy who is thrilled at being allowed to be with them. The sky is grey. The journey out is long. The nets have been thrown into the sea and they wait. There is no memory of talking in the boat. Time seems to have vanished. All that can be seen is the sky, the sea and the boat. The lapping of the water against the boat is calming. The wind hasn't got up yet. The silence is tangible.

After a long time, the father says, "The sea is turning." The two sons immediately haul in the nets. The boy watches the choreography in silence. What he sees is horrible. Many, many fish are caught in the nets. They are all gasping for air. Unable to continue to watch this scene, the boy looks at the sky. Then his eyes run along the sky to the horizon. He notices how the sky and the sea meet. His eyes then run along the sea back to the boat and take in the boat, the men — and he sees the unity of everything. Everything is interconnected. It is hard to find words to express what he saw that day. No words can describe the scene. The amazing aspect of this Happening — that it simply happened, out of the blue, not expected, uninvited, simply present. This scene changed his life. Sixty-nine years later, the man who was that boy still ponders, still churns over what he experienced that summer's day.

Hymie's is a story of perception, of something that went beyond language, despite the verbal color he now gives it as a result of countless retellings. What he experienced at the time, though, was a state of Not Being, of awareness of and connection with all that surrounded him, in a manner that he was unable to articulate meaningfully to other people. He could only say what it was not. Indeed, Wittgenstein suggests that not everything we see *can* be verbalized. Sometimes it can only be *shown*, in silence, without the adornment of words.

There is something primal about the ability to visualize rather than verbalize. To think and communicate visually is to encapsulate a vast array of knowledge without categorization or separation. As Sigmund Freud suggested, thinking in pictures is closer to how the unconscious works than thinking in words, which is more conscious and deliberate. For Wittgenstein, words are discrete, labels that we acquire from a young age to describe what we see. With words, we make linguistic associations with objects. It is an approach that is both reductionist and inadequate when we move beyond simple identification (*this is a table*) to descriptions of the experiential and the emotional (*beauty, truth, justice, love*). A picture can relay a complete story, a word only a fragment of it. As such, Wittgenstein sought not to see things in isolation, instead looking for patterns and connections, paying attention to context and familial relationships, allowing for shifts in perspective, as with the ambiguous images that can be both rabbit and duck.

Inevitably, an emphasis on the visual invokes the perspective of the artist. In that sense, Francis Akpata, who works in private equity — running his own boutique investment consultancy with clients in renewable energy, hedge funds and real estate — might not be the first person to come to mind. However, away from his demanding financial career, Francis is also an award-winning painter, who has developed very different ways of engaging with the world:

> In business, I carry out research, deciding, through top-down analysis, which sector or region to focus on. I then decide, through bottom-up analysis, which company or fund manager is best suited for our objective. I have financial models and business plans to guide the process. I can quantify the probability of success or assess the viability of a fund manager by checking his returns over a specified period. This quantitative process guides my decision. In my artistic practice, on the other hand, all is a magical mystery. Moving between the two is a sublime experience.

Francis began drawing when he was seven. As an adult, he studied drawing and painting in evening classes at the City Literary Institute in London and began to work on landscape paintings. There then followed an urge to paint alternating geometric patterns in primary and secondary colors that would visualize minimalist music. Francis's new work was intuitive rather than formal, with some stylistic overlaps with cubism and expressionism.

Listening to poetry, reading books, or reflecting on words or phrases like *vortex* or *to meander seamlessly*, led me to create abstract paintings where the intersection of angles and various colors have their own rhythm. There are no human figures or landscapes in these paintings. The paintings make those who perceive the world attempt to decipher what the theme is. Abstract painting is the style which most describes my inner feelings and stretches the imagination and understanding of the percipient.

At present, Francis is working on two different styles. His portraiture mixes watercolors and charcoal, with the contrast between these two mediums depicting his subjects in a way that reveals their essence. Meanwhile, he is also experimenting with optical surrealism, whereby viewers are presented with the illusion of depth of movement in his paintings. Francis describes the time he spends painting as an almost spiritual experience, drawing on both his subconscious and conscious mind. It cannot be explained in linear or sequential terms but makes sense to him after the fact, not unlike a pianist who, when improvising, suddenly finds themself playing a harmonious tune.

With my paintings, I try to superimpose rhythm and harmony while achieving a fine balance between the figurative and the abstract. I never start with a preconceived final image in mind. To do this, I have to combine austere rigor with unbridled fantasy. I believe contemplation facilitates revelation. Through contemplation and observation, one is able to grasp the essence of nature and depict that rhythmically. I aim to replicate the osmosis of nature in painting. I want my paintings to be like an optical dialogue. Each patch of color is part of a dialectic process where each surface is trying to establish itself. In my paintings, there is conflict between luminosity and density, struggle between quantity and quality, tension between gravity and lightness. I seek to find a rhythmic balance between the forces at play.

This interplay is reflected, too, in the way that Francis moves in and out of the business world of quantification, numeracy, words, logic and verification, and the artistic sphere of intuition, emotion, subjectivity, visualization and connection. According to author Ted Falconar, in *Creative Intelligence and Self-Liberation*, this is the difference between Aristotelian thinking, which is favored by our education system, and Non-Aristotelian thinking. In *Tractatus Logico-Philosophicus*, Wittgenstein goes so far as to reason, "That the world is *my* world, shows itself in the fact that the limits of the language (*the* language which I understand) mean the limits of *my* world." Art, however, proves itself to be a boundless universal language.

In *Science and Sanity*, the theoretical scholar Alfred Korzybski developed our understanding of Non-Aristotelian thinking, examining how feelings often have primacy over reason. It is a thesis that has been strengthened further by studies in neuroscience. We are predictably irrational beings, frequently moving to action before we have even processed logical thought and consciously decided to do so. Korzybski observes:

> Creative scientists know very well from observation of themselves, that all creative work starts as 'feeling', 'inclination', 'suspicion', 'hunch', or some other unspeakable affective state, which only at a later date, after a sort of nursing, takes the shape of a verbal expression worked out later in a rationalized, coherent, linguistic scheme called a theorem. In mathematics we gave some astonishing examples of intuitively proclaimed theorems,

which at a later date, have been proven to be true, although the original proof was false.

In a 1931 paper — 'A Non-Aristotelian System and Its Necessity for Rigour in Mathematics and Physics' — that was subsequently included in *Science and Sanity*, Korzybski remarked, "A map *is not* the territory it represents, but, if correct, it has a *similar structure* to the territory, which accounts for its usefulness." A map, an image, a string of words, can never fully reflect reality or capture the forms, structures, patterns, shapes, feelings and intuitions, the fusion of subjectivity, objectivity and context, from which our understanding of it is composed. All they can do is provide pointers.

Steven: As a child, for seven years I would take a coach to and from school each day. It was a 13-mile trip in either direction. While this was an opportunity to catch up with friends, or to complete last-minute homework, on many occasions I would just look out of the window, observing the patterns the raindrops made on the glass. I would not be thinking about what I saw but would just look. There was a sense of the mind being at rest. I was not daydreaming or thinking about the future or reminiscing about the past; I was just experiencing seeing. There was a quality of deep peacefulness to this, beyond the chatter of the analytical mind.

By invoking Wittgenstein's words — Don't think, but look! — it is not our intention to dismiss the power of rational thought. Indeed, we need more of it in this confusing world, filled with alternate facts, conspiracy theories and psychobabble. Instead, we seek to remind the reader that we can expand our experience of who we are, going beyond verbalization and conscious thought, embracing the creativity that can be derived from emotion, intuition and visualization. Noticing *how* we perceive allows us to reflect on our perspectives, enabling us to look from different angles and in new ways that can inform and surprise. Through stilling the incessant thinking mind and allowing ourselves to simply look, we can gain greater awareness of being.

LIVING IN STORIES

"We tell ourselves stories in order to live."

Joan Didion, *The White Album*

In 2005, novelist David Foster Wallace began his commencement address at Kenyon College, in Ohio, with a parable:

There are these two young fish swimming along and they happen to meet an older fish swimming the other way, who nods at them and says, "Morning, boys. How's the water?" And the two young fish swim on for a bit, and then eventually one of them looks over at the other and goes, "What the hell is water?"

It's a question that carries the potential to transform us, if we dare to follow its line of inquiry. To see the water, to recognize the water, is to understand that the world we live in is mediated and shaped by stories. To become aware of the story is to become aware of the possibility of alternate realities, of other ways of seeing and being in the world.

By stories, we mean more than the captivating fairytales from childhood, which often revealed hidden truths, or the latest juicy gossip heard from a friend or read on social media. Rather, we are referring to those invisible narratives that shape our culture, our attitudes, and every aspect of our lives. It is our worldview that unconsciously dictates who we are, what we think, our political tendencies, and our opinion of others. Humans need stories just like fish need water, but, unlike the fish, we don't necessarily move through the water. Instead, we can become stuck in our stories, even if the tank is dirty and the water is killing us. In *The Choice*, Edith Eger, a survivor of Auschwitz, writes of the need to "dismantle the prison in our mind."

We are constrained by and suffer because of what is external to us but also as a result of what is internal: that is, the stories and beliefs to which we are in thrall.

Steven: The banging continued on my front door. It was 2 a.m. "Who on earth could this be?" I wondered, half-startled and unsure whether I would be dealing with a crazed intruder or someone in urgent need of help. I walked towards the door and opened it. It was my neighbor Martin, a big, burly man. He looked stressed and pointed to the back of my garden. I didn't need to look, as I could hear it. The tiny brook, which was situated about 20 feet from the cottage, had become a raging river and was close to flooding my home. It was then that I noticed the orange lights of a fire truck. Firemen were laying sandbags along the edge of the river to prevent the banks on the other side from bursting. "Could I have a bag for my home?" I asked one of the firemen. "Sorry mate, we don't have enough," he replied.

The cottage did not flood that night, but that was the least of my worries. I lived with the constant, low-grade threat of flooding, but, more worryingly, also of being given 30 days' notice to knock down my home, as the person who had sold it to me had not secured the appropriate planning permission. It was an incredibly stressful period, facing the prospect of either being homeless or spending thousands of pounds that I did not have to destroy and rebuild the cottage. It all hung on an appeal, and my head was filled with images of bankruptcy, destitution and vagrancy as I worried about what would happen.

It was at this point that I came across The Work of Byron Katie, a meditative practice of inquiry developed by a former alcoholic. I quickly signed up to attend one of her 'Schools of Unlearning' in Germany. Katie had had her own Damascene moment, in the depths of depression, as she lay on the floor of a halfway house watching a cockroach crawl over her body. "Whenever I believe my thoughts," she realized, "I suffer." As she began to question her beliefs, she felt both peaceful and free. From this point, Katie began to turn her life around, repairing her relationship with her daughter, and teaching her simple method to thousands of people around the world. She helped them to unlearn and to unshackle themselves from faulty beliefs rather than amassing more of them.

Katie's main premise is that we all live in stories. When the stories we tell ourselves do not bring us peace or result in effectiveness, we should question them. "Who would you be without your story?" she asks. Her method is a fusion of cognitive behavioral therapy and mindfulness. "All war belongs on paper," Katie claims, meaning that it is important to write down our beliefs so that we can begin to question them. What should we question? Essentially, any belief that causes us stress, including our self-doubts and fears. In my case, this related to the prospect of homelessness and financial ruin.

Katie leads each person attending her course through a series of questions, which examine their beliefs in a meditative way, involving both the head and the heart. The questions challenge the validity of the beliefs, the individual's attachment to them, and how that affects them. In my own case, as I addressed the situation with the cottage, imagining myself with no money or home, I could feel the stress build in my body, as my breathing became shallower and my chest tighter. But, as I was encouraged by Katie to inquire more deeply, I could feel myself letting go, become lighter and more peaceful as I responded to the question, "Who would you be, right now, if you could absolutely not think this thought?"

Over several days, I went through variations of the exercise, managing the stress, challenging the beliefs, identifying what I could do in order to resolve the situation. Since then, I have made it part of my practice to notice when I am stressed, to recognize what belief lies behind this, and to thoroughly question it.

Katie's method has been criticized by some people who argue that it either results in the individual blaming themself, or simply changing their beliefs rather than addressing the situation at hand. However, this was not my experience. I found that from a place of calm I was much better able to deal with the situation, taking appropriate action, rather than being paralyzed by worry. What good did my beliefs do me if they only resulted in suffering and stress?

As we have seen, an essential aspect of Not Being is to not think, but to look, inquire and explore. This is what Katie's method led me to, and I left her course with fewer beliefs to cling to than when I arrived. "Reality is always kinder than the story we tell about it," she says, before elaborating: "If you argue with reality, you lose, but only 100% of the time."

One of the problems with the stories that entrap us is that they tend to be simple and reductionist. Even when based on facts, they are skewed by subjectivity and confirmation bias, filtering out what does not fit with a particular perspective or conform to our prejudices, whether conscious or unconscious. Reductionism and simplification make it impossible for us to make sense of or understand the complex environment of which we are part and in which we live. Like Wallace's fish, we end up lacking awareness of the waters in which we swim.

In 'Fragmentation,' the first part of this book, we examined how the story we currently live in emphasizes disconnection and separation: from ourselves, from other people and from nature. The consequences of this story have left the world in crisis. Not Being is an invitation to explore new stories that involve an identity larger and bolder than anything you have previously imagined; stories of relationships, connection, entanglement and inter-being, in which we perceive the self not as fragmented and apart from life, but *as* life.

When we lack the ability to challenge stories that no longer fit us, we go on believing the water is fine while we boil within it like the proverbial frog. We need the capacity to question our stories and to go beyond the constraints of our beliefs. Through simply gaining awareness of the stories we live in, seeing the water, noticing the filters and the blind spots, we awaken ourselves and can begin to ask, "What else is here? What else has been missed?" To notice the story is to create the initial shift.

We can then develop the flexibility to embrace those who think very differently from us. Not necessarily to agree, but to listen and hear, to discuss and debate, to inquire and learn, examining the nuances that connect, rather than separate, polarized opinions and ideologies. With a fixed mind, there is no possibility for or openness to change. Yet, the opportunity to learn, change and grow is precisely what we need, accumulating other potential stories and narratives rather than living in one alone.

Lucie works for a large management consulting firm in Milan, Italy. She began her journey of self-inquiry when she sought coaching assistance from Anna Simioni, an organizational change and people development adviser, because she was upset that she kept losing her temper whenever her boss contradicted her. "Every time that happened in a meeting, I'd get furious. My face would become hot, and I would snap back at them." Lucie didn't like herself or how she behaved in these situations and wanted to work on controlling her emotions. Superficially, at least, this seemed a relatively straightforward case.

Anna, however, intuited something different. Years of training in an approach developed by transformation consultant David Drake, known as *narrative coaching*, had made her sensitive to the stories people tell themselves. She understood how stories can entrap, shaping how we interpret our experiences and make sense of our realities. We consider the story to be us, to be part of our identity, thereby mistaking the clothes for the body. Rarely do we consider that the story has become worn or no longer fits properly. What once was functional and served a purpose has now locked us into a pattern that is inappropriate for our present situation.

Narrative coaching involves a rite of passage, a timeless and timely way of framing the outer change and inner transition. This enables clients to move through the liminal transition periods when they no longer view themselves as part of the old story, but have not yet ventured into a new one. The client moves through four phases, each marked by the crossing of a distinct threshold. While these phases are often not linear, each threshold can be seen both spatially, as a doorway, a place of transition, as well as temporally, as a movement.

First, the client is invited to *separate* from the outer world of behaviors, embarking on a journey into the inner world of narrative in order to undergo an identity transformation. In Lucie's case, during the first phase, Anna challenged her to reflect on why she reacted the way she did. Lucie's response emphasized her investment in and need to protect her self-image: "I have strong professional self-esteem, and I cannot stand it when my boss doesn't trust my judgement." When Anna probed further, she learned that Lucie's irascible behavior when contradicted was not unique to her interactions with her current boss, but had occurred with a previous manager, as well as with her husband. "How could I stay calm? It's a sign of weakness," she told Anna.

Lucie recalled a particular incident when she had exploded, in front of their son, in response to something her husband had said. Afterward, she felt compelled to explain what had happened to the child: "It's normal for a couple with strong characters to have small fights, but because they love each other, everything will be okay." However, when Anna queried what message this sent the child, Lucie was taken aback when she realized that it normalized conflict, framing it as a sign of strength. Anna's questions made her see the stories she was telling herself and others, making her aware of the negative effects not only on herself but on those for whom she served as a role model.

Anna challenged Lucie to question the stories she tended to cling to, acting as if they were not true, as if the behavior of others was not a threat to her self-respect, as she had come to believe. How would such a shift affect her own behavior and her interactions with other people? Could she remain calm when she felt that she was being contradicted? After a few attempts, Lucie developed gestural and breathing responses to the trigger, discovering that she could now control her reactions.

This was the sign for Anna to guide Lucie beyond the second threshold. In the second phase, the client begins to *individuate* as they overcome the obstacles in their inner world, seeking out what will bring restoration and maturation. These obstacles are what have held the individual back, the stories that have served as a straitjacket. In Lucie's case, she was trapped by her self-image as an energetic and super-committed person, twisted by and caught between the fear that arises in the face of new challenges and her need for control. It was all too easy to become stuck in such a situation. As Lucie progressed through this phase, she moved from a feeling of vulnerability to one of rebirth, learning what was and was not important to her. She further refined her embodied responses to the trigger, adopting a maternal gesture with her hand on her stomach.

The third phase, *re*-incorporation, marks a shift back from the inner world to the outer, implementing what has been gained through exploration and experimentation. At this point, Anna and Lucie drew on a narrative coaching technique known as *five perspectives*, which is designed to help people become unstuck, seeing and responding to their situation in new ways. Anna role-played certain difficult situations with Lucie in order to test out her newly won awareness and ability to stay focused, acting as a demanding colleague, and then as the new CEO, who provided bad news or negative feedback. Lucie was noticeably excited by the newfound freedom from her own old story.

Less is more. I'd never accept that before, but now I want to write it on the front of my office!

In the past, I was like a windsurfer. With a good wind behind me, I was able to go fast. Now, I am more like a dolphin who is able to play on the surface of the water, as well as to go deep and change direction on my own, without the wind or even with the wind against me.

What got in the way when I was windsurfing was the windsurfer itself: *me*. It was my self-esteem, which had always seemed so strong and important yet was easily jeopardized by my fear of judgement. In the past, I responded to criticism emotionally, using armor to protect myself. But this made me heavy, unable to swim like a dolphin.

The final phase relates to *integration*, in which new insights and embodied practices enable transformation towards a new identity. This entails ongoing work, especially as old stories die hard, while it takes time for new stories to stick. Lucie acknowledges that during this struggle to change how we perceive ourselves — and our relationship to other people and our environment — we can quickly revert to old beliefs, habits and behavior. Lucie learned that she had to be patient and invest energy strategically in order to master her emotions.

At this point, Lucie even chose to seek psychological help for her son and herself as they grieved the loss of her mother. She was now able to integrate two apparently different stories — 'I'm strong and can handle challenges on my own' and 'I need help' — into a new narrative: 'I am strong and competent, and if I work on my real priorities, I can ask for help.' Lucie had learned to shift from an either/or perspective to a both/and one, accepting paradox and bridging between the inner and outer worlds. Anna said this of her shared journey with Lucie:

> Often, when faced with challenges, many of us look for techniques to fix issues or manage our emotions. What we need instead is to become more aware of our identities and stories, investigate our emotional states with a different view, and act according to what matters to us. In this state of awareness, challenges can help us to go deeper and become stronger in our multiplicity.

LIFE AS INQUIRY

"The tension between curiosity that leads to discovery and the curiosity that leads to perdition threads its way throughout all of our endeavors. The temptation of the horizon is always present."

Albert Manguel, *Curiosity*

The illusion of the separate self can be challenged in a number of ways. In Lucie's case, her examination of her inner world, her improved understanding of her emotions and their impact on other people, illuminated her own connection to and interdependency on them. There is a need, too, to enhance our awareness of the environment through which we move and of which we are a part. It is not enough simply to journey through, our heads buried in maps, focused on a destination. We need to immerse ourselves in our surroundings, recognizing and accepting our symbiotic relationship with them, as we inquire, explore and discover. We have to open ourselves not only to what is inside us, but to what is apparently outside us and to the relational space in between.

In *Becoming a Practitioner Researcher*, therapist and consultant Paul Barber describes a Gestalt approach to inquiry. This is phenomenological, attending to the direct experience of the environment. It is felt, seen and heard without pause for thought or interpretation. We 'constellate' the rich dynamics of our experience in the moment. According to Barber, such an approach requires "a genuine, interested and non-judgemental" presence, guided by humanistic values. If a picture is worth a thousand words, then, with Gestalt inquiry, experience is worth a thousand pictures. But, how do we pay attention to experience in a way that extends beyond our own subjectivity and is more inclusive? Is it possible to live life itself as inquiry?

Kathleen King is an organizational consultant and the former director of the doctoral program at the UK's Ashridge Hult International Business School. When Kathleen assumed leadership of the doctoral program it was grounded in a well-established theoretical perspective on organizations. Participants were encouraged, if not expected, to adopt this framework as the foundation for their doctoral work. For Kathleen, it was imperative that participants develop their own perspective, grounded in their experience. For too long, she argued, organizational leaders and consultants had attempted to squeeze their experience into reductionist models and frameworks rather than paying close attention to their actual lived experience and the complexities of organizational reality. To counter this, reflective Action Research became the broad methodological umbrella for the program. This required participants to take a profound interest in their practice, their assumptions, their actions, their favored theories, and to be willing to challenge everything they think they know and do. Ultimately, the aim was to contribute to the flourishing of the living world — both human and beyond. It entailed a cyclical process of experience, reflection, conceptualization and experimentation.

> Inquiry, for me, is about suspending judgement, refraining from advocacy, staying curious, especially when I am desperate to leap to judgement — especially negative judgement when I feel attacked, frustrated, angry or bored. It is a way to stay connected in a soft, open way, rather than becoming either disconnected (withdrawal, dismissal, condemnation) or violently connected (verbal attacks, abuse, aggression). The outcome is the possibility of dialogue, of relationship. Another word for it is *ecology*. Action research is an attitude of inquiry, a serious

commitment to suspending judgement and staying curious, to thinking carefully about what I am discovering, and then acting in the world from the basis of what I found out. More of a stance rather than a prescription.

A second important aspect of the program's revised philosophy was a result of Kathleen's conviction that deep knowledge is often hard to express in propositional statements, and can be both explored and represented more readily through art. As the dancer and choreographer Merce Cunningham put it, "If I could say it, I wouldn't have to dance it."

After leaving the business school, Kathleen has dedicated herself to consulting, coaching and research. She has also developed her own artistic inquiry through working with textiles. Kathleen found an outlet for this passion in 'Unspeakable Loss,' a piece that explores the impact of the Covid-19 pandemic, which was displayed at the Sussex Together Festival of Arts at Chichester Cathedral.

Deeply unsettled by the Covid-19 pandemic and by the effects of lockdown, it was inevitable that I would undertake a stitching project. While I was deeply grateful for the privileged position I found myself in — sharing my home with a loving husband, living by the sea, having access to friends, albeit virtually, and to plentiful food — I also followed, with growing disquiet, the sharp rise in incidence and fatality rate of Covid-19 worldwide. I was increasingly perturbed by the bland statistics, which obfuscate as much as they reveal. I wanted to disrupt that blandness, to honor in however small a way the human tragedy behind the graphs.

I chose to embroider an alternative representation of the neat little graphs on scrim, a flimsy material that presented me with more challenges than I had bargained for. This work required me to seek out the daily death toll, and subsequently sit with the reality of what I found for at least a couple of hours every evening. Stitching, however challenging (or perhaps because of the challenge on occasions), has a soothing quality. There is something mesmerizing in the rhythm of the needle going through the cloth and I love the sensuous touch of the materials. It is a way to "lose my mind and come to my senses," as Fritz Perls would have said.

During the numerous hours of creating 'Unspeakable Loss,' I discovered the many layers of my discomfort, my fear, my snap judgement of others, including politicians and the decisions they did or didn't make, as well as friends who held sometimes wildly different views to my own. Stitching helped me to stay with what I uncovered, rather than running for the cover of tempting distractions: novels, movies, TV, wine.

For me, action is an integral part of inquiry. I consider myself an action researcher at heart. Sometimes, that action consists of keeping quiet, sitting still, refraining from reacting. Whatever I think is likely to be the most generative in a particular context. Volunteering for coaching work in the NHS was one of the outcomes of my Covid embroidery reflective discipline. Another was the resolve to be mindful of the kind of energy I sent out into the world. Whatever my instinctive reactions, the world did *not* need more anger, more anxiety, more frustration from a rather privileged person like myself.

If I start from the assumption that nothing in the human condition is alien to me — that every one of the inexplicable, savage, cruel, enlightened, glorious, benign, delightful characteristics I discern in others is potentially also present in me — then it behooves me to stay curious and interested in how the other got to where they are right now, so that I can respond in the most ecological way. Living life as inquiry also keeps me from taking for granted the privileges I experience on a daily basis: a home, food, friends and family.

LIFE AS INQUIRY

By remaining curious, by constantly inquiring, I have learned to notice in myself and in others the ways in which we humans become stuck. I catch myself in the midst of action going merrily around the drama triangle or falling for solutions that aggravate the problem: terrible simplifications, trying harder, shooting the messenger, utopian ideals. These are all rife these days. I catch myself stepping into the polarizing good/bad, right/wrong dichotomies. More often than not, I notice the extent to which my judgement of others is also a projection on my part.

By using inquiry to feed her art, and using her hands as part of her sense-making process, Kathleen found a way to maintain interest, suspend judgement and seek to connect. Where working with textiles has supported Kathleen's own practice of inquiry, other people may find that journaling, meditation, dance, performance or painting encourages their curiosity and enhances their experience of life, deepening their connection to themselves and to others.

COMPLICIT

"How have I been complicit in creating the conditions I say I don't want?"

Jerry Colonna, *in conversation with Tim Ferriss*

Self-inquiry often begins with an uncomfortable question, like: 'What's my part in this mess?' With an inquiring outlook, the first impulse when challenges arise or disasters happen is not to apportion blame to others. Instead, it is to understand what role we have played in bringing about these events, as well as determining what we can do to mitigate them and effect change.

Why does that matter? Now, more than ever, anyone paying attention to issues, whether local or global, can recognize that each of us is entwined in fundamental infrastructures relating to ecology, economics, geopolitics and other aspects of life. While we may complain, for example, about the cost of fast fashion or the destruction of the environment, if we pause to take stock, we will see how our own behavior and everyday decisions about what we eat, how and where we travel, what we purchase, what we discard and when, all contribute to these effects, on our own doorstep and much further afield, both now and in the long term. Whether we like it or not, as entrepreneur and life coach Jerry Colonna suggests, we are complicit in creating the conditions in which we live and contributing towards those that will be our legacy to the planet's future inhabitants.

In the workplace, we are similarly complicit. We create and exacerbate problems, abdicate responsibilities, and expect charismatic leaders to find the right solution and light our way, pointing the finger of blame at them when they fail to do so. Too often, the prevalent discourse around challenges relates to the notion of the leader as hero who, in surmounting challenges, will build a following, transforming attitudes and behaviors along the way. This is what leadership coach Simon Western refers to as the "Messiah leadership discourse," which, he argues, has resulted in conformist, homogeneous cultures, lacking in genuine organizational creativity and, ultimately, subject to a totalitarian style of leadership. Our complicity can deliver not heroism but tyranny.

What we learn is that no one person — including ourselves — can exert control over our lives. All events, opportunities and misfortunes are co-created and shaped by context. They require shared responsibility across a range of different actors. Often, it will not be we who are at the center of the stage. Nevertheless, we are as integral to the events that affect other people as to the drama of our own lives. What we say and what we do matter. They reflect our complicity in the events that unfurl.

Sharon Nash, an organizational consultant and leadership coach based in the UK, has experienced this in a variety of ways. She has depended on self-inquiry — which she describes in an article published in *Organization Development Review* as "a process of profound self-curiosity and discovery which results in a deeply evolving consciousness, cultivated over time, with no hard borders or containers" — to examine a growing sense of disenchantment and to question whether she has been doing the best work possible with her clients, and truly making any difference.

The practice of inquiry invites us to move beyond who we think we are, beyond notions of fixed identity and a separate self. It challenges us to go deeper and wider, to attend to our feelings, thoughts and emotions, and to develop awareness of our actions and their effects. It is a process of continuous unfolding. For Sharon, this began with her noticing a gap between her own self-perception and her action in the world.

FIXED
IDENTITY

As a consultant and leadership coach, Sharon's professional ethos was about "working with authenticity and helping others to come to their awareness." However, through self-inquiry, she saw that her actions were occasionally driven by self-doubt, a need for control and perfectionism. Working with a coach, Sharon began to understand that how she behaved and what she did stemmed from a childhood perception of sibling inferiority and an inherent desire to prove her abilities.

Our identities are shaped by our past experiences, even though our conscious memory can be selective about what it recalls — "more poet than reporter," as the novelist James Sallis characterized it. While past experiences cannot be isolated from current reality, they help us to appreciate how nuanced experiences have shaped our identity, even if those identities cannot be singularly or clearly defined. In Sharon's case, seeing clearly how her identity was shaped by her upbringing enabled her to accept the mixed intentions and forces within her.

As a consequence, she gained greater awareness, noticing how she was a conduit for multiple personas, each exerting their own influence on her. She could no longer think in terms of a fixed solitary self, but recognized a multifaceted identity comprising many selves, embracing self-confidence and self-doubt, a willingness to learn, a fear of making mistakes, and countless other apparently polarized tendencies. This was who she was in all her complexity and diversity: multilayered and multistoried.

The next step in Sharon's process of inquiry moved from *knowing* herself to *being* herself, exploring how her presence impacted those around her. The catalyst was her involvement in a client leadership meeting at an organization that was struggling to implement its business strategy. Sharon had intended to be a quiet and purposeful presence at the meeting, listening, questioning and prompting deeper discussion of the underlying issues that had caused the impasse. However, she found herself assuming a leadership role when the CEO failed to do so, with "my presence shifting between competing modes, wanting to act and holding back, and noticing how that felt, like being stuck in an elevator between floors."

Reflecting back on this unsatisfactory experience, Sharon discovered that she had been fixed in her desire to deliver a good outcome for the client, which had been predetermined prior to the meeting. In effect, she had had a behavioral agenda and, by holding too tightly to her objective, she had ultimately diminished her presence, failing to respond effectively as the conversation strayed from where she thought it should be.

Sharon had assumed authority on behalf of the other people in the meeting, receiving their silent assent. However, this removed her from her intended role of discerning observer, conversation facilitator and coach. Sharon's actions had meant that the people in the organization that she was meant to assist had stepped back and relied on her to intervene, when they should have stepped up and taken the opportunity to learn from the experience.

The Gestalt psychotherapist Fritz Perls once asked, "How is it possible to be unattached to outcome, fully in the moment, and yet have an agenda?" It's a nuanced challenge to be able to hold multiple intentions at once, being both a part of and apart from the client system, while maintaining an open awareness that can attend to what is most needed in the moment. This is especially the case in situations where stakeholders are invested in their own conscious and unconscious agendas. The anxiety level of the whole group rises, and there is a need for someone who is a "non-anxious presence," who can remain emotionally engaged without being reactive, to borrow from the terminology of rabbi and family therapist Edwin Friedman. Such a presence, Friedman asserts, "will modify the anxiety of the entire organization."

Steven: *In my early days of exploring the field of self-development, I was drawn primarily to behavior and techniques. For example, the work of Neuro Linguistic Programming (NLP) gave me specific tools that I could use to shift behavior, which I anticipated, over time, would cause a shift in identity. The work I did with a mature student helped stop her panic attacks but surfaced a deeper issue — that they were a response to past abuse. For me, it was a very early lesson that all behavior serves a purpose, and that we are not simply cogs in a machine but complex systems. When we change or remove something, even an unwanted behavior, it is likely there will be other changes as a result. We should not tinker unless we have the capability to work with the depth of and connections between issues that may arise. If a heavy drinker stops drinking alcohol, for example, the addiction may simply shift to other substances or compensatory behavior. These can achieve the same purpose as the drinking: avoidance of an underlying problem.*

Over time, I came to see that development was less about techniques or tools and more about our very being, about who we are. This was key, especially in working with clients. I began training in psychotherapy, and doing the 'inner work' as well as the 'outer work.' Both paths are equally necessary and valuable. What I noticed was that positive results with my clients didn't come from fancy techniques but in who I was being: present, loving, curious, steady, playful, strict, firm.

There were no prescriptions, but rather being whatever was required in the moment, representing something that had been missing for the client, something they needed to feel and experience or that I, as a therapist, needed to feel and experience in relation to them. A key phrase that struck me profoundly during my training was, "We make a difference through our Presence." The simple fact of being myself could be the most powerful intervention possible.

Sharon arrived at a similar conclusion. To stay present and assist her clients, she learned that we need to stay aware of our unconscious thoughts and assumptions. She now asks herself these questions both before and during any interaction or event:

What assumptions am I holding about how I need to show up in this situation?

How does my intent to impact this particular situation get spelt out to my clients?

How tightly am I holding onto my intent and how is that affecting my presence?

Critical self-reflection, accompanied by feedback actively sought from others, has expanded Sharon's self-understanding and made her open, present and effective in her client work. She is more aware now of how beliefs can serve to filter and distort, more wary of the pitfalls of becoming too closely aligned with sophisticated frameworks, more adaptive to the shifting sands of human interaction. Genuine self-inquiry requires profound curiosity and quiet attentiveness to the effect we have on the world around us, to our complicity in events wherever we happen to be standing on the stage.

IMAGINAL KNOWING

"Anything will give up its secrets if you love it enough."

George Washington Carver

What is color? What is the nature of light? Philosophers and natural scientists have pondered these questions for millennia. From the time of Aristotle until the Enlightenment, there was a widely held assumption that pure light was fundamentally white and colorless, and that colors came from a mixture of light with darkness. It was only in 1704, when Isaac Newton published *Opticks*, his second major book of physical science, that this understanding changed. Through experiments with prisms, Newton demonstrated that light is composed of different spectral colors.

Where Newton opted for theory and explanation, however, Johann Wolfgang von Goethe — who straddled both the sciences and the arts — offered an alternate scientific approach, less dependent on detached observation and inferential reasoning. Goethe's method stays with the immediacy of perception and, only with great hesitation, reveals any explanation. In his *Theory of Colors*, he describes different phenomena, exploring the nature of color and its perception by humans. What he outlines in terms of experimentation can be undertaken by anyone and does not require specialism or scientific expertise.

Since before the Enlightenment, science has tended to be influenced by the clockwork model, in which the universe is viewed as an intricate mechanism, with every piece subject to laws that govern its behavior. In this sense, the key task of scientific endeavor is to figure out what those laws are. Of course, reality is more complex than this, as reflected in Goethe's more tentative approach to color. Nevertheless, there remains a belief among Newton's 'descendants' in the scientific community that, with sufficient time, it will be possible to arrive at a unified theory of everything. Progress may not be easy, they suggest, but it is possible and desirable.

Implicit in this Newtonian view is a story of separation between the observer, the observed and the observation. Nature is objectified, fragmented into discrete units that can be observed and measured. Indeed, the objectivity of conventional science demands distance; researchers are required to maintain a non-interfering distance from their experiments so they do not contaminate the results. The impact of this approach still resonates in the way we live and work today. For example, a common market research practice involves customer focus group interviews in which researchers find ways to extract and unveil insights without being too close to the subject. Here there is a sharp divide between intellect and feelings, between objectivity and participation.

Reality, in its richness and variety, is neither revealed nor understood through a single means of inquiry. It has to be explored and illuminated in different ways: Newtonian and Goethean, objective and subjective, outer and inner. One method requires the development of a particular critical faculty: imagination. It is a form of *imaginal knowing* that approximates what Ralph Waldo Emerson described in his essay, 'The Poet,' as "a very high sort of seeing, which does not come by study, but by the intellect being where and what it sees."

There is, in such a situation, an emotional involvement with what is experienced, a loosening of objectivity, an entanglement, regardless of whether what we contemplate is an animal, a plant, a planet, a computer system or another human being. There is an anthropological dimension to this approach. It is similar, too, to what Craig Foster underwent as he observed, interacted with and, ultimately, was educated by an octopus.

IT HAS TO BE

EXPLORED

& ILLUMINATED

REALITY

IN DIFFERENT

WAYS

The closer you are to a phenomenon, the quieter you need to be — physically, mentally, emotionally — in order not to disturb it. As the physicist Arthur Zajonc observes:

We must pause to reflect before speaking, quietly engage the issue inwardly before acting, open ourselves to not knowing before certainty arises, and so we live for a time in the question before the answer emerges.

When we are comfortable with Not Knowing, opening ourselves to a relationship with what we are learning about, something about our sense of self shifts. The boundaries between the observer and the observed, between the acts of observation and participation, begin to blur. This was what Barbara McClintock, a Nobel Laureate in biology, experienced when she immersed herself in the study of maize, which informed her understanding of genetic transposition.

When pressed for her secret, McClintock spoke of the maize not as *objects* but as *beings*. This required becoming so familiar with them, through direct observation, that she was able to detect the slightest change, noticing the environmental impact, the traces left by the wind, the damage inflicted by insects. In effect, she had to empathize with the plants she observed, to know them intimately — every single one of them — developing a highly refined "feeling for the organism."

What McClintock felt, she later reflected, was a form of sacred communion akin to ecstasy. In *Scientific Studies*, Goethe notes that with such depth of inquiry, "Every object, well contemplated, opens up a new organ of perception within us." From this intimate participation is born imaginal insight and creative breakthroughs. In McClintock's case, this involved a convergence of the rational and the mystical, of science and spirituality. She sought not to replace the scientific method but to supplement and complement it, attaining, in addition to new knowledge, what her biographer Evelyn Fox Keller refers to as "the highest form of love, love that allows for intimacy without the annihilation of difference."

GO DIGITAL

*"Touch comes before sight, before speech.
It is the first language and the last,
and it always tells the truth."*

Margaret Atwood, *The Blind Assassin*

The acquisition and application of knowledge is both mental and sensory. It can depend as much on manual dexterity as on the intellect. Matthew Crawford, author of *The World Beyond Your Head* and *The Case for Working with Your Hands*, among other books, has embodied this in his work. Crawford holds a doctorate in political philosophy and was the executive director of a Washington think tank. He chose, however, to leave this behind him, subsequently earning a living as an electrician and as a motorcycle mechanic.

Symbolically, at least, Crawford embraced not only the head but the heart and hands as well. His is a story that echoes many of the principal themes in Robert Pirsig's *Zen and the Art of Motorcycle Maintenance*, in its fusion of philosophical musings, passion, technical knowledge and craftsmanship. A major turning point for Crawford occurred when he was still a student at the University of Chicago, seeking the guidance of a master motorcycle mechanic while still working on a dissertation about eros in Ancient Greek political philosophy.

The entanglement of his different interests led him to understand how we experience life's vitality, something he would regain later in his career when he brought together his expertise as a motorcycle mechanic and his work as a writer. Like many other manual craftsmen, Crawford fell in love what his hands get to touch, mold and shape. Working with his hands offered another way to know and experience the world.

As with artisanal craftspeople and those involved in cuisine or manual sports like tennis and hockey, it is necessary to maintain deeply and narrowly focused attention on what you do. A short-order cook or a glassblower doesn't have the luxury and freedom to choose what to do. Yet, that very constraint of being keyed into the demands of a busy kitchen or a sweltering forge simultaneously limits and energizes them. They are fully immersed without much distraction because, in those moments, they have voluntarily submitted themselves to what is in front of them. Instead of living in the head, they sense the heat of the flames at the grill or the grip of the glassblower.

By contrast, Crawford laments the conditions that confront many modern-day workers, who (at least in the pre-Covid times) have been confined to steel-and-glass towers, engaging in so-called *knowledge work*. Here, they find themselves immersed in a different kind of digital occupation involving ones and zeroes, with everything they do mediated by glowing screens. For Crawford, the prevailing failure to appreciate skilled manual labor is a symptom of something much worse: a narcissistic refusal to wrestle with the material world of unpredictable objects. A mechanic will take time to sense the condition of an object, turning it over in their hands, listening to it, orienting themselves like a doctor becoming attuned to a patient's vital signs and condition. In both cases, the interaction is immediate, intimate and very much alive. In *The World Beyond Your Head*, he writes:

The clearest contrast to the narcissist that I can think of is the repairman, who must subordinate himself to the broken washing machine, listen to it with patience, notice its symptoms, and then act accordingly.

In Crawford's view, it is not through the imagination or turning inwards that we should live our lives, but by turning outwards, by applying ourselves to, acting in, and developing our relationship with and affection for the world around us. The practice begins with paying close attention to what is not *us*. Such practice will count on different organs of cognition: our eyes, ears and hands. Senses precede reasoning.

Crawford stresses that "there is a moral imperative to *pay attention* to the shared world, and not get locked up in your own head." It is not that we should wholly reject our sense of independence. Rather, we should always question it, valuing our relationship with other sentient beings and inanimate objects, touching and interacting with them, recognizing the effects of design on what we do and the choices we make, and gaining awareness of how our independent selves are embedded and entangled already in a world founded upon interdependence.

Khuyen: I didn't grow up experiencing a lot of touch. In my Vietnamese family, touch was alien. My single mom took care of our food and schooling, but we rarely touched each other except for when I held onto her riding on the back of her motorcycle. Even when I touched things, I rarely paid attention to them. Weights in the gym, for example, were handled in order to make me stronger and improve my self-image. They were a means to an end. Nothing more.

In school, I worked hard and did well in logic-oriented subjects. In college, I majored in Computer Science and Philosophy mostly out of intellectual curiosity. Thinking hard about interesting problems was satisfying but also stressful. I felt airy, ungrounded, and was often anxious. The body and senses were considered secondary to the mind. The body was simply a fleshy vehicle for the mind's endless pursuits.

It finally dawned on me, though, that thinking alone was both limited and limiting. Curiosity couldn't be confined to the intellect alone. While the mind makes sense of things, it first requires sensory input. Touch, then, is as much part of the sense-making process as anything that occurs in the brain. They are mutually dependent, mutually informative, as aspects of experiential inquiry.

My own body, my own skin, were the sources of my most transformative learning experiences in college. Dance, physical theater, improvisation, sensuality, sexuality — all of these prompted a whole new way of being in my formerly nerdy self. Even though I was awkward as I underwent them, a part of me knew there was something innate, ancient, yet fresh about the dance, touch and contact.

I began to explore the sense of touch further, taking classes, paying more attention to it, reading about it, recognizing the language of touch and its importance in my experience of and interaction with the world.

Through touch, sight, imaginal knowing and awareness of the stories I lived in, I was able to gain a richer experience of life, of being.

MEMENTO MORI

CHAPTER 8

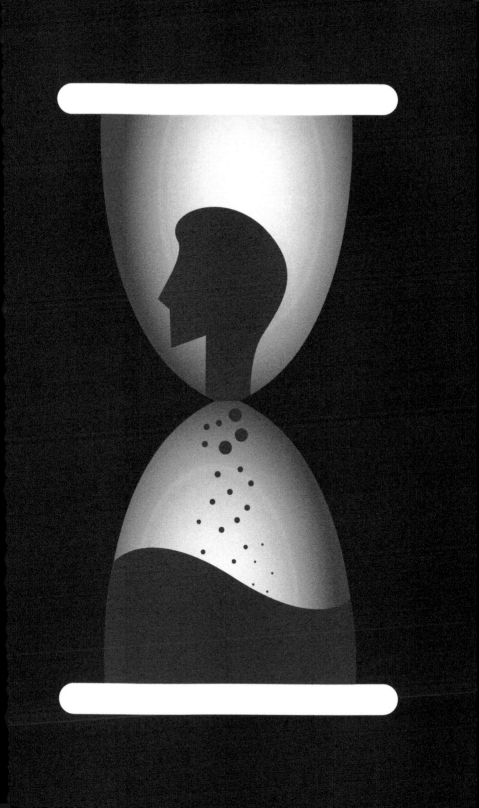

BEAUTIFUL ILLUSION

"The master had preached for many years that life was but an illusion. Then, when his son died, he wept. His students came to him and said, 'Master, how can you weep so when you have told us so many times that all things in this life are an illusion?'

'Yes,' said the master, wiping away his tears while they continued to course down his ancient cheeks, 'but he was such a beautiful illusion!'"

Solala Towler, *Tales from the Tao*

According to the author Joan Tollifson, drawing on her simultaneous experiences as a cancer patient and as the caregiver for her terminally ill mother, then in her 90s, death marks the end of self-improvement. Aging and dying provide further insight into the process of When Things Fall Apart: the dissolution of old identities, being with the unknown, letting go of absolutely everything.

Aging and dying, like awakening, are a great stripping process, a process of subtraction. Everything we have identified with gradually disintegrates — our bodies, cognitive skills, memory, ability to function independently. Eventually, everything perceivable and conceivable disappears.

The fact is that we don't like to talk about aging and death, at least in Western culture. While growing old, decline and death are natural and inevitable, we do all we can to avoid confronting them head on, making use of euphemisms that make our own demise and that of our loved ones seem less raw and final: *resting in peace, passing away, meeting their maker.* We encountered the impact of grief when we met Ryan Pereira in Chapter 3. In Ryan's case, he had to undergo a period of meaning-making, coming to terms with the loss of his brother and father, and making a conscious decision to make the most of the time he had available to him. The Dalai Lama once observed of his fellow man, "He lives as if he is never going to die, and then dies having never really lived." Ryan, conversely, remains determined to enjoy the journey as fully as possible, avoiding any anxiety about the final destination.

We can see the avoidance of decline in our market-based society. The products available to us range from dyes that disguise greying hair, Botox injections and cosmetic surgery that reshape our bodies and tighten our skin, and hormone replacements and little blue pills that retrieve the vigor and sexual vitality of youth. Celebrities who, with the assistance of the surgeon's knife, defy the passage of time are glorified, while the cardiovascular, stretching and diet regimes espoused in books and on social media and television by fitness and wellness gurus are slavishly followed. After the workouts and breathing exercises, supplements are consumed, cold showers and ice baths taken, all in pursuit of longevity and the avoidance of illness.

While there is nothing wrong with wanting to live a healthy life for as long as we can, ultimately, the promise of advertising is founded upon a lie. It promotes the idea that we can always be young and healthy, brushing over the reality of decline, an unraveling that occurs When Things Fall Apart, where there is illness and pain and loss, where we are no longer able to control our bodily functions, remember what happened moments ago, or live without the support and intervention of others.

We essentially return to infancy, reversing roles, becoming dependent children once again. Tollifson elaborates:

Old age is an adventure in uselessness, loss of control, being nobody and giving up everything. That sounds quite dreadful when we have been conditioned to believe that we must be *somebody*, that we must strive to get better and better, that our lives must have purpose and meaning, that above all, we must be useful and productive and always *doing* something and *getting somewhere*.

The struggle against decline is also prevalent in organizational life. Occupied with the implicit and often unquestioned agenda of growth at all costs, conversations about loss and death in many workplaces are often avoided and, if mentioned at all, are found in short sentences at the bottom of announcements. In the essay 'The Diabolization of Death,' professor of organizational development Burkard Sievers said, "As long as survival is written on the banners of our organizations and enterprises, there is just no space for the standard bearer's potential death. 'The show must go on!'" Such an assumption is rarely questioned, and people carry on as if it were true. Deep down, we all know that we will die, and that the organizations with which we are familiar will disappear. As theoretical physicist Geoffrey West demonstrates in *Scale*, our companies and even our cities are subject to the same patterns of life and death as organisms. Indeed, the longevity of businesses is becoming shorter and shorter.

Behind the fear of death is the fear of losing our identity. When viewed as an ongoing process of ego destruction, life can be thought of as a series of 'mini-deaths,' reflecting its impermanence and the many identity shifts and losses we undergo while it lasts — relationships, employment, status, independence, dignity, respect. Life, we discover, is punctuated by death, which is ever-present. Standing on stage unable to deliver our well-rehearsed speech. Exiting the office, having been dismissed from our job. Bringing a marriage to an end. Moving into a care home. These are all mini-deaths of one sort or another, experienced every day by huge numbers of people. Yet, with the final and conclusive death, there is no longer anything to fear, no consciousness, no ego, none of the anxieties and misgivings that assail us during our waking lives — a permanent state of anesthesia.

Having awareness of our death, accepting it without allowing it to overwhelm us, can enrich our lives. Entangled as we are with all living systems, we live in the company of both birth and death at all times. It is not only our own selves, but everything around us that is subject to cycles of demise and renewal. Not Being, as we have seen, exposes the abstraction, the myth, of separation, revealing how we are indivisible from the whole. The atoms that comprise our bodily vessels are borrowed temporarily before being recycled into something else, always present, always part of something complete and unbroken.

This is not to say that our emotions and the grief we deal with when confronting the everyday reality of death should be belittled or bypassed. Quite the contrary. We *should* notice how precious life is and attend to it more fully, recognizing its impermanence even as we do so. It also means that we *should* be open to the gift of the moment, rather than holding onto some glorious past or fantasizing about some indeterminate future. The moment will continue to unfold — emergent, unknown, and potentially beautiful. Each moment, each life, provides a microcosmic insight into the whole, as Tollifson observes:

> Every living being is a unique and precious expression of the universe, a unique point of view, a unique and unrepeatable pattern of energy. When someone we love dies, they are gone, never to return, and one day, this life we are experiencing right now will end. In so many ways, death is the greatest wake-up call there is.

Nobody is more aware of this reality than Simon Western. Simon is the organizational consultant and coach whom we encountered briefly in Chapter 3, when he supported Lynne Sedgmore through her leadership transition. Like Ryan Pereira, though, Simon has been carrying with him the effects of grief for many years. Just over a decade ago, Simon's son, Fynn, was knifed to death, at just 23.

The two had been very close. Simon, a single parent, had tried to fill his son's life with adventure, despite money struggles, ensuring that they found pleasure in the small things, like picking apples, sneaking into the zoo and jumping onto barges. He also organized overseas travels together, visiting China, Russia, Turkey, Nepal and the United States, even trekking to the Annapurna base camp in the Himalayas when Fynn was only seven. Their mutual love was palpable. Then, suddenly, Fynn was no longer there.

Simon's own life changed dramatically. He lost his job and suffered suicidal thoughts. His grief was all-consuming.

Facing the loss of Fynn felt physically like I had just woken from a car crash each and every day. My body, mind, and spirit had been traumatized. I was battered and bruised. Trying to escape the sadness one evening, I went to a music show. I sat there choking, feeling claustrophobic, trapped between people with my emotions running wild inside, experiencing the terror of my uncontrollable grief. Sitting among happy people, I was a lost soul. I gasped for breath, desperate for some stability. There was nothing left but to hold on for the next few minutes, to try and breathe. Then to escape into the night air and walk alone, walk to nowhere, for there was nowhere left.

Everyday items and events triggered memories: smells, clothes, birthdays, Christmas, anniversaries, TV, the sun's rays. These memories were haunting, loving, terrifying, uplifting. What made his grief even more difficult was the guilt of burdening friends and family, forcing them, however unwittingly, to accompany him on this journey.

As the parent of a murdered child, you are everybody's worst nightmare. Losing a child is their worst fear. Losing a child through violence adds to that fear. God be praised for those who stand by us during the traumatic early months, during the first couple of years. Eventually, it all changes. A grief fatigue often takes hold: people who cared, still care, but they have lives to live. Now you are safe, they think you have moved on. They drift, and you have to find new ways to cope. People think there is some kind of closure but, in my experience, there is no closure — and I do not desire it.

Simon appreciated how important family and friends were, helping him survive and persevere. But he also understood that his was a burden that few could really share. Loneliness and isolation were always nearby. He compares living with grief to a high-wire balancing act: denial and distance from our grief creates numbness, among other problems, while too much attachment to our loss makes it difficult to live fully today. The grief is always there, and it is necessary to keep shifting in order to maintain equilibrium.

I struck a bargain with myself. I took risks to live fully. I got married, I lived in a new country, I worked for myself, I had other children. Just as Fynn would have wanted me to. I try to live honestly, and that means facing the grief with courage, and allowing Fynn to continue to live in and through me.

There is an inexplicable guilt, a shame attached to having lost a child. There is a hidden pressure to hide your loss. But I don't want to hide Fynn, to brush over his existence, or to bury my feelings. To deny my grief leads to a kind of living hell.

While society privileges happiness, success and material wealth, Simon's lived experience was that without vulnerability there is no strength, without sadness no experience of real joy or beauty.

When we light candles and smile at sunrays, my children, Albert and Lily, experience a transcendence. They speak of Fynn. They feel something beyond the material, an everlasting spirit. I think it will serve them well. I told the children that when the sun shines over Galway Bay, it is Fynn's way of saying hello. Now, when walking or in the car, the children will often call out, "Hiya, Fynn," when the sun appears from behind the clouds, or, "Fynn, you're shining too brightly in my eyes."

The paradox and gift of grief that Simon experienced was that "the more absent our lost children are, the more present they become. When we miss them the most, they are so tenderly and painfully close." Fynn is still Simon's constant companion. Given that Simon didn't try to flinch away from Fynn's death, people often asked him if he believed in God, or an afterlife, but these questions always bemused him.

For me, these are the wrong questions. I don't know what I believe in, but I do know what I experience. I experience Fynn with me all the time, and I experience moments of grace, small transcendent moments every day, that have saved my life, guided me, and lit up my soul.

I learned very early on to be open to moments of grace that would sustain me through despair. The kindness of a stranger when crying in a public place, bird song, a flower, the sun's rays, a heron catching a fish. When a deer jumped out of a forest glade, I immediately recognized Fynn's spirit jumping with joy into my life.

When Simon met his wife, Agata, he experienced a deep, real happiness for the first time since Fynn's death. It was a happiness that he truly believed he had lost forever. This was a life-changing moment of grace. Faith, for Simon, isn't a question of beliefs but of noticing the small moments of grace that quietly come each day.

You don't have to believe anything. Just experience the love that comes through moments of grace, in tiny glimpses at first, and the love slowly grows. There is no manual, no right way to grieve. But there are companions that can help us on our unique journeys. Be open to these companions so that your family and friends can sustain you with love. So that your lost child will always be your closest companion. So that your faith will allow moments of grace to hold and guide you on this journey. Then love will overcome.

THE ANCIENT MARINER

*"We always get together to bury
our dead. And then to bring them
back, to remember what their lives
were like, afterwards."*

James Sallis, *Moth*

Adapting to death and managing grief have been thread-
ed through Rupert Callender's life story, too. Rupert is the
co-founder of The Green Funeral Company (GFC), which was
established in 1999 and is based in Devon and Cornwall in the
UK. The company offers an ecological alternative to traditional
funerals, focusing on humanity rather than orthodoxies and
ceremony. GFC has helped hundreds of people through the
traumatic days following a death, ensuring a meaningful and
emotionally rewarding funeral experience.

While none of us come from traditional funeral backgrounds,
we were moved to become funeral directors through our beliefs
and experience of bereavement and its aftermath. We proudly
call ourselves undertakers so there is no ambiguity about what
we do. When we first meet you, we are unlikely to be wearing
suits. We don't have a fleet of hearses and limousines. We don't
employ bearers. We don't have a standard funeral. We don't
use euphemisms. We don't consider faux-Victoriana and a
mournful expression to be an assurance of respect and dignity.

Rupert spent much of his childhood in the hospice where his
mother worked. His approach at GFC is very much informed
by the caring, humanistic philosophy of the hospice movement.

Grief entered my life at seven, with a brisk parade of bereavements that I was, as was the custom of the time, excluded from. It never left. It robbed me of those feelings of immortality with which most teenagers unthinkingly weave their way gleefully and ignorantly through danger. I was always aware that people could and did just walk out of the door, mid-sentence, never to be seen again.

I was not invited to their funerals, particularly the most important one, that of my father, the first and hugest of my losses. My absence from that, and the feelings of fear and anger that then accompanied me, have been among the biggest drivers of my life.

The grief that Rupert was not able to express for his father was not buried, but would resurface years later when his mother passed away while he was still in his 20s.

Grief can be postponed, feelings buried. We adapt, form a carapace that protects us from the world, deflecting emotions, keeping us safe and numb. It builds slowly as the years of childhood pass, and, if we notice it at all, it is to mistake it for armor or a shield, a thing of good.

But there was a hard lesson that I learned early about the brutal unfairness of life and the biting existential wind of death. When my mother died, the carapace cracked open, and I realized that it had not been a shield at all but a structure that had hobbled my development.

We become distorted within the carapace. We are as tender as a soft-shell crab and seek refuge in the comforts of self-soothing denial, physical pleasures, numbing habits, distractions.

It is an experience common to us all, not just to those of us who were bereaved as children. Our first death can become encased in emotional amber, clearly visible, but untouchable. When it is cracked open, we find ourselves deep in retrospective grief.

We realize, to our shock, that we are playing catch-up, that each death reignites the painful flames of the previous one. If we do not attend to this situation, it becomes our lifelong fate: putting out the fires of loss that smolder in our past. This is how I found myself as an undertaker. Fully orphaned by the age of 25, I understood what I faced, the backlog of grief I had to deal with.

Rupert feels that he was incredibly lucky to find a way to work out the grief that he was experiencing by becoming an undertaker himself. At the time it was easy to do, he recalls, requiring no more than "fervor and naivety" in an industry that was not highly regulated. Most undertakers, he found, followed a formulaic service, which, although sentimental and sympathetic, lacked the rawness and authenticity required for true remembrance and healing.

My entire career as an undertaker has been about gently leading people away from the mistakes I made, the avoidance of the death at hand. I want them to engage with it so that, unlike me and so many others, they can confront the death before them instead of being held captive by the death behind them.

One of the hallmarks of GFC's work is to ensure that the funeral ceremonies are stripped down and shorn of the artificial, avoiding meaningless praise of the dead or obfuscation of the reality of their lives, faults and all.

It is a huge risk, this mining deep for the truth of our characters, this unveiling of our lives and our faults, which stand in plain sight but which so often we conspire to ignore.

I do this for people I have never met, an outrageous liberty, but somehow, due to the relationships we have created with a family, my portraits of the dead are not cruel and judgemental but tender and spookily true.

This is because we share one thing: our humanity. The lives of the dead reflect back on us all and give us meaning and insight; a narrative trick that perhaps we lost at the same time as church ministers lost their authority.

But the truth of our lives was never God's, nor a priest's, but something we all carry deep within our hearts and recognize when it is brought gently to the surface.

Having been a guide with a clear gift for helping others with their own grief, Rupert is not somebody who is at peace with death or in any way tries to hide its impact with clichés or cheap sentiments about living life more fully as a result.

None of it makes me drink any deeper from the bowl of life. I still fear death and think of it every day. I fear the grief that awaits me, and the grief I leave in my wake. I am no cheerleader for death. I don't think it sharpens the character. But it is my vocation, burnt into me through experience, and opened to me through luck and destiny. It has been my way of life for 21 years now, and I can see no other future. I am the Ancient Mariner.

Although death has not sharpened my experience of the everyday, it has opened doors to me to extraordinary peak experiences. I have been healed of my own suppurating grief by being allowed to accompany others in their darkest moments, experiencing first-hand the enormous communal well of love and strength that is available to us all, whatever we feel about our own courage or shortcomings.

Love is the law, and compassion is the direction we all naturally turn towards, as long as our distortions and wounding are accommodated. This accommodation is part of our work as undertakers. Acceptance and forgiveness are our salves.

I am deeply grateful for death giving me a way through life.

Recently, Rupert has become involved in a memorial project with Bill Drummond and Jimmy Cauty, former members of the British electronic band The KLF. In 1994, the duo's K Foundation oversaw a performance-art initiative in which one million pounds sterling, in a pile of 50-pound notes, was burned in a disused boathouse on the Scottish Island of Jura. The ashes from this fire were then turned into a brick. Their new project focuses on bricks of another kind.

Drummond and Cauty contacted Rupert, seeking a partner to build a memorial in Toxteth, Liverpool, site of riots in 1981 following long-standing tensions between the police and the local Black community, which resulted in one fatality and multiple injuries. This will be a unique memento mori: a pyramid, 23 feet in height, built from 34,000 bricks, each of which contains 23 grams of cremated, powdered bones. A mix of the personal and the anonymous.

It will not be completed in any of our lifetimes. Yet, somehow, it feels the work of my life. We began the project a couple of years before the coronavirus pandemic, and it seems as if we had a prescience about the need for a shared secular memorial to help us through these times.

EXPRESSION

EMBRACE

"The knowledge of fear can help make us free."

Audre Lorde, *Man Child*

Ryan's, Simon's and Rupert's encounters with grief have taught them about the need to embrace trauma, to face it head on and accept it as part of their stories, as part of who they are. According to Thomas Hübl, founder of the Academy of Inner Science and author of *Healing Collective Trauma*, the notion of trauma itself is synonymous with separation. To give ourselves over to trauma is to separate ourselves from others, from our environment, from our present context. As Rupert suggests, we have to be careful about becoming enslaved by the traumas of our past. Our ability to confront and integrate is important to our future well-being and interconnection with others. We have to address the inner fragmentation that can affect body, mind and emotions.

Many of our fears are unconscious, prompting automatic, emotional responses that have little apparent relevance to our current situation. In fact, Peter Levine, a pioneer in the field of trauma healing, argues that many of our emotions are recycled from procedural memory — our bodies retain the imprint of past trauma, even if we have no conscious recall of it. Unexpectedly, our reactions can be visceral, overwhelming and seemingly irrational. We have sudden sight of an aspect of ourselves with which we are unfamiliar; a trace of one of the mini-deaths we previously underwent.

Gabor Maté is an expert on trauma and childhood development. He explains that there is a fundamental, evolutionary tradeoff for all humans between *authenticity*, which is about being in touch with ourselves and expressing what is true for us, and *attachment*, which is about maintaining connection with our early caregivers and, later on, with other people. Mammals are more involved than other creatures in caring for and nurturing their offspring. Of all the mammals, humans invest the most time in this process. Attachment between parent and child is essential to the survival of the young, who adapt to their caregivers. As such, Maté suggests, attachment trumps authenticity.

To lose or threaten such attachment, therefore, is to create trauma. Extreme independence, separation, distrust of others, bottling up our emotions, and an unwillingness to seek help can be unwelcome outcomes of this experience. Alternatively, there can be a compulsive regard for the emotional needs of others, or the rigid fulfillment of duties or roles, at the expense of our own interests and well-being.

Home Nguyen, whom we last encountered as a young refugee in Chapter 6, recounts an illuminating anecdote that reflects the interplay between and rebalancing of attachment and authenticity.

> Mikaela is the daughter of a dear friend of mine. I first met her around 15 years ago when I visited her family for a weekend in their house in California. She was about five years old at the time, with a mass of curly brown hair, big blue eyes and a look of constant curiosity, fascinated by everyone and everything she encountered.
>
> When I introduced myself, she was delighted to hear my strange name. "Home as in a house," she murmured to herself. Over the weekend, we developed a strong bond, singing and dancing, making funny faces, playing hide and seek, just enjoying each other's company. The weekend passed by like a dream. But on Sunday afternoon, when I told her that it was time for me to go, initial disbelief gave way to despair. Tears rolled down her face and she began to shriek, "House, don't go!"

The intensity of her response took me by surprise, even as I found it endearing to be called House. I had never seen anyone cry so fully, her lips stretched, her body shaking. When she screamed, "House, House, I love you, don't go," I realized how moved I was too, promising her that I would visit again soon.

Then, it was suddenly over. When her older brother ran by, inviting Mikaela to play with him in the garden, she released my hand and chased after him, briefly turning back to wave enthusiastically and call out, "Bye, bye, House. I'm leaving!"

The memory of that farewell lingers today. As an adult, it was inspirational to see how someone could be so open to their emotions, fully letting the intensity of the moment take over, then vibrantly bouncing straight into the next moment. So many adults keep those feelings in check, doing themselves harm, eventually seeking therapeutic assistance to heal emotional wounds. They cut themselves off from the larger current of life with all the beautiful, terrifying, and lovely moments it offers. How can we rediscover the capacity to let life in like Mikaela did back then?

Levine, as a result of his close study of the animal kingdom during the 1970s, noticed the constant shift between the fight, flight and freeze impulses when threatened by predators. The bodies of the animals he observed had to store up energy to prepare for either confrontation or escape. But, once the threat had passed, such energy had to be discharged. He discovered that many mammals achieved this discharge by shaking or trembling. Yet, this is something that humans rarely do. Instead, the energy associated with stress and trauma is locked up in our bodies, without any outlet. Such repression of natural impulses and genuine feelings contributes further to our sense of separation.

Mikaela, at the age of five, though, was in touch with her own experience and expressed it without reservation. Hers was a way of being that comes before the learned behavior of 'second nature,' observing and mimicking what the adults around us do, adapting to their responses and corrections. We learn what is socially acceptable, not necessarily what is natural or good for us. But, as Home found, authenticity can influence and motivate others in a way that is even more compelling than the grandest vision or the most inspirational speeches.

How might we dance more skillfully and consciously between attachment and authenticity? How do we achieve a better balance, find a middle way, between the repression of our emotions and their fullest expression, to the discomfort of others? How do we learn to switch from what is stressful to what is joyful, letting go, finding release, permitting our bodies and minds to rest and recover, embracing what we feel while not succumbing irrevocably to those emotions?

INITIATION

"Sometimes it takes darkness
and the sweet confinement
of your aloneness
to learn that anyone or anything
that doesn't bring you alive
is too small for you"

David Whyte, *Sweet Darkness*

There can be no genuine breakthrough without the death of an old way of being. Many of us have, at least once in our lives, experienced a nagging intuition that something about our current way of life has to change. It's more than a simple lifestyle switch. An entire way of being has to end. The inessential has to be stripped away and we have to open ourselves to the new.

The historian of religion Mircea Eliade observed in *Rites and Symbols of Initiation*:

Whenever life gets stuck or reaches a dead end, where people are caught in rites of addiction, possessed by destructive images, compelled to violent acts, or pulled apart by grief and loss, the process of initiation presses to break through.

Here, death is to be welcomed and is not to be viewed as a negative experience. The empty tomb is not the end but rather the womb of change. Eliade continues:

In dreams and dramas of initiation, death represents change for the entire psyche and life of a person. It means change inside and out, not simple adaptation or switch in 'lifestyle.' Initiation includes death and rebirth, a radical altering of a person's 'mode of being.'

Inspired by the seasons and the lunar cycles, our cultural traditions are filled with tales of death and destruction followed by rebirth and regeneration. Orpheus descends into the Underworld to retrieve Eurydice. The Phoenix, like Dionysus, rises from the ashes. Ragnarök, the ultimate destruction, is followed by fertile renewal. In *The Golden Bough*, a groundbreaking study of comparative religion and mythology, anthropologist James Frazer associates the stories of Dionysus, Osiris, Dumuzid and Inanna, Adonis and Aphrodite, and Jesus, among others, with fertility rites and vegetation cycles, as well as with each other.

These stories are archetypal, representing the arc of human experience and reflecting the various transitions required to move from one stage to another. In 1909, ethnographer Arnold van Gennep termed each of these transitions a *rite of passage*, involving a significant change in status, a movement from one social group to another, marked by rituals and ceremonies of initiation considered fundamental to the growth of the individual as well as to the development of the community.

We still have these rites of passage and initiation processes today, marking the beginning of adulthood, the entry into and practice of a particular faith, marriage and civil partnerships, the progression from one stage of education to another, the shifts from apprenticeship to journeyman status to mastery, and induction into tribes, organizations, clubs, gangs, military corps and sports teams. During the modern era, though, these rituals have tended to become occasions for consumerism and excess, losing both their meaning and symbolism.

As people experience the series of mini-deaths that demarcate the different stages of their lives, they follow certain steps that signal the initiation of change and its eventual fulfillment.

LIMINAL SPACE

To begin with, the separation from the old self is symbolized by divestment and cutting away. Buddhist monks and nuns, for example, or military recruits, have their heads shaved, submitting themselves to their new orders. Civilian clothing is also discarded in favor of outfits that signify belonging and conformity: uniforms, cassocks, business suits, sports kits.

The initiate now finds themself in an ambiguous, in-between, liminal space; a bardo. This is where they navigate a carefully orchestrated ordeal, testing the limits of their resources. Through that experience, which is often painful and causes a breakdown of their previous way of being, they eventually emerge into a new self and a fuller life. Richard Rohr, a Franciscan priest, and author, observes of those who successfully undergo initiation:

> Instead of avoiding a personal death or raging at it, they went through a death of their old, small self and came out the other side knowing that death could no longer hurt them. They broke through in what felt like breaking down.

This mirrors Ha Tran's experience. Ha is the co-founder of Authentic Live and Learn (ALL), an organization with a vision for a loving and compassionate Vietnam. She has often found that in order to teach effectively, she has to practice what she preaches. This led her to participate in a weeklong nature quest in a forest a few hours away from the city where she lives. Ha arrived at the retreat with big expectations, hoping to use this time away from work and family to find out more about who she was and what she was meant to do with her life.

After five days of mental preparation and relaxing her body, Ha was led to a four-square-meter section of the forest that was far from anyone or anything else. She would remain on her own, fasting for two days, freeing her stomach from the process of digestion, creating space for feelings and emotions to surface. At first, she was excited to be on her own, studying her surroundings — the tiny leaves, the few trees in her immediate proximity, the lines of bark on their trunks. However, the novelty soon wore off. Hours passed and everything seemingly stayed the same.

I was growing restless. There was nothing here. Every minute felt longer, making me impatient. Hunger came and went, but the hardest thing to deal with was the boredom. Being out there was boring me to death!

That first night I mostly lay awake, watching the moon replacing the sun replacing the moon again.

There was nothing, absolutely nothing, about this boring, tiny square of land. How could I have expected that it would reveal something to me? Either I had too much faith or was too stubborn or simply had no other choice. Whatever the case, I waited and waited in growing despair.

Around noon of the second day, I remember hitting rock bottom. My mind had failed to entertain me, and my body had grown weary of simply fumbling around. I had given up on whatever it was that I was hoping for: a revelation, truth, or big idea about who I am or what this whole shebang is. I was very much in despair.

There was no guidance, no one to turn to or confide in, no one to provide solace or disrupt her sense of loneliness. Ha was at her wit's end, depleted physically and emotionally. It was then that the most unexpected and, at the same time, most ordinary thing happened: an ant crawled slowly across her forearm.

In that moment, which was like a slow-motion movie, a sense of love swelled up all over me. It was not unlike the feeling I had when I held my first child. Tears streamed down my face and my body began to tremble while the ant continued walking on my arm.

I experienced so much love for everything. For myself, for the ant, for the trees, for the whole wondrous and comical surrounding. Everything that was, was made of love and from love. It wasn't an abstract idea anymore, nor was it a passing emotion. It was an experience, a reality, that penetrated through my whole being. I must have cried for a long time, tears of joy, of reconnection, of love for the world and this very self.

Ha stayed in that deeply joyous state for the rest of her time in the forest. Afterward, she spent a long time on her own digesting the experience, hardly interacting with the rest of the group. She felt a renewed and visceral connection to life and its vitality.

With rites of passage, even the longueurs, impasses, obstacles and dead ends are never accidental. Their successful negotiation is essential to progress. As in Ha's case, they help us to fall apart and achieve transformation. We have to place trust in both intent and intuition, allowing the ritual to take its full course. As the educationalist Parker Palmer reflects in *Let Your Life Speak*:

> Treacherous terrain, bad weather, taking a fall, getting lost — challenges of that sort, largely beyond our control, can strip the ego of the illusion that it is in charge and make space for true self to emerge. If that happens, the pilgrim has a better chance to find the sacred center he or she seeks. Disabused of our illusions by much travel and travail, we awaken one day to find that the sacred center is here and now — in every moment of the journey, everywhere in the world around us, and deep within our own hearts.

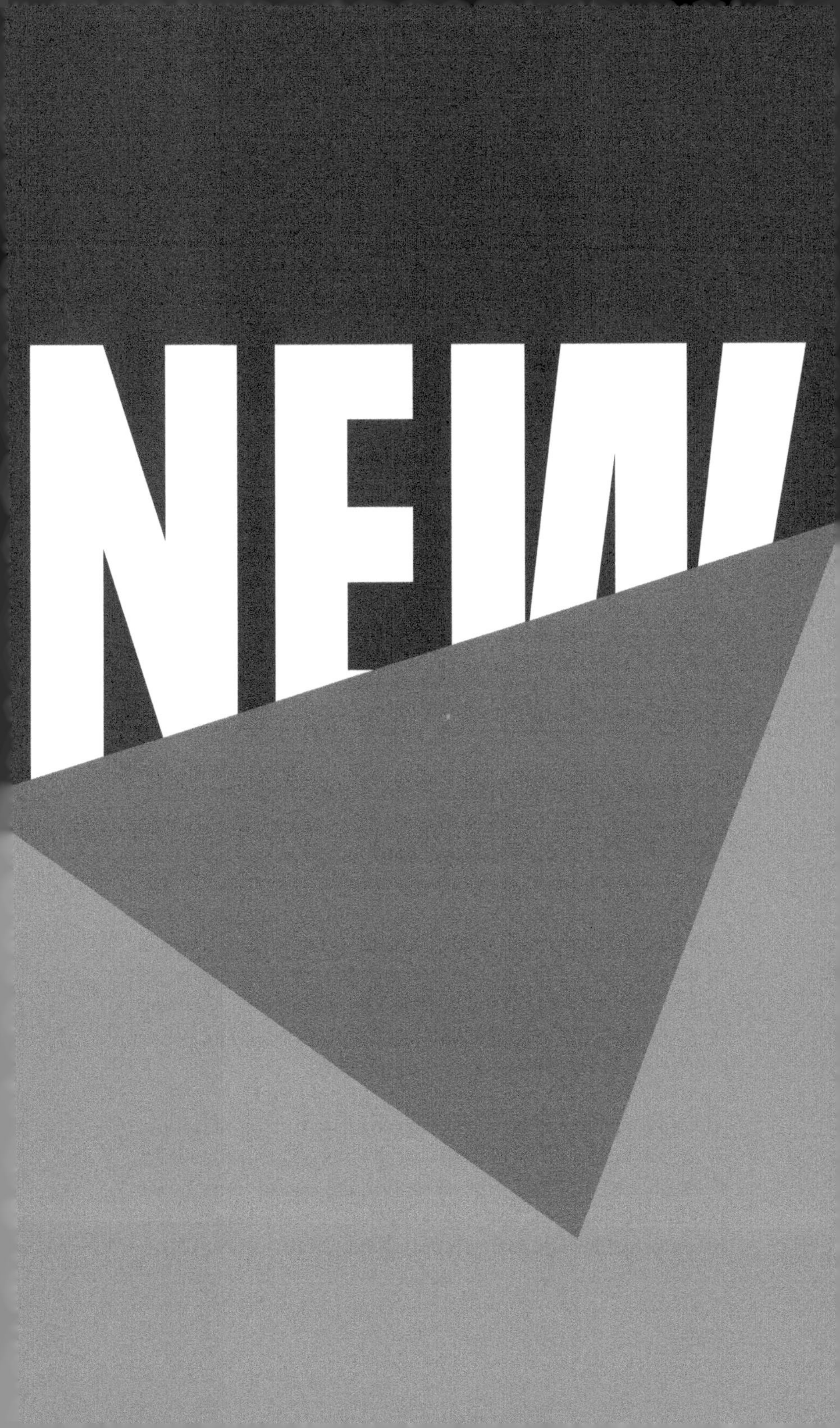
NEW

REINVENTION

"Every crisis is the protagonists' opportunity to kill off their old selves and live anew. Their choice is to deny change and return to their former selves, or confront their innermost fears, overcome them and be rewarded. They can choose death, or they can choose to kill who they were in order to be reborn."

John Yorke, *Into the Woods*

As we have seen, an intrinsic part of transformation involves the destruction of current ways of knowing, doing and being, before the new can be born. This applies as much to organizations as it does to individuals, as demonstrated by the turnover of listed companies in the major exchanges. Companies disappear with increasing regularity, either through design or because they are unable to respond to disruptions quickly enough, displaced by competitors, negatively impacted by changes in consumer demand or government regulation, or simply victims of historical events like the global coronavirus pandemic.

The term "creative destruction" was coined by Austrian economist Joseph Schumpeter in 1942 to describe how organizations can dismantle established processes to make way for new, more productive methods. It derived from his observations of the manufacturing industry, prompting him to describe creative destruction as the "process of industrial mutation that incessantly revolutionizes the economic structure from within, incessantly destroying the old one, incessantly creating a new one."

Schumpeter's theory challenged the idea of continuity and homeostasis. Instead, it posited that economics and markets were organic and dynamic in nature, subject to constant reshaping and replacement as a result of innovation and competition. Schumpeter argued that assumptions, as well as processes, need to be destroyed to free up energy and resources for innovation. Over time, creative disruption became a term that was applied to wider examples of business disruption, especially concerning game-changing technologies enabled by the internet, which had a significant impact on retail, the media and the finance sector. While disruption destroys some businesses, new ones are simultaneously created by it.

Organizations that disrupt themselves and their industries not only sense-make and adapt to present challenges but prepare for future ones in an attempt to ensure their survival and increase their longevity. The challenge for established companies — rather than start-ups — is one of a dual transformation: the need to acknowledge and manage the decline of the existing business, while simultaneously developing an emergent business. This takes courage, looking forward, making tough decisions, and investing in areas that may not see a growth in the short term. IBM is a well-known example of an organization that has gone through the process of creative destruction on numerous occasions since its origins in the early 20th century. The company frequently reinvented itself, shifting its focus from mechanical weighing and timekeeping devices to computing to business process outsourcing to strategic consulting to the cloud, artificial intelligence and infrastructure.

At the level of both the individual and the organization, there is an S-curve trajectory that is followed. The idea was developed by sociologist Everett Rogers in his 1962 book, *Diffusion of Innovations*, to explain the rate at which new ideas and technologies are adopted, from gradual uptake to explosive growth to stagnation. More recently, Charles Handy in *The Second Curve*, Whitney Johnson in *Disrupt Yourself* and Geoffrey West in *Scale* have used the S-curve to illustrate the life cycles of companies, cities, organisms, identities and roles. Those with foresight can anticipate the need to change, to pursue creative destruction, before the S-curve begins to flatten out. Leave it too long, though, and the moment is missed, with decline and obsolescence inevitable for the organization, and boredom, ossification and, ultimately, irrelevance for the individual.

Anushia Reddy has held senior executive roles in the UK for 25 years. Before moving there, she had lived under apartheid in South Africa, where she was born.

> I lived in a white suburb under the Group Areas Act, which was prohibited, yet made possible by my parents, who defied the boundaries with the support of my entrepreneur mother's Jewish business partner. The need to learn in the flow of life was drummed into me by my father. It was a currency for a sustainable future within and across borders; something that could contribute to reducing unemployment, social exclusion and inequality. The dominant philosophy at home related to the dynamic interconnectedness of things and the importance of collective goals. From all of this grew my fascination with what lies behind the best and worst of human behavior and its impact.

When she was 17, Anushia began to study psychology. The sudden death of her father, who believed strongly in the benefits of education — and had his own aspirations to become a doctor closed off to him because of lack of money — motivated her, giving her a sense of purpose. Her reliance on scholarships to pay for her education further intensified her focus, and she eventually graduated with distinction. Having written directly to the human resources lead at a financial services organization that she wished to join, she then participated in an accelerated development program, which entailed frequent change in terms of what she did and who she worked with.

I was promoted quickly and within a few years found myself in senior management. By this time, I was disillusioned with psychology, which seemed to be more about generating profit and shareholder return rather than also improving the lives of people and the communities we live in. My husband, now a professor and consultant in neurocritical care, with a mindset of being in service of others, was keen to expand his contribution. With this came questions about a possible move to the UK and whether we would thrive in this environment, which was considered at the time to have surplus availability of highly skilled people.

This was a major transition for both Anushia and her husband. They had to let go of the familiar — their home country, their professional and support networks — and start life on a completely different continent.

It took Anushia four years to register as a psychologist in the UK. In the meantime, she remained on a traditional career trajectory, undertaking a range of talent, leadership and organization development roles, while also gaining experience working with different boards of directors. She also became part of a 'future of work' consortium, participating in projects of a strategic nature, scenario planning for tomorrow's business practices and the implications of new ways of working.

I started to build on the early foundations of lifelong learning to mitigate skill obsolescence and to intentionally shift away from the now collapsed three-stage approach of education, work and retirement. I challenged myself to reimagine how I could respond and contribute to changing market needs, making tomorrow *today* by identifying the skills to build my own career resilience and long-term employability.

All of this was happening at a time when the new world of work promised opportunities for many, while also posing a threat to many who could be displaced without reskilling becoming a business imperative. I felt like I had come full circle because unemployment, social exclusion, inequality and poverty were at the heart of people's concerns about the future, and this was the context of my roots in South Africa.

At the same time, the global workforce was becoming increasingly unwell, costing trillions of dollars in lost productivity. This was now being voiced by the World Health Organization, governments and businesses, as well as across disciplines way beyond psychology.

Anushia believes that the future of work is about the future of human beings. She realized that she could help create a sustainable future through a holistic approach to well-being. This meant dedication to learning about a new field, spending evenings and weekends studying. Anushia modeled the dual transformation of organizations, investing more time in what she saw as her future career.

I started to plot my path in a deliberate way, exploring what this might look like in five years if I committed fully rather than tinkered around the edges. I set in motion a number of time-bound goals, sharing them with colleagues so that they would hold me accountable. I continued doing talent strategy and executive development work, and this portfolio became my way of funding rapid, in-depth research into well-being and resilience across multiple disciplines. As a result, I was able to access a vast range of the less-accessible journals and books, as well as invest in programs in neuroscience, cognitive behavioral therapy, acceptance and commitment therapy, and resilience. I could also engage with and learn from experts in well-being and resilience around the world.

Soon her immersion in the topic bore fruit, with Anushia invited to advise one of her clients on their approach to resilience. This propelled her to converge the broad work she had done and make decisions on an approach that had the possibility not only to build resilience but to sustain well-being and strengthen the performance of individuals, teams and organizations as a whole. Before long, Anushia was designing, developing and delivering a range of solutions.

As I delivered workshops to different audiences, I noticed the difference it was making to people and how rewarding I was finding every experience. There continues to be tremendous learning and insight. The feedback from others — including leveraging my husband's medical neuroscience skills — has enabled me to stay agile and confirm that I will always be a work in progress as I build this new portfolio and anticipate what's next.

Constant change is a given. But, remaining conscious of creative destruction allows us to pay attention to what is moribund and seek out opportunities for reinvention and renewal. While we may not be able to predict the future, we can do what we can to prepare ourselves to meet it.

STREAM ENTERER

"I've never once thought about how I was going to die," she said. "I can't think about it. I don't even know how I'm going to live."

Haruki Murakami, *Norwegian Wood*

We don't tend to live our lives in awareness of our own death, until, that is, we are forced to. However, not being aware of death doesn't mean we don't want to know more, especially about our own. In the essay, 'I Die, Therefore I Am,' Philip Cozzolino and Laura Blackie reveal the findings of a survey in which they asked people if they would rather not know that they would die someday. Only a quarter responded affirmatively. To the surprise of the researchers, the majority of people revealed that they would rather wrestle with the tension inherent in their awareness of death than be totally blind to it. To confront death, and survive, leaves us with a new perspective and grateful for the lives we previously took for granted.

Cozzolino and Blackie are among a group of people who have contributed to the growing field of Post-Traumatic Growth (PTG) study, not to be confused with the study of Post-Traumatic Stress Disorder (PTSD). They have documented many specific areas of growth when life-changing events cause us to face our own mortality. They include an increase in the desire for self-direction, closer relationships, and reorganized priorities that reflect a new appreciation of life.

Importantly, it is how we confront the fact of our death that matters. Abstract reflections on death, referred to by researchers as 'mortality resilience,' have been shown not to have that great of an effect on an individual later on. Death, it seems, has to be faced at a visceral level, through endangerment or serious illness, for real learning and PTG to occur.

Steve Rowe is a dedicated martial artist, having trained for over five decades and attained the level of ninth dan — the traditional highest skill ranking — in both karate and kung fu. Steve is an international tai chi coach, a third dan in Iaido, second dan in jōdō, and first dan in jujutsu. He is chairman and chief instructor of Shi Kon Martial Arts and the Martial Arts Standards Agency. Steve owns a martial arts center in Chatham in the UK and has spent much of his career in the security sector, training European police, special services, presidential bodyguards and security personnel.

After a week leading a martial arts summer seminar in the Jizerka Mountains region of the Czech Republic, Steve was taken ill while traveling back to the airport in Prague. He found that he could barely move, and required the assistance of his friends to get from the car to check-in.

I felt so bad that I had to use a wheelchair to get to the plane. The plane journey was a nightmare. At Gatwick Airport, I was unable to get into the car to take me home and was in a state of collapse. An ambulance was called. It took two hours to get me into the ambulance because by this time the pain was so bad that I was in tachycardia arrest. I thought I was going to die.

Steve was taken to Surrey Hospital, where he was diagnosed with sepsis, a life-threatening reaction to serious infection. Despite the care he received, the situation continued to deteriorate, even after two surgical interventions. While waiting for a third, his infection levels became even worse, convincing Steve that were he to undergo another procedure at Surrey, he would die. Instead, Steve found a top private surgeon willing to treat him and, in the absence of an available ambulance, persuaded a friend to drive him directly to the private hospital. There, his family was informed that Steve was in renal failure and that there were only 24 hours left to save his life.

So, there I was lying in my bed at death's door. I had spent most of my life in search of who I really was, studying martial arts, meditation and healing practices. I was wondering, how do I prepare myself to die? I knew that I had to allow the flood of emotions to pass. They did not belong to me, and I had to recognize that they were the natural survival emotions of my body and its software, the thinking mind.

Deep breathing gradually calmed Steve's mind, body and emotions. He found that he could empathize with the emotions and worries of his family and friends, too, even as they tried to conceal them from him. He had to keep going deeper into the calmness, moving beyond his thinking and emotional self.

The pain was terrible. I had to keep reminding myself to acknowledge and accept it but not take ownership of it. I didn't need to make it worse by having an emotional reaction to it. This was certainly an occasion to put all that training to the test. So, where was I? What was actually dying? My body, my thinking mind, my emotions, for sure. I had to be able to sit in the part of me that went beyond that.

When the Chinese talk about finding immortality and someone being an immortal, they mean a person who has gone beyond that part of themself that lives and dies. A *stream enterer* is a person that has entered the stream of consciousness that binds the universe, the silence, the stillness, that is always there behind all things.

In that hospital bed, through the countless surgeries that followed and all the complications that have occurred since, Steve found his peace.

I found the part of me that was absolutely silent and still. I was in ICU with checks every few minutes, beepers and alarms constantly going off, and people running around. My baseline was silent and still. I was sitting in the wordless mind. The part of me that constituted my entire being as a human baby before I knew my name and learned how to talk. Through this wordless medium, I could commune with nature. I knew its language, I understood what joined me with the animals, and what humans were trying to say behind their crafted words and expressions. Everything had changed. There is a huge difference between knowing *about* a subject and actually *knowing* it.

You cannot know what something is like unless you experience it directly. Conjecture rarely gets it right. A near-death experience is not something I would wish on anyone, but you see people who have experienced it transforming their lives when they have survived. What I have taken from it is not just the value of every breath, but the intensity required to pierce the shell of the illusion of life, to discover the truth of who we really are, and the mindfulness required 24/7 to be able to maintain that still, silent peace that sits behind the fabric of life.

Confirming the shift that occurred for Steve, Cozzolino and Blackie assert that rejecting the reality of death in our lives is akin to denying a true part of who we are. While that can provide short-term peace, it eventually leads to an inauthentic conception of self. Through their research, Cozzolino and Blackie discovered that those who are likely to keep death at an abstract level, tending to deny its concrete inevitability, find less meaning and fulfillment in their lives, worrying about what they are missing out on rather than enjoying the moment. It is only in the light of death that we can fully address our being.

IT IS ONLY IN THE **LIGHT OF DEATH**
THAT WE CAN FULLY ADDRESS
WHO
WE ARE BEING
IN LIFE.

ENDING WELL

"Our wagon is prepared,
and time revives us:
All's well that ends well;
still the fine's the crown;
Whate'er the course,
the end is the renown."

William Shakespeare, *All's Well That Ends Well*

In the 2009 movie *Up in the Air*, Ryan Bingham, the character played by George Clooney, fires people for a living. He is the new Organization Man who doesn't have an office but travels to the offices of others to deliver his work. Bingham works for a talent-management-solution outsourcing company that lends him out to people who, in his own words, "don't have the balls to sack their own employees." When corporations need to downsize quickly but hate the mess, he flies in and breaks the unwelcome news. For many people, getting fired from a job is akin to a small death. Firing someone, especially someone to whom you are close, creates confusion, hurt and emotional turmoil for both employer and employee.

But how painful is such an ending, really? As with visiting the dentist, it is often the anticipation of pain rather than the fact of it that causes the most trepidation. Buddhism distinguishes between 'primary suffering,' which includes the universal human experiences of birth, aging, sickness and death, and 'secondary suffering,' which includes all the stories, drama and mental turmoil we experience on top of it. What is the cost of avoiding endings, of avoiding death, whether physical or psychological?

Handled poorly, these endings can scar, their effects enduring for years. Nevertheless, avoiding them, not taking action, often results in a situation that becomes so intolerable that ending is the least painful option.

Steven: During the global financial crisis of 2007–8, I was working for an investment bank. I remember receiving a call in the late afternoon at the end of the week. It was my manager, who was working from home. "I'm really sorry to tell you this, but your job has been made redundant," she said. Her remorse seemed genuine, but it did not make the news any easier to accept, especially when delivered over the phone. I was told to pack my belongings and not to return to the office. Officially, I was on garden leave.

After the initial shock, the disbelief, I was furious. The process seemed so unfair. I even considered going to an employment lawyer to find out what my rights were. My girlfriend, though, reminded me that I had been unhappy in the role and that this might be the opportunity I needed. For the past six months, I had worked part-time at the bank while trying to write more and develop myself as an educator. She was right: redundancy was an ending that I needed. It may not have been on my terms or what I expected, but it forced me to move on, to stop being stuck between two roles, and to commit to the development of my own company.

Reflecting back, it was the best thing that could have happened to me. Of course, that is certainly not what I felt at the time. The truth is that I've always had a bad relationship with endings, even with extended leave-taking from a group of friends. If things have to end, I like them to be over and done with, quickly and neatly, almost unacknowledged, with no lingering or protracted farewells, no denial that things are over.

I realized the power of ending well while training as an organizational consultant. It was necessary for participants to consider the transition points, the beginnings, middle and endings. What I learned was that many of us don't attend to endings well, even though they are a critical part of closure. When we achieve something, there is a tendency to quickly move on to the next thing to do, without pause or celebration. However, if something is left unfinished, this creates an open loop, which is known as a Zeigarnik effect.

The mind, though, always seeks closure. You can see this in everyday examples. If you see an incomplete image, the mind will automatically seek to complete it. Attending to endings well, especially by celebrating them, leads to less psychic energy being invested in the past, making more energy available for present and future projects.

Ending well and embracing the loss that accompanies endings helps us commit to the moment, to whatever comes. Rituals can help with endings: burning, tearing, releasing into the sea or the air, clearing out the old, making space for the new. Good endings are less about letting go, more about offering up thanks.

Daniel Beaumont is in his early 30s and hails from Kendal, in the English Lake District. When he was 21, Daniel moved to Australia, and then spent several years working his way around the world, visiting over 50 countries. He would be curious about the people he met, often making friends with his hosts, hearing their stories about love, loss and regret, but also about what made them happy.

Daniel and some of his friends discussed an alternative to the nameless hotels and hostels they were used to, drawing on their own travel experiences, and creating a genuine community offering. They wanted to bring people together not only for lodging, but to learn from each other, to share food, and exchange stories and knowledge. Podstel, Daniel's first business, was intended for both travelers and the local community, bridging the tourist–local divide.

I've dedicated the best part of eight years to building a hospitality business. Podstel is part hostel for travelers and part café for locals. It is all about community, bringing people together from all over the world in Bucharest, Romania, to share, learn and connect. Building Podstel wasn't an easy feat. Over the years, I put a tremendous amount of effort and motivation into growing the business, underpinned by an ambitious vision to grow and expand the concept, first to multiple destinations around Europe, and eventually around the world.

On a gloomy morning in the middle of March 2020, the hospitality and travel industry was brought to an abrupt halt by the coronavirus pandemic. From one day to the next, the business that Daniel had poured so much energy, effort and passion into over the years faced an existential crisis.

Prior to the pandemic, Daniel was gearing up for a smooth exit: to sell the business and move back to the UK to start a new chapter in his life. However, things did not go to plan, and the possibility of losing his business during the crisis was very real. What he hadn't anticipated, though, was the battle he was about to enter into with himself.

My first reaction was panic, denial and confusion. I scrambled, doing everything I could to keep the business afloat despite revenue plummeting to zero. I recall feeling incredibly helpless and out of control, riddled with anxiety. Looking back, it was clear I was in pain. Podstel had dominated my life for many years, and my identity and self-worth were tied into the project. But with the business on life support, coupled with lockdown restrictions, I panicked. I felt lost and fell into a state of numbing purposelessness for months. It was a slippery slope. I isolated myself from people, often feeling disconnected from reality, struggling with intense feelings of guilt, shame and deep anxiety about the future.

After months of worry, rumination and irrational thought patterns, I was tired of aimlessly planning for an uncertain future that was impossible to predict, given the turbulent nature of the pandemic. It was here, in the depths of my exhaustion, that I finally realized that all that I could do was surrender, accept that the future was outside of my control, and try my best to embrace the present.

While Daniel was not in control of the events that were happening, he decided to shift his perspective. Yes, there was real loss, but what impact would it have in the longer term? He could appreciate both the impermanence and the preciousness of his situation.

I asked myself, "Will what I am going through right now matter ten years from now?" The answer was a resounding *No*. It was clear that it was no longer necessary to expend valuable energy worrying about something as transient as the future of my business. I realized time was precious, and time spent worrying was futile. It was time I could never get back. This brought my attention to the fragility and impermanence of life, encouraging me to be honest with myself and reassess what I valued.

Daniel realized that he has been blindsided by business and that there were much more important things to be grateful for, which he had neglected over the years. His mind kept rolling back to the same themes: well-being, friends, family, serving others. He realized that these had all been suffocated by the seductive and never-ending pull of business, arbitrary measures of success, and the lure of progress at all costs.

By looking at my situation from a different perspective, I began to see that although what I was experiencing was painful and difficult, there were lessons to be learned and precious seeds of blessing to be found in what I was going through. Although comfort, stability and an identity attached to my business was alluring, the pandemic accelerated changes that I knew in my gut should've happened years ago. It encouraged me to look within and reorient myself towards what is truly important in life. It has shown me the power of acceptance, and, when faced with a high degree of uncertainty, the need to be kind, compassionate and patient with myself.

Above all, I now know that there's no bad ending. When one chapter closes, another one opens. It's not the situation that causes a painful experience, but rather my perspective and the way I choose to look at what I am experiencing. Therefore, in the future, when faced with ending a difficult situation, I'll remember to ask myself one simple question: "What are the seeds of blessing in what I'm going through right now?"

After the journey with Podstel, introspective travel adventures, living in three different countries and, most importantly, meeting and listening to the stories of thousands of people from all kinds of backgrounds and cultures, I came to one simple, but profound conclusion: *Home is where the heart is.*

In some ways, learning to end well starts by recognizing the fluctuating nature of our experience. We become more intimately in touch with life as it freshly unfolds moment to moment. Whatever arises is welcomed and let go quickly, rather than clung to. We realize that everything ends, and we can either resist that fact or be grateful for it. Endings can resist conclusive answers — and that is okay.

CHAPTER 9

CONTEMPLAY

TRICKSTER

"He knows neither good nor evil yet he is responsible for both. He possesses no values, moral or social, is at the mercy of his passions and appetites, yet through his actions all values come into being."

Paul Radin, *The Trickster*

Sun Wukong is a mythical monkey king who features in the 16th century Chinese novel, *Journey to The West*, by Wu Cheng'en, as well as in numerous other fables, movies, television series and games. Wukong is often rebellious and almost always unpredictable, with the capacity to move at great speed and shape-shift into an array of animals and objects. He is a mischievous prankster who is himself occasionally on the receiving end of divine trickery, often with disastrous consequences. In one story, Wukong tricks his way into heaven, demanding equal rank with all the gods he finds there. He is appointed 'Director of Animals,' dedicating himself wholeheartedly to horse husbandry, only to learn later, to his fury, that this is the lowliest of positions. Enraged, he challenges and defeats the strongest among the gods, disrupting the heavenly order.

How did a character with such temperament become so popular and resonant, not only in Asian culture but globally? One answer is that Wukong — like other mythical figures, such as Loki, Hermes, Iktomi and Anansi in, respectively, Nordic, Greek, Lakota and West African and Caribbean folklore — represents an important in-between liminal space. He embodies the portion of our human experience where the good and the bad are hopelessly entwined. Such figures are known as tricksters. They are neither good nor evil, neither above nor below.

In his introductory note to *The Trickster: A Study in American Indian Mythology*, anthropologist Paul Radin offered this characterization:

Trickster is at one and the same time creator and destroyer, giver and negator, he who dupes others and who is always duped himself. He wills nothing consciously. At all times he is constrained to behave as he does from impulses over which he has no control.

Tricksters play with and traverse boundaries, disrupting orders not for any personal gain but simply for the fun of it. As Lewis Hyde explains in *Trickster Makes This World*:

The boundary is where he will be found — sometimes drawing the line, sometimes crossing it, sometimes erasing or moving it, but always there, the god of the threshold in all its forms.

The trickster, then, muddles polarities, upending established categories regarding what is right and wrong, useful and useless, young and old, opening the world to new possibilities. Indeed, the energy associated with the trickster is especially relevant in times of disruption and transformation. They have a catalytic effect either on the individual or on the collective, their agility and adaptiveness providing a welcome alternative to personal intransigence, organizational rigidity and societal decay. Wherever there are borders or boundaries, including in terms of identity, there is the potential for the trickster to play.

The trickster views the world askew, finding humor in the most unlikely of situations, while introducing a degree of seriousness to their boundary play. This is an archetype that embodies paradox. The trickster is an agent of change, introducing a different way of being and perceiving. Through mischief, the trickster comes alive and enlivens the world. Their duplicity, their doubleness, is the source of an absurd humor that goes beyond entertainment and causes genuine surprise, not least to themselves, opening up the possibility of multiple truths.

In the case of performance artist Amichai Lau-Lavie, founding director of Storahtelling, a New York-based Jewish theater company, humor emerged in the form of an alter-ego drag character. This was the aged Hungarian widow Hadassah, who outlived six rabbi husbands and became a sex and marital advisor to the ultra-orthodox elite. Over time, Lau-Lavie used his performances as Hadassah as a form of ritual, further blurring the boundary between what is funny and what is serious, while providing what he called "first aid for spiritual seekers." In an unexpected turn of events, Lau-Lavie himself became a rabbi. He now leads Lab/Shul, an artist-driven, pop-up synagogue in New York City.

The trickster energy that Lau-Lavie drew on in his performances as Hadassah is also essential to Reverend Leng Lim, when coaching his leadership development clients in America, Europe and Asia. The lightness he seeks himself by stepping back, letting go, reflecting and relaxing through massage allows him to notice, to explore and, sometimes, to tap into breakthroughs quite by chance. He finds that the path of relaxation and the provocation of the trickster benefit his clients as well.

> One time, I was coaching a client, a French executive. He was a very competent and smart person who knew how to get things done. Like many of us, but perhaps to a greater degree, he would get very tight and caught up in his mind, especially before important meetings. This stressed him greatly and affected his performance. He knew he had to loosen up but didn't know how.

> On this particular occasion, even without seeing his face, I could sense from his monotonous tone on the phone a kind of lifelessness. Yes, he was dealing with important work matters and serious challenges, but there was something missing.

In that moment, I felt an impulse to poke around a bit. He was a little taken aback when I interrupted.

"Could I ask you a politically incorrect question?"
"Sure."
"Do you enjoy sex with your wife?"

I risked blurring the line between what is professional and personal, what is acceptable and what is not. He paused for a good five seconds. The question came as such a surprise, he hadn't even queried it. I could explain in hindsight why it was a reasonable question to ask, but to be honest, at the time, I didn't know where I was going with it.

"Yes," he replied eventually. His tone lightened up all of a sudden. "Yes, I do. Very much." He sounded freshly in love, irrationally passionate. It turned out that he found it relaxing not having to be his usual, serious, professional self in those intimate, playful moments.

I asked him, "Do you notice how different you sound? Just from your tone alone, you seem more alive."

"I don't know. I'm just happier."

People can do all kinds of things to try to change their state of mind. Sometimes we just need to dare to talk about the juicy stuff.

"Do you think you make better decisions when you are happier like that?" I laughed with him, bringing us back to the topic of his work.

> Often, to be duped by the trickster is to rediscover life. The trickster's energy is a powerful counterpoint to inflexibility and staleness. The new perspective, the challenging or surprise question, can open us to a different way of being.

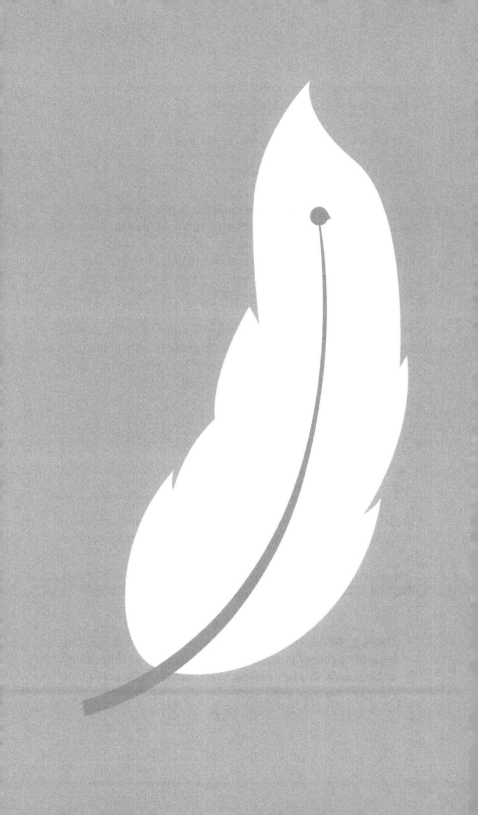

LIGHTNESS

"Her drama was a drama not of heaviness but of lightness. What fell to her lot was not the burden but the unbearable lightness of being."

Milan Kundera, *The Unbearable Lightness of Being*

Buddhist monk Jack Kornfield recently recounted a story to entrepreneur and lifestyle guru Tim Ferris on his podcast. Years ago, he was one of several people traveling through rice paddies with his teacher, Ajahn Chah, on their way to a village to collect alms. When they came across a large rock, Ajahn Chah asked his companions, "Is that boulder heavy?" When they replied affirmatively, he responded with a smile, "Not if you don't pick it up." As with the trickster, the question and elaboration here serve as a wake-up call, as a reminder not to become stuck in habitual patterns of thinking and seeing. It is possible to acknowledge and accept all the rocks we encounter in life — those we love and those we fear — but to hold them lightly, not permitting them to weigh us down.

As we saw previously, when we encountered Maria Garcia Tejon and learned about her transformative experience of motherhood, it's not easy to hold things lightly. As with Maria, Kerry Radcliffe has had to learn how to interweave motherhood and her professional life, choosing which rocks to pick up, which to leave on the ground, which to hold lightly, which to let go. Kerry, a faculty member at New Venture West Coaching School in California, is an executive coach with extensive experience in the field of leadership development. Her personal transformation began at the age of 33, with the birth of Mia, her first daughter.

For years, Kerry had suspected that she lacked the primal urge to nurture, while also fearing the prospect of post-partum depression that had afflicted her mother when she was growing up. This latter fear was exacerbated by the fact that Kerry had herself experienced periods of depression throughout her life. The birth of Mia opened up a new relationship with the world.

> I could not believe how powerful my body was, nor how connected I felt caring for Mia, or how much healing was happening in the mirroring and the closed loop she and I had together.

> You are constantly emptying yourself, not just in terms of food and sleep, but also regarding expectations and self-image.

There were many times, though, where Kerry's energy levels were so depleted that she thought it impossible to continue being the loving mother she aspired to be. Yet, to her constant surprise, she would find herself restored in completely unexpected and marvelous ways. Sometimes, gazing at her sleeping baby led her to an inner coherence that she had never experienced before.

For a long time, Kerry had harbored a sense that something was missing or wrong. Now, Mia's presence both broke her open and made her feel whole again. It was a feeling that became more profound with the passage of time, as she embraced the vulnerability of being a caregiver and the impotence she experienced when observing her child's independent develop-ment. Beneath it all, however, there was a deep joy derived from being more sensitive to life, appreciating each moment without clinging to it.

Kerry's transformation as a mother — adapting to the unexpected and to the demands of someone dependent on her — also carried over into her professional life. This was especially the case with her coaching work, her delivery of a leadership development program for a French fashion house, and her new understanding of the concept of service. It showed in her sensitivity and willingness to trust the goodness in people while still pushing them to be better, as well as in her attentiveness to the needs of the people she was helping. She had to let go her previous 'professional overachiever' identity, where she would seek to be faster and better than colleagues, subsuming her own inclinations in order to meet other people's expectations.

In *Home Is Where We Start From*, psychoanalyst Donald Winnicott explores how important it is for a child to fully express themselves rather than being constrained or having to learn too early in their lives to adapt to the whims and demands of their caregivers. He also notes how anxious parents would often share their misgivings with him, worried that they were not parenting correctly and could inadvertently inflict emotional or psychological harm on their children. Winnicott would reframe their worries, helping them understand that not only was parental perfection unachievable, but that it would fail their children, leaving them unprepared to negotiate life's vicissitudes and uncertainties.

For Winnicott, the job of a parent is to divest the child of the illusions of parental perfection, making them see that it is not always the parents' role to meet their demands, and thus gradually enabling their self-sufficiency. The aspiration is to be a 'good enough' parent, who will taste both success and failure, responding in the moment to the best of their abilities. This situation was enlivening and liberating for Kerry, in her professional work, as well as in her private life. She could now see that while she underwent change herself, the people with whom she interacted did too. Everyone had to adapt. Consideration of context was essential, and it was inadvisable, impossible even, to impose a one-size-fits-all solution.

Kerry drew on these insights in her leadership development assignment with the French fashion house. She sought to develop a more supportive, nurturing, familial environment in the organization. Kerry began to experiment with building a tight-knit community of stewards, training coaches to carry out one-to-one work across all levels of the company, providing professional guidance and pastoral care in service of the common good. Such work felt creative and thrilling, and she found that it nourished and energized her for close to a decade. Then, she walked away.

The tragic death in a car accident of a close friend and colleague, who left behind an 11-month-old baby, prompted Kerry to reassess what was important to her and what she could let go. She had learned the power of non-attachment, experienced the capacity to fully engage in something, and attained the wisdom that if you are able to hold that same thing lightly, over time, it will continue to grow on its own. We don't have to carry every heavy rock we encounter with us in perpetuity. Yet, as Kerry argues, what we touch in life can be "flavored" by our love — lightly given and lightly worn.

SERIOUS PLAY

> *"Play's original purpose was to make*
> *a pledge to someone or something*
> *by risking one's life. "*

Diane Ackerman, *Deep Play*

According to game scientist Bernie de Koven, writing in *The Well-Played Game*, "Play is the enactment of anything that is not for real." That is not to say that play is not taken seriously, for it often involves putting something important at stake, and it can affect us viscerally. In fact, there are people who can be so emotionally invested in play that they cry with joy, for example, when their favorite sports team wins an important match or despair when it loses. They are fully engaged, throwing themselves into their play as if their lives depended on it, even though they know that not to be the case. Play is about that capacity, albeit temporarily, to ignore reality, suspend disbelief and entertain alternative possibilities.

In *Deep Play*, poet and naturalist Diane Ackerman emphasizes the essence of play not as a specific kind of activity but as an attitude, a *choice* that can be made.

One chooses to divest oneself of preconceptions, hand-me-down ideas, and shopworn opinions, chooses to wipe the mental slate clean, chooses to be naive and wholly open to the world, as one once was as a child.

In this sense, play is not determined by the content of what we do, but it can be applied with freshness and lightness to the task at hand. With play, exploration and receptiveness to the new replaces tightly held knowledge and the tendency towards confirmation bias and predetermined outcomes. Play, then, has significant parallels with the concept of inquiry, which we examined in Chapter 7. Play can be serious, fundamental to both insight and creativity, regardless of setting or context.

Johan Roos has taught strategy and leadership, and consulted with corporations, for three decades. Since the start of the new millennium, he has led or been part of the leadership team at five academic institutions in four countries. For Johan, corporate practices like strategy development and change leadership should be emergent and engage peoples' capacity to imagine. They cannot be constrained by procedure and conventionality.

> Relying only on plans and data means that we're often not ready for the unexpected, simply because we have not in our minds pushed the boundaries of what is thinkable and what might be possible.

Johan has long believed that better outcomes can be achieved where people are freed from the traditional linear approaches to business management. In the late 1990s, he began to experiment, starting with the participants in a leadership seminar. Instead of relying on flipcharts and slides, they were invited to assess a tricky case study using LEGO bricks of different shapes and colors. While initially resistant to this approach, eventually they dared to play with the blocks, constructing, dismantling, trying out different structures that reflected what happened in the case study. The results were startling. The participants came up with unusual solutions to problems, interacted good-humoredly with one another, and became deeply engaged through their "serious play" with the LEGO bricks.

After his initial success, Johan further developed the approach, working alongside his colleague Bart Victor on an executive program for the top 300 managers of the LEGO Company itself in 1996–97. Following a year of experimentation, they presented their findings to Kjeld Kirk Kristiansen, the owner and CEO of LEGO. He was taken aback by what they had learned, and soon greenlighted a project to develop LEGO Serious Play products. In 2001, LEGO launched Real Time Strategy, its first such product, and offered it to experienced facilitators and consultants. At the same time, together with Kristiansen, Johan established the independent Imagination Lab Foundation in Switzerland.

Johan found that when people played seriously, the focus of strategy conversations shifted fundamentally away from consideration of company vision to prioritization of identity. The bricks in their hands were helping them deconstruct and assess their shared corporate journey and reconsider where they wanted to go next, and why. "Now, they were asking questions like 'Who are we, here and now,' 'How do others see us, here and now,' and 'What do we want to be, at our best?'"

There was nothing frivolous about the play. It was leading to deep analysis and complex thinking as solutions were sought. Consistent with complex adaptive systems theory, participants had the opportunity to explore the interconnections and interdependencies between natural and social systems, observing the impact of even the smallest of changes and their disruptive effects.

Johan noted that there were several important shifts that participants experienced. First was the move from abstraction to deep, multifaceted inquiry, involving a sensory, tactile dimension often absent from business conversations. Second was a shift in perspective from the particular and narrow to the holistic and big picture, taking into consideration environmental context as it affects both the individual and the organization. Having a concrete, 3D LEGO construction allowed people to step back, to gain perspective, or lean over, to change their vantage points. It offered something that flat, paper-based and screen-based models could not do. This was a catalyst for what game designer and author Jane McGonigal terms "ecosystem thinking" in her book, *Reality is Broken*.

It was amazing to watch and carefully facilitate groups building and talking about elaborate physical representations of their company in a larger ecosystem. They freed themselves from traditional models, language and dogma about what was important. It was gratifying!

The third transition related to how the participants interacted with and spoke to one another, using the LEGO bricks and figures to inform constructive challenge of one another. The use of these pieces to mediate conversation made the situation lighter, more open, more imaginative and less threatening than it could have been in a formal corporate meeting.

The process brought subjective views to the forefront. The metaphors and storytelling are powerful sense-making tools. People like to start by depicting the identity, then look at the outside. Modeling interactions caused people to heed them carefully.

Serious play had given rise to a new approach to strategy development, and so much more. With play, the participants discovered, came the 'risk' of being changed not only organizationally but personally, too. Serious play could challenge a firmly established sense of identity. It could undermine and strip away who you thought you were, opening you up to mystery and emergence, leading you from the linear path to one of obliquity, from the known to the unknown.

IDENTITY YOGA

"When you realize the story you're telling is just words, when you can just crumble up and throw your past in the trashcan, then we'll figure out who you're going to be."

Chuck Palahniuk, *Invisible Monsters*

Is it possible to play with and stretch our identity stories in the same way that we stretch our bodies? Charles Davies, a creative consultant, trainer and coach, has helped hundreds of people bring more clarity to their work. In a previous role as a magazine editor, Charles worked to help contributors write better stories. He discovered that the best stories were those that were alive for the writers themselves. What surprised him was how long it would take for them to arrive at that version of their own story.

Charles was no different himself. After two decades in a variety of jobs — including journalist, stand-up comic, songwriter, environmental campaigner and barista — he began to notice how many troubles in the workplace arose out of a misunderstanding of how work *works*.

Initially, I thought work was supposed to be something people did to make a living. Over time, though, I came to realize that work is something you do to meet a need. When the work doesn't meet the need, then it won't work. Once you are clear on the need, you will naturally work on what is needed.

Charles saw that this general principle could be applied to any story we tell to, or about, ourselves. As with Lucie's experience being coached by Anna, discussed in Chapter 7, the trick was to notice which stories would be most constructive, most helpful, making us feel most alive, and to identify which stories created tension, making us feel stuck. Charles refers to the process of noticing, of rewriting stories, of releasing the tension that stands in the way of creative flow, as *identity yoga*.

> I don't need a goal. Because I know there is always a tension, and when I don't know what it is trying to say and not listening to it, it will hurt. All I know is that I want that hurt to stop. What do you do for the pain to stop then? You listen.

As with other forms of yoga, the root of this practice is a simple set of moves that anyone can do, although there will always be more to discover. It starts from the fundamental notion that we all invest a lot of energy in telling and crafting stories about ourselves, through the things we say, the clothes we wear, the people we socialize with, and what we do. Our identity is a story collection that helps us make sense of who and what we are. Frequently, however, these same stories inhibit us, preventing us from coming fully alive. It is then necessary to revisit and pull apart the stories, breaking them down into their constituent parts, stretching, massaging and reshaping them until the tension is dissolved and we no longer feel stuck.

As historian Michael Puett and journalist Christine Gross-Loh suggest in *The Path*:

> Instead of thinking of ourselves as single, unified selves who are trying to discover through self-reflection, we could think of ourselves as complex arrays of emotions, dispositions, desires, and traits that often pull us in different and contradictory ways. When we do so, we become malleable. We avoid the danger of defining ourselves as frozen in a moment in time.

IDENTITY
STORY
I

IDENTITY
STORY
II

IDENTITY
STORY
III

Following in Lucie's footsteps, in her interactions with Anna, we can learn to recognize and question our stories. We also have to develop the capacity to tinker with and challenge them when they don't seem useful. This means developing a quality of non-attachment to them — the opposite of detachment or separation. When we understand that the concept of a separate self is an abstraction, we begin to question how separation or detachment from the whole can even be considered a possibility. Rather than try to detach from what we don't like, we can become curious and explore it, examining how it functions in our lives, how it serves or hinders us.

In *The War of Art*, screenwriter Steven Pressfield explores the concept of resistance. His argument is that with any creative process, especially when we are doing something new, there will always be resistance. This may take the form of procrastination, feelings of unworthiness, or even self-sabotage. The same is true when we take on new identities, such as becoming a parent for the first time, teaching our first class or writing our first book. Rather than succumb to the voice of resistance, we can be curious about its motivations, questioning what it is trying to protect. Resistance can be a signal to explore further, rather than something to be combatted or ignored.

When we are caught up in an identity or behavior, we feel like we cannot choose. We find ourselves engrossed in a psychological dynamic that learning specialists Robert Kegan and Lisa Lahey term "a competing commitment," building our resistance to change and instigating behaviors that can sabotage our own work or relationships, as well as those of other people. We want to act, but for some reason find that we cannot. Charles himself experienced this during the coronavirus pandemic, when he was willfully ignoring his ever-growing email inbox, prioritizing whatever else needed to be done. He had to follow his own identity yoga practice, becoming attuned to his own needs, contextualizing the management of email in relation to them, and then choosing to attend to the task with what he described as "clarity, purpose and joy."

With the recognition of choice comes more freedom, a realization that we are not tied to any specific story about who we are and how the world works. We can see that obligation can be worn lightly. We can discover that in every difficult situation there is potential for humor and absurdity. This is especially so when we play with the words that describe the situation, substituting, say, 'Here now' for 'I am,' or adding a negative word like 'not' to a statement. Nevertheless, with radical freedom comes radical responsibility. There is a need, Charles argues, for absolute clarity when choosing. You have to be aware of the consequences of what you choose to do, and that can be frightening.

As we listen more and notice the subtle misalignments in our stories, our lives become simpler. Knowing that all we need is already available to us, we can now listen closely to the pain that directs us to what is required, trusting that the next step will reveal itself.

Khuyen: When I was struggling with writing and feeling a lot of resistance, I decided to try the identity yoga approach. I started with a simple statement: "I am writing this book by showing up every day to write." What felt right, however, was rendered absurd when I added a negative word: "I am writing this book by not showing up every day to write."

Yet, I knew, from my instant reaction, that the story implied by the initial statement was causing me pain. When I listened to that pain, I began to see that there was the potential for so many different stories.

Perhaps I could show up every other day and, in between, socialize with friends and dance. The point was that I didn't have to stick with the version of the story that was troubling me. I had committed to co-authoring a book, but how I accomplished it could take many different forms. I had choices, albeit with responsibilities.

INFINITE GAME

*"There are at least two kinds of games:
finite and infinite. A finite game is
played for the purpose of winning,
an infinite game for the purpose
of continuing the play."*

James Carse, *Finite and Infinite Games*

Niki Harré is a professor of psychology at the University of Auckland in New Zealand. The distinction between finite and infinite games has fascinated her throughout her academic career. This is reflected in the publication of her book, *The Infinite Game*, in which she argues that infinite players relate to the humanity in each other, while finite players, constrained by the roles they have adopted or have been assigned, relate to each other as allies, pawns, spectators or competitors.

In academia, Niki has found that finite games abound. Whether seeking grants to support research, attempting to have papers published in prestigious journals or applying for a promotion, there are fixed criteria for winners, thereby limiting the possibilities for all players. Research is at the epicenter of finite games for university academics. This is where competition is the fiercest, monitored in Niki's homeland by the New Zealand Performance-Based Research Fund (PBRF), which was established in 2003.

Every six years, each academic must produce a performance portfolio of work and accolades. In such a system, the most valuable 'wins' are publication in major peer-reviewed journals that are cited by other academics. Despite the rhetoric, genuine originality and innovation are curtailed by the prioritization of research over teaching, administration, or the introduction of transformative change to the university system. Moreover, there are established ideas that are difficult to shift regarding what qualifies as quality research worthy of publication in the top journals.

To Niki's increasing frustration, the established approach to research on social issues has created something of a closed loop. Papers are read by a small circle of academics, and the findings they contain have limited (if any) societal impact. This prompted her to follow a different route, publishing a book, *Psychology for a Better World*, rather than a peer-reviewed article. This led to numerous invitations to talk at events and opened up conversations with people from diverse sectors, all of whom were working towards social change. However, the book, first published in 2011, did little to boost her PBRF grade in the following round, as Niki had anticipated.

This is an indignity, and if my grade is lower than I hope, I will feel that indignity to my core, like a lead weight nestled inside. I will, however, hold the resulting shame and doubt close, private; because as a 'senior academic' I should be at the top of my (their) game. But, I also look on that book as a move motivated by infinite values as I understand them, and do not, ever, regret the time and energy it has taken.

Niki felt strongly the contradiction wrought by the finite game, especially as someone who advocates for social change and, at the same time, is deeply embedded in an academic institution that is competitive and highly individualistic. "We must speak and act out against the worship of research," she argued, "even as we ourselves long to be research stars." She decided that she could only involve herself in research and other activities that were about more than just the end goal. "I made a pact with myself a long time ago that I would enter a finite game only when I can see the infinite space."

Niki's determination was put to the test when a paper she had finely crafted, after years of research, was rejected by a journal's editor. While some of the feedback she received was constructive and well reasoned, she still found that she was being regulated by the gamekeepers, and not permitted to stray beyond the tried and tested, or to wander beyond the boundaries of long-established frameworks. Conforming was a struggle. Yet, the study was too important to simply let go. Instead, she wrote an email questioning the decision.

To Niki's genuine surprise, the editor agreed that rejection of her paper had been made in haste. He was open to reconsider. On this occasion, the finite game had been trumped by the infinite game. "Infinite players," history and religious literature professor James Carse observes in *Finite and Infinite Games*, "do not *oppose* the actions of others, but *initiate* actions of their own in such a way that others will play by initiating their own."

In many fields, from business to religion to environmental activism, work is often described in terms of a 'battle for change' or 'competition for resources.' The underlying assumption is of separation and scarcity — of time, money, people, equipment, materials. When people are certain of who they are, of the validity of their vision, and of the steps required to achieve it, they often descend into a struggle to win a finite game, competing with others who are equally certain of the 'rightness' of their own ideas.

The finite player, then, narrowly focuses on victory at all costs, delimits themself, conforming to a closed, rule-bound system. For the infinite player, however, the aim is to keep the spirit of play going, remaining open to changes, no matter how unwelcome they initially appear. It is the unknown, the new, that surprises, nourishes and energizes us. To embrace the infinite game requires us to be alert enough in the moment to notice and nurture what matters to ourself and others.

For Niki, this ongoing process of discovery begins with noticing what she reacts to. As someone who is involved in climate change activism, for example, she knows that it is not the likelihood of her own demise or scenarios relating to global extinction that inspire fear and compel her to act, but concern about the kind of world that her children and their children will inherit. She understands what motivates her, what falls within and outside the boundaries of the finite game.

Indeed, the finite game is unavoidable to some extent, for society necessarily requires order and structures. However, there are ways through what Niki terms "STARs," or *small tiny acts of resistance*, that creatively, playfully and sustainably disrupt and challenge, opening up alternate avenues to get things done. Being an activist within the system is not easy, but embodying such paradoxical stances, and catalyzing change where possible, can make life seem worthwhile.

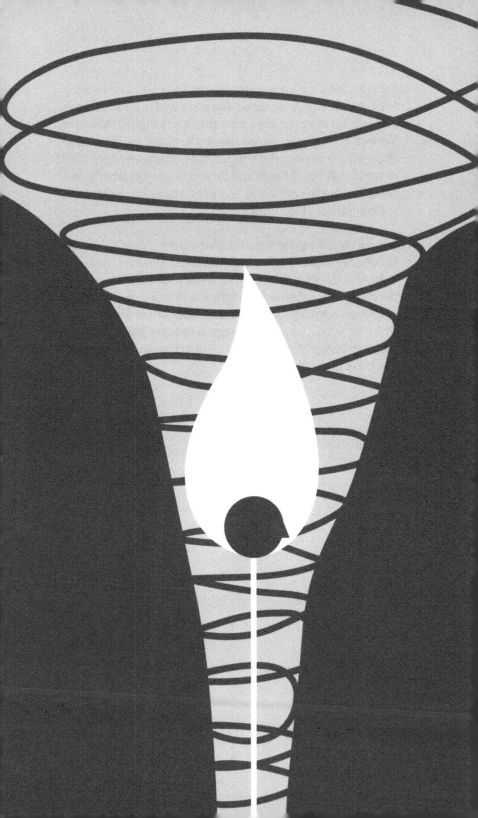

EQUANIMITY

*"Out beyond ideas of wrongdoing
and rightdoing,
there is a field. I'll meet you there."*

Rumi, *A Great Wagon*

How do we navigate the continuums between competing poles, acknowledging the validity of each of them, maintaining balance, continuing to function, and then finding a 'transformational third way' — a true integration of both? This necessarily brings a shift in perspective and identity.

Charles O'Malley is a senior advisor to the United Nations Development Programme (UNDP) and founder of the Responsible Leadership Forum. He designed and launched Big Issue Invest, one of the UK's leading social impact funds, and has dedicated his career to catalyzing positive social and environmental change in business and wider society. Charles has seen many initiatives to address environmental and climate-related issues come and go, with the deadline to achieve critical targets sliding out from 2020 to 2030 and beyond.

I view these changes with a wry smile. I understand that it's very helpful to have dates that mobilize people to action, but I don't really believe them. Whatever the presenting problem — plastic pollution or climate collapse — they all pose an existential threat. But there isn't some kind of utopia where something gets permanently fixed. In my early career, I believed that I had a purpose, something important to fix, something that could define an era, but I now realize that I am just part of a never-ending story. The story of life on earth, our solar system, the universe, is unfolding continuously.

Charles's pragmatism reflects his own journey towards effective action, at the heart of which is equanimity. He grew up in a Catholic family and, from the age of 11, was a boarder at Ampleforth College, which is run by the Benedictine Order.

Since childhood, I've always had a strong sense of purpose. Having the Abbey next to our school gave me a sense of something bigger and greater than myself. I studied there until I was 18. The college's unofficial motto — 'We prepare our boys for death' — was in stark contrast to schools whose mottos were along the lines of, 'We prepare our boys to succeed.' Yet, what it did do was emphasize that we should live our lives fully, so that we find ourselves fulfilled when we do die. Ultimately, death can arrive at any moment.

Charles enjoyed a successful career in accountancy, investment banking and venture capital before transitioning to sustainability and corporate responsibility. He was always aware of his deep sense of vocation, focused on service and contribution. But, in later years, he became increasingly aware that his sense of balance, equanimity and detachment was most likely an effect of disassociation and numbing. This he attributes in part to his separation from his family as a school boarder and to being born the child of parents of the war generation who learned to compartmentalize their feelings in order to survive. He had adopted their ways of coping.

I thought it was equanimity, but really it was numbness and disconnection. I did not feel the highs and lows. I lived in my head, quite disconnected from my feeling self. I think this was an adaptive strategy for survival, but the nature of reality is that we are fundamentally dependent on relationships to survive. The idea that we are separate is a complete illusion.

Charles's work, then, was an attempt at reconnection, underpinned by a deep and subconscious longing to rediscover parts of himself. For too long, though — as a mission-driven person, advocating for social and environmental change — he could externalize his energies, crusading on behalf of a worthy cause, endeavoring to make the world a better place. At the same time, this distracted from the need for him to do the internal work, permitting himself to feel pain and grief, and healing himself, too.

In his 30s, Charles was introduced to a form of group psychotherapy known as Systemic Constellations. This focuses on unconscious processes, highlighting patterns of relating that exist beyond the individual, including family systems, organizations and cultures. Charles found this approach to have profound healing effects, achieved over an extended period of time rather than in the short-term. He has had to develop patience, recognizing that there are no quick fixes. Instead of the five-year-plan cycles that he has been accustomed to at the UNDP, with their clear objectives and funding, he has had to place more trust in life's ebbs and flows, in its innate wisdom, certain that he will be able to do what needs to be done when it needs to be done.

The sense that I exist is very difficult to let go. If I was attached to my own identity, that could be very depressing. The idea that I have some fundamental external existence separate and indivisible from the whole is laughable. I can let go of any attachment to my own importance, my own work, and what I do. There's a relaxing into a sense of what's here, what needs attending to, what am I invited into now, a journey into the body as a compass, when the mind wants a map. The body tells me which direction to turn towards, it notices what feels satisfying, mine to do. There is a level of simplicity and a growing trust that my body knows; things become even simpler.

There is a cultural value that somehow grief, loss and sadness are bad, and need to be fixed. That we need to always move towards joy and ecstatic experience. I believe that, because I came from a numbed and disconnected background, my work is to open up to grief, loss and pain. To allow, accept and include it. When I do that, there is more possibility that joy comes through that.

Joy is not something that can be grasped, but it comes from an opening up to experience. It cannot be predetermined.

The ultimate experience of equanimity is to completely surrender and face the abyss: death, death of self, and this idea that there is anything to be done. It does not mean you are not active. It means that you patiently wait for whatever presents itself to be attended to. There is less striving, more trust in your own safety. I move from defended to opening up.

> Charles describes this significant shift in himself in terms of permission, acceptance, attending to what is happening, connection and inner peace.

In a very real sense, the earth has always held me. I had a fear I was on my own, but I never was. The air has always given me oxygen to breath, the earth has always held me, the sustenance was always there. Relaxing, I experience the intimacy of all experience; a slowing down gives a deeper sense of contact and beauty. I think of the scene in the movie *American Beauty* where the young man films a plastic bag swirling and caught in the wind. Being so present that in the moment, everything is beautiful.

> Charles now brings this equanimous stance to his work. It avoids the emotional or spiritual bypassing often encountered in activism.

Equanimity, for me, means that everything is included. As a facilitator, especially for difficult conversations and heated discussions on complex topics, it is important for me to hold the space, ensuring that everything is okay. That allows things to unfold before us and then our task is to allow it, meet it with respect, welcome it, without shutting it down.

CONTEMPLATION

CONTEMPLATION

"Solitude is independence.
It has been my wish and with the
years I had attained it. It was cold.
Oh, cold enough! But it was also still,
wonderfully still and vast like the
cold stillness of space in which
the stars revolve."

Hermann Hesse, *Steppenwolf*

The word *contemplation* is often associated with reflection —
and sometimes more negatively, associated with inaction. Its
roots can be traced back to the Latin word *templum*, which
originally meant 'an area to receive the signs,' but is more
commonly translated as *temple*. To contemplate, then, is to
mark out a space for deeper observation in order to discover
what is fundamentally true and important. In this sense,
contemplation is integral to an active, engaged, productive life.

Samir Rath is the CEO of Blue Fire AI, an award-winning
fintech start-up with offices in Singapore, Hong Kong, London
and Toronto. He has run global algorithmic trading businesses,
worked for the Singapore government as a macro-economist
and been active in building start-up communities around
the globe. When he is not working, Samir can be found on a
motorbike traveling the Silk Route, having previously traversed
Japan, Chile and Argentina. At first glance, he does not fit the
stereotype of 'a contemplative.'

Samir's notion of contemplation is founded upon his educational experiences, and an ongoing ability to understand multiple concepts while remaining curious about the relationship between them. Samir attended an experimental school where, in addition to the standard subjects like math, science and English, he was also able to experiment with woodworking, typewriting, playing music and painting. Given the variety of experiences, the eight-year-old Samir began to question the role of and the relationships between these different disciplines, wondering why they were important and why he should care. He demonstrated the innate ability of children — as identified by organizational systems research Peter Senge — to detect connections and interrelationships.

Samir illustrates his multifaceted perspective with reference to relationships. When a couple first gets together, they are naturally playful. Their interaction is unplanned, and the experience is emergent and spontaneous rather than premeditated. Nevertheless, a relationship also requires some structure, with agreed-upon commitments and an investment of time, energy and care by both parties. Through relationships, a couple helps one another grow, which, at times, requires challenge and a degree of discomfort. All these elements have to be held together in easy fluidity. Thinking about them all simultaneously is difficult, and actually embodying them even more so. Samir elaborates:

> Why so complex? Most people, even as mature adults, cannot hold these things in their head together. That's what I mean when I say that it's so important for contemplation to have the ability to hold different concepts without needing to merge or simplify them. Or, to determine what is right or wrong.

From his parents, Samir learned to blend both contemplation and action in his work. His father, a psychologist by training, with extensive experience in health-related policy, taught him a fundamental lesson: that there are many different kinds of people in the world, which makes it impossible to find a single solution that can address all problems. Therefore, in order to connect and share with as many people as possible, while preserving respect for human dignity, there has to be some kind of principle, an abstraction, to help guide our decisions. His mother, meanwhile, was involved in putting health policy into practice, making it concrete, observable and measurable. She was concerned with the micro-impact of every single action, which meant that every piece of data mattered. Samir learned from her that while principles and concepts matter, nothing changes without action.

His parents' careers illustrated a symbiotic relationship between contemplation and action. While the spaciousness required for contemplation allows for deeper insights to emerge, someone needs to act in the first place, planting the seeds that will eventually grow. Nevertheless, contemplation itself enables the clear and direct observation that fuels effective actions on the ground. As his own career has developed, Samir has learned to both draw on and differentiate between his use of analytical skills and contemplation.

Analysis aims at an answer or a better solution to a given problem, such as making a faster car or more money. Contemplation, on the other hand, is about understanding and appreciating reality and perception for their own sakes.

In this sense, contemplation is concerned with 'fundamental truths.' Contemplation points us to the space before words, before forms. In contemplation, we consciously pose a question, idea, phrase or image, and let our minds roam free, without the organization that comes from linearity, analysis and logic. It is necessary to relax our mental grip, to stop grasping for immediate answers. The aim is not to find a single, right answer but to open oneself up to possibility, holding multiple concepts at once, arriving at something that wasn't there before.

For Samir, the rhythm, the ebb and flow between intense analysis and spacious contemplation, has evolved and become smoother over time. He is able to preserve quiet periods where, physically, he does nothing, taking time off in the evenings and at weekends. He also takes longer breaks from the office every three months, either traveling to a different location, spending time outdoors or, during the pandemic, setting aside one room where work is not permitted, where he can engage in what engineering professor Barbara Oakley calls "diffuse thinking." As a mentally intense person, Samir knows firsthand the importance and challenges of unstructured time and space for contemplation:

> If your time is structured you cannot hold your own space, because your brain just jumps to the next task, the next deliverable, the next whatever.
>
> When I'm in the woods or outdoors, my brain and my breathing changes immediately. I breathe slower. It doesn't matter what's going on in life. Everything just slows down.
>
> When you're in nature, at least for me, I'm constantly reminded of how insignificant everything we do is. This is really meaningless. I mean, from a grander scheme of things, it's chaos. It's just randomness. Any meaning that comes to it comes from our mind, because we need a narrative. We need meaning in our life to move forward.

This oscillation between meaningfulness and meaninglessness is what the computer scientist David Chapman refers to as "patterned nebulosity." Our experience of meaning can be like a cloud pattern, looking like an elephant in one moment, then something indecipherable in the next. Contemplation expands our capacity to hold that kind of paradox — about ideas, concepts and even multiple versions of ourselves. Samir's example shows us the need to switch constantly between the potential revealed by contemplation and the action that will help make a difference. Meaning can come when we fill our lives with both.

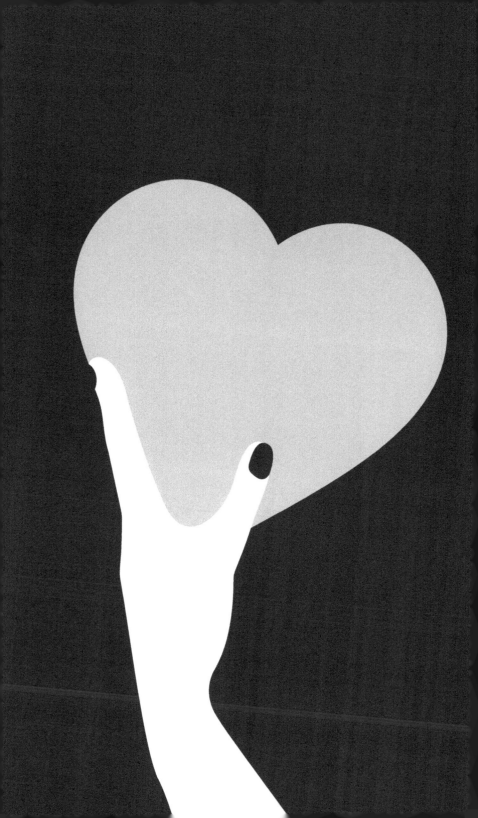

GIVE YOUR SELF AWAY

CHAPTER 10

GIVING

"Rings and jewels are not gifts, but apologies for gifts. The only gift is a portion of thyself."

Ralph Waldo Emerson, *'Gifts'*

One of the dominant narratives of modern capitalism is the story of self-interest, exemplified by the Chicago School of Economics and Milton Friedman's exhortation that the primary goal and moral duty of a corporation is to maximize shareholder profit. By extrapolation, the inference is that individuals have a moral duty to maximize their own interests, putting them above those of other people. The established economic model depends on both our rationalism and our self-interest.

In *The Virtue of Selfishness*, philosopher Ayn Rand explores this concept of rational egoism in depth. She argues that for a rational person, their own life has the highest value, rationality is considered the highest virtue, and their ultimate purpose is happiness. Rand was critical, therefore, of the ethical doctrine of altruism.

> The issue is whether the need of others is the first mortgage on your life and the moral purpose of your existence. The issue is whether man is to be regarded as a sacrificial animal. Any man of self-esteem will answer: *No*. Altruism says: *Yes*.

Rand challenges us to confront the motives behind our giving, the beliefs we hold, and the moral assumptions and shadow dynamics that are a feature of what appears to be altruism. In *Oneness vs. the 1%*, environmental land rights activist Vandana Shiva has written equally scathingly of philanthropy:

Compassion arises naturally from connectedness and the consciousness of being interconnected. It is not the philanthropy of billionaires as their billions are made through the violent economies of extraction and because they use their billions and philanthropy to create more markets and make more money. Above all philanthropy is not compassion because it assumes that money is the only human currency.

Given all that we have learned about the myth of separation, predictable irrationality and the shortcomings of *homo economicus*, could it be that the neat division between helping ourselves and others is not as polarized as it first seems? We know that excessive consumption, achievement and self-improvement has failed to deliver the happiness we sought. But what of enlightened self-interest that emphasizes mutuality over personal financial gain or other forms of individual reward?

If you have traveled on an airplane, you'll be familiar with the emergency safety instruction to put on your own oxygen mask before assisting fellow passengers. While it is true that we are unable to help other people if we are incapacitated, the general theory that we will be most happy when attending to our own needs before those of others has been found wanting. The race to create and distribute vaccines during the global coronavirus pandemic illustrates the point. National governments have sought to ensure the immunization of their own citizens, but this is not sufficient to prevent the spread of the virus. In an era of global travel and mass migration, citizens of all nations need to be vaccinated in order to contain the disease. Our fates cannot be decoupled. We may be in different boats, but we share the same stream. In *The Spirit Level*, economist Richard Wilkinson and epidemiologist Kate Pickett argue that, no matter the context, from vaccine rollouts to wealth distribution, equality benefits everyone.

There is evidence, moreover, that spending money on other people rather than on ourselves is a greater source of happiness, as documented by psychologist Elizabeth Dunn and marketing specialist Michael Norton in *Happy Money*. When it comes to giving, though, there is a tendency to value more highly those objects, tasks or relationships in which we have invested time and energy. Investments that go beyond money result in greater emotional satisfaction. In their report, 'The Happiness of Giving,' researchers Wendy Liu and Jennifer Aaker suggest that when people are asked to donate time rather than money, their charitable contributions increase, with time carrying emotional meaning rather than mere economic utility for them.

Michael Banks knows all about giving and receiving, from the perspective of being the recipient of a donor. Born in the suburbs of London, Michael was sent to boarding school when he was 11-years-old — a miserable, traumatic experience that nevertheless seeded his mission to make a positive contribution in life. After graduating from Reading University in the in the mid-1970s, Michael's urge to make things better took him to Peckham Adventure Playground, where he worked primarily with criminalized Jamaican youth in an area of London that was considered particularly violent and depressed at the time. In addition, Michael helped establish a community bookstore and newspaper, as well as serving as a union leader.

After three years of rewarding but extremely stressful work, Michael left to join a pioneering and progressive group of companies, intent on proving that the integration of spiritual practices and principles into business could yield great success. Eventually, he became a senior trainer for the organization before emigrating to the United States in 1989. There, starting from scratch, he soon established himself as a leadership expert, working as a consultant to American Express, among others, before joining the consulting firm KRW International.

Early in the new century, Michael found himself starting afresh yet again. His marriage had collapsed and his lucrative role at KRW was no more, following the fallout of 9/11. Yet, Michael found himself happier than he had ever been. A two-dimensional life on the corporate treadmill had been replaced with newfound freedom. He moved across the country to the San Francisco Bay Area, took up his long-abandoned passion for playing cricket again, fulfilled a lifelong ambition to perform his own spoken-word pieces to live audiences backed by professional musicians and, at the age of 50, met the love of his life, Karin Jordan, a fellow English émigrée.

Things were good for several years, but then worries about high blood pressure, headaches and cramps prompted Michael to have a medical checkup. When he called the doctor for the results two days later, he was shocked.

"It looks like you have stage three chronic kidney disease," the doctor explained. I went blank. I was shocked because you don't expect that. The next thing I know I'm with a nephrologist in a San Francisco hospital, and he's saying we can try to save you losing your kidneys with strong medication.

Initially, Michael explored alternative medicine and practices, but he noticed that, as a result of his disease, his body felt much colder than normal. After a few months, his symptoms became worse.

I had no energy so I would have to pull up in my car outside my home and just sit there for fifteen minutes behind the wheel, numb, paralyzed. Eventually, I went to sleep on a Wednesday and slept through all of Thursday. On Friday afternoon, Karin insisted on taking me to the doctor, who called my nephrologist, and I was sent straight to the hospital. My kidneys had failed. It was really serious, and I was put on dialysis.

At the time of Michael's diagnosis, the waiting time for kidney transplants in the US was about seven years. Even then, most transplants are from cadavers, which usually are not as successful as transplants from live people. Michael's own situation was further complicated by the fact that the poison in his system had damaged his heart, too. When Karin questioned what she could do to help, he asked her to donate one of her kidneys to him.

Although Karin agreed, there were a number of hurdles to negotiate, not least relating to the complexity and emotions of such a decision, the medical tests for compatibility, and informing family members and friends of their plans. There were potentially life-changing consequences for Karin that she needed to take into consideration, and for which she received counseling. Michael and Karin also sought advice from another couple who had been through a similar situation.

While Karin was willing to give part of herself away to Michael, there were also practical challenges the couple faced. Michael had health insurance for the operation, but the hospital would not carry out the transplant without having proof of payment to cover the cost of the aftercare. Michael explains that he had to let go of his ego in order to be able to ask for support.

> We did a fundraising exercise which was extraordinary. We had about 150 people who donated various amounts of money and we raised $65,000. There are many lessons there. The generosity of people was extraordinary. There were people coming out of the woodwork from my past that I hadn't spoken to for decades. Then there were people who donated even though I knew they couldn't afford to. One friend, who had very little, gave me £1,000.

In *Gotta Kidney?!*, a book Michael wrote to help others prepare for and manage experiences similar to his own — including a chapter written by Karin to add the donor's perspective — he recounts the operation's success. Today, both Karin and Michael are healthy and happy together years after the event, active in raising awareness about organ donation and providing information and support to donors and recipients.

The cover of *Gotta Kidney?!* shows a ribbon-tied kidney, emphasizing its status as a gift, a gift of love. In conversation with Michael and Karin, it is their mutual love and gratitude that powerfully colors their recollection of what they went through together — asking, giving, receiving, sharing — and the full lives they now lead. As their book's subtitle indicates, theirs was a journey that took them "from fear to hope and beyond."

ARTISTIC TRUTH

"Art remains the one way possible
of speaking truth."

Robert Browning, *The Ring and the Book*

Art has the potential to transform people's lives. This is the powerful lesson that Judith 'Jude' Kelly learned by dedicating her own life to the arts. Jude is a theater director and producer responsible for more than 100 stage productions. Between 2006 and 2018, she was artistic director of the Southbank Centre in London, Europe's largest center for the arts. In addition to working in London's West End, Jude has overseen productions for the Royal National Theatre, the English National Opera, the Chichester Festival Theatre and the Théâtre du Châtelet in Paris. In 2010, she was the founder of the Women of the World Festival (WOW), an annual celebration of achievement and a feminist awareness-raising movement focused on the obstacles that confront women and girls. Since 2018, she has served as the first director of the WOW Foundation.

Jude's love of theater dates back to her childhood in Liverpool. She remembers listening to the Nutcracker Suite as a six-year-old child, dancing and jumping around enthusiastically, while identifying with the Sugar Plum Fairy. Jude loved to make up stories and would put on plays in her back yard with the neighbors' children. Her passion for music and storytelling at Quarry Bank School was encouraged under the guidance of John Lennon's former headmaster, Bill Pobjoy.

I was always fascinated with how the story was being told, not just being in the story. If it involved boys and girls, girls could never be the hero or the knight. They could only be tied up and rescued. Often, they didn't even have a speaking role. I remember being angry about it, even though I had no idea of gender politics at that age. Stories are images of feelings. As a child, I could get out and think, but not *own* the story.

During her early childhood, Jude lived in a multicultural, inner-city area of Liverpool, with immigrant communities from China, the West Indies and Ireland. When her family moved to a more affluent area, the absence of diversity and the stories from those other cultures were the first things that Jude noticed and missed. While her ballet lessons took place in the West African center, the room itself was full of white girls, making Jude acutely aware of the community beyond the center's walls in which she felt more at home. Art, she realized, carried the potential to connect rather than separate; it could shape an identity.

Infants and children have always used expression as a vehicle to communicate their feelings. Art is certainty and doubt, knowledge and mystery, mirrored back to yourself. I explore my feelings and show that content in art. It is that feeling that is created when you see a sunset or take a picture. You want to share it. So, it involves both self-recognition and social recognition. From ancient Greek gatherings in the theaters or African tribal ceremonies, all societies have used art to strengthen community identity. If this becomes monocultural, it can be insular.

According to Jude, people make art by exploring what they want to explore, and when they present it to others, it enables them to participate and respond. Artistic practice then becomes communal rather than a solipsistic, individual pursuit. People respond both individually and collectively, while the artist is always seeking the maximal moments of resonance. Jude, who lives a highly active life in public service, has never drawn a boundary between her public work, her family and her introspection. All are integrated.

My childhood colored my passion for social justice and my desire to make stories. The art industry legitimizes the solo artist — the visionary, making something for their own elegant purpose. The more you are interested in democratizing, the less legitimate your art seems to be. There is a feeling that selling yourself, you'll do better with a conventional route, while not doing this sets you back. There are moments as an artist when you just want to wallow in text. People don't only invest in theater but in the context in which art will happen.

Jude's art has served as a means to express her passion for social justice, continuing a long-standing tradition of art activism. During the 1960s and 1970s, for example, the feminist movement used art for personal expression and revelation, exercising both social and political influence. In Jude's case, beyond her activism, she has always seen her work as something that she *wants* to do rather than as something she *ought* to do.

I don't know how much choice comes into it, your heart, your sense of purpose. Why me for this project? Your experiences, including negative experiences, are huge pieces of knowledge and wisdom. Some of these things have forged me. The lack of rights of others dismayed and humbled me, prompting me to focus not only on what happened to a person but to the system. Lots of people don't have a purpose because they don't see why they matter. That larger you, that you can discover and offer to other people. This includes and goes beyond gender, skin color, class. It is the validating of themselves.

At the same time, Jude argues that it's important to give yourself and others permission to *not* be of service.

This is often a burden that is put on women. For example, white men are not asked to represent white men all the time. Some people are frightened of owning, say, their femininity or their skin color. So, how can you change the occupation in the arts? It boils down to our values and our stories, to liberate us from the stories we tell ourselves, and others about ourselves. We need to speak to people who feel guilty, to help them understand entitlement and how you can use it.

At the heart of her passion for the arts is the way in which Jude values diversity. It's not only about promoting equality for women to benefit in the arts. Jude also recognizes that when women are not flourishing and contributing their stories, men are stripped of and denied knowledge, while society as a whole is poorer. In ancient times — and perhaps in modern times too — rulers were surrounded by 'yes men' who sought to protect them and the power they represented, rarely challenging their worldview or the narratives they used to describe it. Jude, however, has dedicated her life to speaking truth to power, helping women in all their diversity tell their stories.

Jude's own experiences highlight both the importance and the limitations of following your passion. In their study of the benefits and perils of art-making, *Art & Fear*, working artists David Bayles and Ted Orland observe that "making art now means working in the face of uncertainty; it means living with doubt and contradiction." There is a constant need to balance risk and reward, self-expression and socio-political context, messaging and entertainment, critique and compassion. "The art you make," argue Bayles and Orland, "is irrevocably bound to the times and places of your life." For Jude and her peers, their aspiration is to use their art to capture a truth, to educate even, without perpetuating the same societal conditions that their art is attempting to disrupt.

WE ARE EACH OTHER

*"The time will come
when, with elation,
you will greet yourself arriving
at your own door, in your own mirror,
and each will smile at the other's welcome,
and say, sit here. Eat.
You will love again the stranger who was
Your self."*

Derek Walcott, *Love After Love*

Volunteer tourism typically involves someone from a developed country traveling to and volunteering services in a less developed country. The volunteers experience life with local people, enjoying the cultural experience of being abroad while helping out. Although the practice gained in popularity prior to the global pandemic, it has not been without its critics, who detect an undertone of colonialism and hero-rescuer dynamics behind the benevolence. They highlight how local dependence on the donated services can be established, while the structural issues that cause and perpetuate poverty may not be tackled at all. Some question the motivation of volunteers, too, wondering whether the desire to feel good about oneself, about your own kindness and generosity, outweighs the actual service to others. To do genuinely important work, we need to disregard the approval of others.

In *Let Your Life Speak*, educator Parker Palmer reflects on hearing the term "the ungrateful poor" being uttered by Dorothy Day, the founder of the Catholic Worker movement. This was someone whose long-term commitment to living among and serving the poor of New York's Lower East Side had inspired him. He struggled to reconcile such a dismissive phrase with the charitable work he so admired. Then it dawned on him that Day really meant:

Do not give to the poor expecting to get their gratitude so that you can feel good about yourself. If you do, your giving will be thin and short-lived, and that is not what the poor need; it will only impoverish them further. Give only if you have something you must give; give only if you are someone for whom giving is its own reward.

When I give something I do not possess, I give a false and dangerous gift, a gift that looks like love but is, in reality, loveless — a gift given more from my need to prove myself than from the other's need to be cared for.

The motivation to give does not come from guilt, nor from being ashamed about your privilege, nor from wanting to prove yourself to be a good person. Generosity is an expression of love, which cannot be forced but only awakened and nourished.

Jolanda van den Berg is the founder of the Niños Unidos Peruanos Foundation, which has transformed the lives of thousands of street children in Peru over the past three decades. An émigrée from the Netherlands, mother of two children, social entrepreneur, philanthropist and businesswoman running a series of boutique hotels, Jolanda's expansive life defies all reductive labels.

From childhood, Jolanda was always an independent spirit who made decisions not through rational thinking but from her heart, dependent on how she felt. She was a non-conformist, refusing to pray at kindergarten, frequently running away, wanting to be recognized as her own person, leaving school at the age of 16. As a child, Jolanda would observe other people and notice whether what they were saying matched how they were saying it. Usually, it did not.

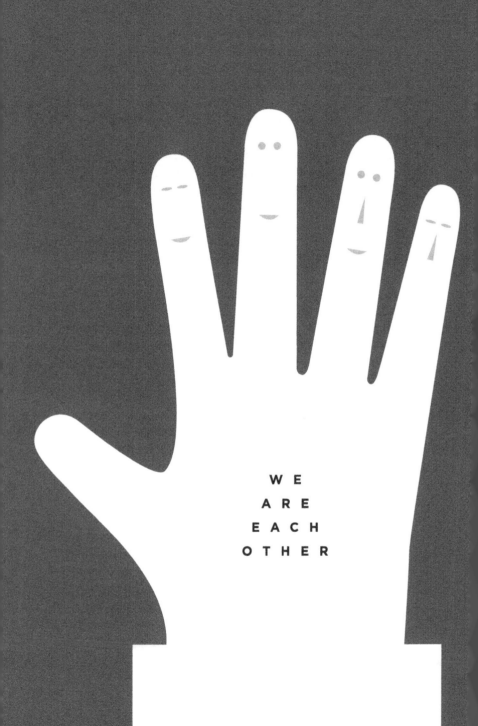

WE
ARE
EACH
OTHER

I was fascinated by the way people believed their own stories. My father was bipolar and was only diagnosed when he was 18. His condition made it complicated to know what he was feeling and what his mood would be, so I learned to observe, even if I could not prevent what was happening. Awareness became a refined and automatic skill.

One of the ways that Jolanda anchored herself and coped with her father's bipolar condition was through her rich imagination. She also established a close relationship with her grandmother, who had worked the land potato farming during the Second World War.

My grandmother appealed to me as she was authentic, she didn't fit in a box. She was strong and people did not understand her. People would say she was not a nice person, but that she was like a king. She did not have rules, and that made me feel free. She was a free spirit, not fitting in in any way.

After her father's death, Jolanda felt disconnected from life. She knew something needed to change. Although she did not know it at the time, her journey to Peru in 1995 to see the pink river dolphins signaled the start of that change.

While visiting Cusco, Jolanda was captivated by the children she met playing in the streets. Some had torn clothes, some were working, shining shoes, carrying heavy loads, or hawking wares to tourists. "I saw in their eyes something that touched me deeply," she recalls. "A strong feeling of recognition and resonance. Something happened to me and I really wanted to be with them." Jolanda would buy far more postcards from them than she could ever send and, twice a day, found herself getting her shoes polished. One day, after attending early morning mass, Jolanda stayed after for an hour, not speaking but feeling something well up inside her.

I was not thinking, "Those poor children, I have to help them." This was a calling. I needed to be with them. It certainly was not something that had been on my agenda beforehand. At the time, I had two jobs in the Netherlands, working in IT during the day and as a sports instructor in the evening. Neither involved children and I didn't even like to look after children. I had a free life, a car from my company, and everything was perfect. Yet, I knew my life was about to change.

This form of calling — something one cannot *not* do — points us to what the minister Frederick Buechner calls "the place where your deep gladness and the world's deep hunger meet." Referring to the visceral knowledge that accompanies these moments of recognition, human potential author Gregg Levoy writes in *Callings*, "Saying yes to a call tends to place us on a path that half of ourselves thinks doesn't make a bit of sense, but the other half knows our lives won't make sense without."

Within six months, Jolanda was back in Cusco. When she landed, she had no plan, no job, no Spanish, and little money other than donations from friends back in the Netherlands. But, her purpose was clear: if she could help even one child, that would be enough. Gradually, she got to know the children in the street, playing football with them, listening to their concerns.

Within a few months, Jolanda had adopted two boys from the street. After nine months, this number had grown to 12, with the youngsters accommodated in apartments. The Youth Court awarded her parental control of the children, many of them pre-teens, until they turned 18. The youngest child was only three years old; his mother had been imprisoned for killing his father in self-defense.

We lived life as a family. It was beautiful and difficult. My main offering to the children was meeting their need to be *seen*. I wanted to ensure that they had love and care, that they could go to school, that they could be children without having to

work or take on other responsibilities. My purpose was to give
them a place where they could be children, where they could
play, where they could forget about everything and everyone,
and just be.

Donations started to pour in, but often with conditions attached,
with the money intended for the purchase of specified items
or gifts. Jolanda felt that such obligations undermined the
independence of what she was creating with the children. To
make the model more sustainable, it would be better to establish
a business. A no-strings donation of $100,000 enabled her to
establish the first children's hotel, Niños Hotel Meloc, in a
refurbished colonial building in Cusco in 1998. This catered to
tourists while bringing in funds for the Niños Unidos Peruanos
Foundation. Each room was named after a different child and
decorated with their artwork and stories. Jolanda made sure
that the business created local, paid jobs. Her own talent as a
designer and the hard work of the staff ensured that the hotel
was a huge success.

Soon, the hotel had generated enough profits to allow Jolanda
to open a children's restaurant, which provided two meals a day,
six days a week, for youngsters from vulnerable backgrounds,
as long as they attended primary school. Many of the children
who came to the restaurant had been abused or came from
violent backgrounds. The restaurant began to offer a range of
other services, including self-defense classes, sports activities,
skill-development opportunities, dental treatment and other
health check-ups. At the heart of it all was unconditional love
and affirmation of the children's own dignity.

In subsequent years, two more boutique hotels and four more
children's restaurants have been opened, as well as two libraries,
a small cinema, a sports hall and a hacienda for horseback riding
outside of Cusco. The needs of over 600 children are met as
a result of income from the hotels, as well as donations from
around the globe. The initiatives also employ 80 local staff,

who receive both salary and benefits. Jolanda looks at everyone involved in terms of family, refusing to distinguish between those who are in need and those who do something in response.

> I see no one is *doing* anything. For healing or helping, you need to look at someone who needs healing or helping. That concept does not exist for me. There are no distinct givers or receivers. No victims, no heroes. We are each other.

SURRENDER

> *"To love a specific person, and to identify with his or her struggles and joys as if they were your own, you have to surrender some of your self."*

Jonathan Franzen, *Liking is for Cowards. Go for What Hurts*

Giving ourselves away doesn't necessarily mean giving ourselves to a grand cause, aiming to fix the system and change the world. Sometimes, it's the opposite: to give up the cause, and commit to something more real, more specific. Such was the case for Jonathan Franzen, the American novelist, and his ongoing relationship with the work of environmental conservation. Recalling how he began this shift in his early 20s, Franzen writes in 'Liking is for Cowards. Go for What Hurts,' a 2011 opinion piece published in *The New York Times*, "I liked the natural world. Didn't love it, but definitely liked it. It can be very pretty, nature."

For many well-educated Western teens and 20-somethings, it's become common, almost fashionable, to express dissatisfaction and rage at the state of the world. Environmentalism, as Franzen readily admits, had an obvious appeal when he reached this age. The young were inheriting the mess of previous generations and could bemoan the existential crisis into which they and the planet had been plunged. Doing something — anything — in the face of such overwhelming odds and in support of worthy causes could go some way towards assuaging a collective sense of guilt.

Steven: When I was 18, I took two years out before going to university. I ran youth retreats, volunteered at an Alzheimer's respite care home, and also worked at a homeless shelter, living in a community with other volunteers. During this time, I explored the possibility of a religious vocation with an order known as the Vincentians, which was dedicated to service of the marginalized.

The priest whose role it was to help me discern if I had a religious vocation questioned me about my relationships with friends and family. To my shame, I realized that, while I could be loving and patient with strangers and dedicated while volunteering, I was less patient and generous with my time when interacting with those closest to me. The priest summed up my situation with the phrase "street angel, home devil."

From this, I learned a valuable early lesson. While I could dedicate myself to the service of others in the wider community, it could and should not come at the expense of those closest to me. In fact, that was where the real challenge lay. It's easier to give yourself to a cause than it is to engage in the grittiness and responsibility that comes with close relationships. These should never be taken for granted. Rather than the grand gesture, the real challenge is to start closer to home.

In Franzen's case, the more he learned about what was wrong — population explosion, ocean trash, deforestation, desertification — the angrier he became. Confronting the wrongness of the world drained him. To prevent himself from lapsing into rage and despair, he tried to keep a tight rein on his environmental consciousness, limiting himself to annual charitable donations. By the mid-1990s, Franzen had made a conscious decision to stop worrying about the environment, acknowledging that there was nothing meaningful he could do to save the planet, and that he would rather get on with the things he loved.

Not long after coming to terms with his environmental despair, Franzen found himself dealing with a painful divorce, as well as his mother's illness with colon cancer and subsequent death. Birdwatching became a source of comfort as he dealt with his grief. "Little by little, in spite of myself, I developed this passion, and although one-half of a passion is obsession, the other half is love," he recalls in *The New York Times*. The obsession resulted in a meticulous list of birds seen and kilometers traveled to see new species, whereas the love was experienced viscerally. "Whenever I looked at a bird, any bird, even a pigeon or a robin, I could feel my heart overflow with love," he says in his opinion piece. Years earlier, in 'My Bird Problem,' published in *The New Yorker* in 2005, he had confessed, "What I felt for birds went beyond love. I felt outright identification."

Franzen's newfound love of birds compounded his grief, carrying with it traces of his relationship with his mother, as well as the legacy of his youthful environmental concerns. But what had been abstract in the past, relating to some vague notion of a planetary future, had now become more concrete and urgent. His love of the avian species had transformed how he looked at the problem, providing specificity and focus. Through his surrender to this love, Franzen had discovered the essence of giving our self away. He could recognize that the other — person, bird, being — was every bit as real and important as he was. This was a wordless revelation, a felt experience of bottomless empathy.

When we accept the risk of being fundamentally changed by what we encounter, our self-centeredness will eventually have to fall away. This was Franzen's experience. No longer merely liking nature in the abstract, but loving a specific and vital part of it, he began to be concerned about the environment again. The forests, wetlands and oceans were no longer just scenery from which he took pleasure, looking at them or venturing into them, but were the natural habitats for the birds he loved. He was vested in their protection and their longevity. To stand aside and bear witness to their ongoing destruction was unconscionable.

As Franzen began to get involved in bird conservation and learned more about the many threats that birds face, he discovered that it became easier, not harder, to live with those difficult emotions. From that place of love, the usual concerns about safety, self-image, mortality and survival slowly fell away. Love, Franzen recognized, was the only way to meet the world's impossibly daunting problems. As he observes at the close of the piece in *The New York Times*:

> When you stay in your room and rage or sneer or shrug your shoulders, as I did for many years, the world and its problems are impossibly daunting. But when you go out and put yourself in real relation to real people, or even just real animals, there's a very real danger that you might love some of them.
>
> And who knows what might happen to you then?

SURRENDER

BELONGING

"We are in fact relational beings in a world where everything affects everything else and, as a result, to care for others is to care for ourselves."

Daniel Christian Wahl, *Designing Regenerative Cultures*

Kenny Mammarella D'Cruz is a successful facilitator who founded MenSpeak. His work consists of creating small groups in which hundreds of men have shared in psychologically safe environments their hopes, fears and feelings of vulnerability. Many have experienced, either first-hand or through their relationships with others, the dislocations and disconnections of modern life that have given rise to mental health issues, suicides, college dropouts and criminality among young men. MenSpeak offers a space in which social masks and performance are set to one side, and people can talk openly about what concerns them, as well as be respectfully challenged and questioned by other participants.

The mutual sense of care that Kenny has created for others stands in stark contrast to his own experiences as a child refugee moving to the UK from Uganda. Both of Kenny's parents were born in East Africa but, as they had South Asian heritage, found themselves persecuted under the dictatorial regime of Idi Amin. Known as the Butcher of Uganda, Amin was a military officer who served as national president throughout the 1970s and was behind thousands of extrajudicial and ethnic killings. Kenny and his family were forced to flee the country.

My father was smuggled to Italy from Uganda. Once we were reunited, we moved to his refugee camp, then to a small town in Wales. We were the only non-white family in the community. As a family, we were traumatized and on the edge. We had no money or knowledge of how to cook, clean or look after ourselves. So, we kept our heads down and just survived. We didn't really want for much, we didn't really have much, and we couldn't really talk about what we had been through because we were still going through it. If one of us had cracked, then we would all have cracked, and that might have been the end of us.

Just before we fled Uganda, I remember my father telling me, "You might never see me again and you are now the head of the family. You have to take care of your mother and brother." From that moment on, at seven years of age, I went on duty.

The stress took its toll on Kenny and was compound by his experience of bullying and racism in the refugee camps. Suffering from PTSD, he developed various mental health issues, including obsessive-compulsive disorder, Tourette syndrome, trichotillomania, twitching and grunting, and body dysmorphia.

I was pulling my hair and picking at my skin. Pretty much anything to try and relieve the anxiety and try and maintain control when I experienced chaos inside me. I dealt with our situation by internalizing everything, putting on a good show, and being there as much as I could for my mother and brother — a habit I developed when my father wasn't there. My father was depressed, trying to find work. Once he did, he was very busy and generally emotionally unavailable.

I learned not only from this experience but from my earlier life, too, that men were not to be trusted. At some level, I felt like my father had abandoned me. But also, I had become enmeshed with my mother, godmother and grandmother. I was their golden boy and it felt great. The downside, though, was I felt like I was responsible for all their emotions and well-being. I couldn't do anything wrong because I couldn't bear being told off or rejected. I had to get it right and remain their wonder child.

Because of Kenny's caregiver role at home, he found that he couldn't really play with the other kids. He belonged with neither the adults nor the children. Fearful of rejection, initially he also was careful not to be associated with men, who were demonized by his female-dominated family.

As I grew up, I overcame most of my mental health issues. I learned how to be present, how to calm myself down. I controlled my PTSD, stopped twitching and grunting, and began to present a normalized mask to the world. Working with Mother Teresa, with dying men in Calcutta, helped me get over my obsessive-compulsive disorder. By my late 20s, I had a successful marketing and publicity company. All my dreams appeared to have come true. I felt it was time to put myself before the needs and expectations of others for a while.

Serendipity, a sense of adventure and new friendships led Kenny to Fiji, Singapore and Australia, where he worked and traveled for the next five years.

On my return, I hooked up with my old male friends, though something was missing. They were distracted by money and power addictions, love and sex addictions, drug and alcohol addictions. Anything that distracted from themselves. I guess they took one fork in the road and I took another. Mine had more passion, maybe more purpose and soul-searching. I needed to share depth and excitement for life with them. So, I called a meeting of a dozen or so of us in my front room and said to them, "I don't know what a men's group is, but I'm starting one now. You're all in it. I will still go raving with you and hang out like we've always hung out, but I need depth as well, and if you can't meet me here, then you're probably going to be chucked." The sad thing was I remember telling a couple of them, through sheer frustration, that I miss them more being with them, here and now, then when I was abroad thinking about them.

Kenny's invitation for others to join him had an unexpectedly positive response. Soon the group was too large to be hosted at his home. People heard about his men's groups, told their friends, who told their friends, and before long the idea had coalesced into something with ground rules, check-ins and structure.

Today, I hold about a dozen men's groups a month. A few men still come along who were at that first meeting. In addition, I train others to facilitate men's groups, including other men, women, therapists, coaches and anyone else who wants to learn how to do it. With Covid-19 and social isolation, I've held small, weekday meetings over lunchtime to help keep men calm, connected, safe and sane.

The groups are different to therapy and other personal development groups, because they are as near to daily life as possible. People get to explore the truth and really get to know not only who they are but who they no longer need to be. It's non-hierarchical, so I'm not the leader at the top of the pecking order. We all learn from each other's experiences, successes and failures. We also get to share our fears and fantasies. We live beyond our histories and explore who we are, what we want out of life, and support each other as we grow into a new life.

While the idea of support groups for men may seem like a very specific niche, Kenny has discovered that they attract a wide variety of people. Some participants feel they have outgrown their lives; others who have been very successful and crossed off everything on their bucket list still feel empty inside. Many are going through some form of change or transition, such as imminent parenthood or career changes, or simply find themselves at a crossroads, needing to make life choices. Some want to fall in love but feel unable to do so. The groups also attract men who, like Kenny, have encountered difficulties relating to other men, having lacked positive male role models early in life or been sent away to authoritarian boarding schools.

The members of a community, argues executive advisor Charles Vogl in *The Art of Community*, must feel that they are invested in each other's welfare, showing mutual concern for one another. Such perceptions matter. According to Vogl, "Communities function best and are most durable when they're helping members to be successful in some way in a connected and dynamic world." What had begun as a meeting group triggered by Kenny's concern for his friends, then, had rapidly evolved into a genuine community of men.

> These days there are a lot of leaders of men around, who aim to turn boys into men with their initiations, training, howling in the woods, nakedness and stuff like that. Men who've been there and done that show up at MenSpeak, as well as men who've moved through the pick-up artist community, or various social, sporting, religious and twelve-step communities. Personal development books and therapists refer men to my groups as a bridge to a calm, grounded, connected daily life. We connect with our authentic selves and test-drive who we think we really are, receiving invaluable feedback, before following our hearts into daily life.

While the groups may seem like indulgent 'talking spaces' to the casual observer, Kenny's experience of their impact is significantly different.

> I know for a fact that these men's groups have saved several lives. The isolated learn to take part with boundaries. The abused or abusive break taboos and talk through their issues and are met in that toxic energy before transforming it into creative expression.

Kenny's story shows us that while our experience might be one of fragmentation and trauma, healing can occur by coming together in community. Either in physical space or online, accessed through modern technologies, it is possible to find or create our own communities, the places where we belong. Kenny's efforts have continued throughout the coronavirus pandemic with the establishment of a charity, introduction of an accreditation program to certify practitioners, operation of supervision groups and launch of an app. MenSpeak graduates have gone on to establish their own meeting groups, while others have downloaded free materials to inform their own approach. Kenny used his personal wounds to heal not only himself but to give something away, in which hundreds of lives have been and continue to be transformed the world over.

THE TWO HALVES OF LIFE

> *"One cannot live the afternoon of life according to the program of life's morning; for what was great in the morning will be of little importance in the evening, and what in the morning was true will at evening become a lie."*

C. G. Jung, *The Structure and Dynamics of the Psyche*

The idea that life was composed of two halves was first outlined by the psychologist Carl Jung. He described the first half of life as constructive, like erecting scaffolding that climbs upwards, in which we build up our sense of identity, security and importance, marking our place in the world. This half is often equated with having an achievement orientation, seeking external success or validation, developing our ego.

This urge to create and to make our mark, often equated with the vigor of youth, is a necessary stage of development. As we have seen during the course of this book, however, there usually comes a point when we discover that our sense of self and the foundations on which our scaffolding is built are not as stable as we first thought. Loss, suffering and changes in responsibility can all cause us to question our assumptions, to scratch away at our positive self-image, to assess our lack of fulfillment.

In the second half of life, we start to dismantle the scaffolding. Life becomes less about finding meaning or purpose in our external successes or achievements. Instead, we look for a deeper source of purpose, often linked to the service of others.

This half of life involves more unlearning. We set aside habits and beliefs we have picked up, letting go rather than acquiring more, questioning what really matters to us and what our lives mean for others.

In *The Second Mountain*, journalist David Brooks draws on Jung's concept and uses the mountain metaphor to examine his own life transitions. He characterizes his story as being symptomatic of a culture that emphasizes individualism and success. Brooks describes how, when on the first mountain, he was an insecure overachiever, a workaholic and a failure in his marriage.

I achieved far more professional success than I ever expected to. But that climb turned me into a certain sort of person: aloof, invulnerable and uncommunicative, at least when it came to my private life. I sidestepped the responsibilities of relationship.

A society that privileges the first mountain, Brooks argues, leaves people feeling alienated, chronically dissatisfied and divided. Their moral and cultural foundations are rotten, which is mirrored by what he called "the rot we see in our politics."

After divorcing from his wife of 27 years, Brooks describes a transitional period in which he not only missed his children, living alone in an apartment and felt ashamed at his failure at marriage, but began to wonder about what he could learn from those who "do commitments well." While hiking in Aspen, Brooks read a Puritan prayer, which proved to be a turning point — a *metanoia* — helping him sense "the presence of the sacred in the realities of the everyday."

Brooks suggests that there are people on life's second mountain who are there not because they have attained a certain age or passed through a particular rite of passage, but because they have chosen to commit themselves to something. They are less concerned about themselves than about dedicating their lives to others. For Brooks, these are people who see that there is something greater than the pursuit of happiness. Their own joy is found in service to others, in community and in public good.

> Happiness comes from accomplishments; joy comes from offering gifts. Happiness fades; we get used to the things that used to make us happy. Joy doesn't fade. To live with joy is to live with wonder, gratitude and hope. People who are on the second mountain have been transformed. They are deeply committed. The outpouring of love has become a steady force.

Jojo Fresnedi is in his 60s and lives in the Philippines with his wife, Rhodora. Jojo was born near Manila, in the town of Muntinlupa, which is the location of the national penitentiary. Despite lacking the resources of wealthier peers, he excelled at school, college and university, usually attaining the highest grades.

> My life was driven by achievement. After graduation I joined a global beverage company, but I still retained the mindset of being the best, conscious of not being outworked by my peers, and always looking for opportunities to shine.

Jojo's talents and strong work ethic were noticed by his firm, and he was quickly promoted to become the youngest supervisor, director and then vice president in the company, running leadership development for them regionally. Today, Jojo considers this drive for achievement to have represented his life's first mountain. Then came a significant shift.

> When my first daughter was born, it was almost as if I had an epiphany. The moment I held her in my arms, I knew that nothing else would be more important than this. It marked a shift in the gravity of my life, not immediately, but gradually and steadily.

Having spent 20 years in his company, Jojo was offered the opportunity to retire early. He was only 39 years old, and an expat based in London. When he received this offer, Rhodora's career was taking off, and he saw an opportunity to switch from a focus on employment to a role as supportive husband and father.

Can you imagine a senior executive, who was used to staff reporting to him and making important decisions, suddenly learning to cook, being busy dropping off and picking up the children from school, spending the evenings helping with homework? You won't believe it, but those were the most fulfilling years of my life!

When Jojo was offered another job a few years later, he was asked by the company's president what his biggest accomplishment had been in his life. Jojo immediately replied, "Raising three wonderful kids as a house husband." He began to doubt the suitability of what he had said immediately after the interview, but was called by the president that same day, who offered him the job and revealed how impressed she had been by his response.

As Rhodora's career climbed to even greater heights, the family had to relocate again, this time to Singapore. Corporate success for both Jojo and Rhodora entailed a globetrotting lifestyle, which meant that they were unable to spend much time together. With the approach of their 50th birthdays, they decided another shift was required in their lives, which would allow them to spend more time together and do meaningful, rather than merely financially rewarding, work.

On their return to the Philippines, Rhodora began to work for a foundation dedicated to 'building a healthier Philippines.' She was involved in a variety of projects, which included promoting inclusion for people with disabilities. Jojo also volunteered his time, running a leadership boot camp twice a year that helped doctors supplement their specialist health knowledge and practice with leadership and management skills.

This was personally fulfilling to me as it was about working to help people, not helping a corporation make more money.

While there's nothing wrong with the latter, there was a deep sense of purpose knowing that we were making an impact on doctors, many of whom served poor villages in rural areas.

Jojo and Rhodora then developed a program called Life Re-Designed, with the aim of helping people like them, who were experienced but didn't want to retire in the typical sense of the term. Instead, they were addressing those second mountain questions: Where do I go from here? What is the contribution I can make at this stage?

One project arose from a conversation Rhodora had with a horticulturalist over dinner, when she mentioned her love of sunflowers and the fact that she owned land in the south of the Philippines. She then had the idea to combine this with her passion for inclusion. In 2018, Sunshine Farm Philippines was established, employing people with disabilities to grow, harvest and sell sunflowers, providing them with sustainable and meaningful work. A social media phenomenon that attracts many visitors, the farm now has 22 people with disabilities on its staff.

Rhodora didn't hire people with disabilities to grow and sell sunflowers. She's growing and selling sunflowers to hire people with disabilities. This is the purpose of Sunshine Farm Philippines: to plant seeds of hope. For people with a disability, hope is a job.

Jojo and Rhodora now spend a lot of time coaching and mentoring others in their community, and are both engaged in a variety of projects. They are still achieving success, but the main difference since they returned to the Philippines is that they have given their selves away. Their lives are about others, about togetherness as a couple, and togetherness in interaction with those they serve. Past knowledge and experiences have been harnessed in service of current practice. Two mountains have become one.

MODERN ELDER

"I think as one grows older, one is appallingly exposed to wearing life instead of living it. Habit, physical deterioration and a slower digestion of our experiences, all tend to make one look on one's dear life as a garment, a dressing gown, a raincoat, a uniform, buttoned on with recurrent daily (tasks)… for myself I found one remedy, and that is to undertake something difficult, something new, to re-root myself in my own faculties… for in such moments, life is not just a thing one wears, it is a thing one does and is."

Sylvia Townsend Warner, *Letters*

Aging means changing. However, while our bodies may atrophy, that doesn't mean that all aspects of our lives decay. In fact, the opposite may apply. Indeed, our lives can become richer, as we reconcile ourselves to — and cease to resist — the inevitable. As we age, we can learn from our experiences, become less anxious, more patient, and develop greater compassion for ourselves and others as we encounter life's triumphs and failures. Importantly, as we become frailer, and more dependent on others, the myth of self-sufficiency becomes increasingly evident to us.

Chip Conley is someone who has sought to counter those who conflate 'becoming older' with 'being elderly.' He questions and challenges a culture and society that privileges the beauty and energy of youth to the detriment of those of more advanced years, unpacking a multitude of negative stereotypes. At the age of 52, having previously founded and run Joie de Vivre, a chain of 52 boutique hotels, Conley became a senior executive at the youthful Airbnb. More recently, he founded the Modern Elder Academy in Mexico.

The global financial crisis that started in 2007 was a significant turning point for Chip and many of his peers. These were people under severe strain as they saw businesses that they had invested their lives in take a nosedive. Chip sold his hotel chain in 2010 and found himself at a loose end, knowing that he still had much to offer, but not finding the fulfillment he desired in his entrepreneurial 'side hustles,' which included Fest300, an online magazine that covers art, music and cultural festivals worldwide. Many of his contemporaries, though, were truly suffering — four people close to Chip, including one who had the same name as him, took their own lives.

> I remember that his death really devastated me. This guy had a light inside of him. It hit me that we were in a stage of life that perhaps was at its darkest, the bottom of the U-curve, but there were no rites of passage, no signposts or tools to help people navigate this period. As I listened to the eulogy with our shared first name being spoken out loud, I thought this could be me. At the time, I was also in a dark place in my life. With my business going down I was also contemplating suicide, hoping for a car crash, something to happen so I could change my life. I just didn't know how to.

Chip's identity had been so invested in his old business that he didn't know how to let it go. What he discovered, however, was that this period of emptiness — painful as it was When Things Fell Apart for him — also created an opportunity for him to shed his old identity and evolve. "I based my work in full trust that from this fertile void would emerge clarity and beauty," he recalls. "Serendipity would have its way with me."

Serendipity arrived in the shape of Brian Chesky, the co-founder and CEO of Airbnb. In 2013, Chesky was struggling to scale his fledgling business, addressing the same concerns as other tech start-ups like Uber, which were seeking to leverage the opportunities enabled by the social web while navigating the pitfalls of an uncertain economy. Chesky had just read Chip's latest book, *Peak*, and wanted to seek his advice.

Things moved quickly after the initial contact. Chip delivered a talk to the Airbnb leadership team about understanding hospitality. Over dinner, he was then invited by Chesky to advise the company on how to grow, coming on board as head of global hospitality and strategy. For Chip, the two principal issues were that he was double the average age of his new colleagues and, in joining the tech world, with its coded language and unique culture, he was venturing into what seemed like an alien planet.

Chip struggled initially, not quite knowing how to advise those who seemed to know so much more than him, especially in relation to the products and language of information technology. However, he began to notice that people were turning to him for different reasons. They valued his good judgement, the way he could convey unvarnished insights, the emotional intelligence he could bring to meetings, his holistic thinking, and his emphasis on stewardship and the wider responsibility to both the company and society.

Joe Gebbia, one of Airbnb's co-founders, summarized the situation well when he nicknamed Chip 'The Modern Elder,' explaining that this sage figure was as curious as he was wise. What the company required, Chip began to see, was a *wisdom* worker rather than yet another *knowledge* worker.

Curiosity opens possibilities and wisdom distills what's essential. I came to realize that while people are living longer, power is also moving downwards. You can see this in the youth of tech CEOs. Those who were born digital natives are the ones with the skills that will shape future global industries. This has led to a lot of confusion on how to deal with the age gap, and it also represents a great opportunity for society if we are able to leverage these differences.

In the 19th century, there was no concept of adolescence. There was childhood and then adulthood. Later, Stanley Hall's research and 1904 book established the concept of adolescence. We came to see there was an important transition period in between the two: puberty, where hormones and identity changes. So, we created schools and tools and other ways to help with that.

In the study of gerontology, it's now been discovered there is also a similar transition space we encounter later in life as we move from middle age into old age. This threshold space is called *middlessence*. In the past, it may only have been associated with crisis — as the popular phrase *midlife crisis* attests — but actually it's something far beyond trivial. My research shows that there has been a 50% increase in midlife suicides over the past 20 years. This is a public health issue.

Like Chip, in order to discover the gifts of middlessence and beyond, we need to question the many assumptions and prejudices that exist about being old. One relates to the association of memory loss with old age. In *Counter Clockwise*, for example, Harvard psychologist Ellen Langer recounts a visit with her 88-year-old father. He won a card game they played together by remembering every card that she picked up. When he later went for a swim, he let her know how many laps he had completed and how many more he had left to go. Nevertheless, in the evening, he bemoaned his memory problem, resigned to this being a necessary part of old age. When challenged, however, he was unable to be specific about how memory loss was affecting him.

Langer argues that forgetfulness, rather than being a sign of aging, may instead indicate that certain information is not worth remembering in the first place, and that a subconscious decision has been made to disregard it. The more experience we have, the wiser we become at making such choices. Alternatively, apparent forgetfulness can be suggestive of complete and intense immersion in the present. That is, absolute focus on an activity to the exclusion of all else, similar to the experience of 'flow,' as described by psychologist Mihaly Csikszentmihalyi. This is a state that disregards age and can be experienced by anyone, from an infant to a pensioner.

Chip's work since 2018 with the Modern Elder Academy not only values the wisdom of those who have navigated middlessence, but also celebrates the two-way flow of knowledge between the young and the old. While it is always gratifying, to paraphrase actor Jack Lemmon, to send the elevator back down, facilitating the learning and progress of others, it is also never too late to learn something new.

We used to think knowledge was like gravity, like an apple falling to earth: knowledge would pass from the elder to the younger. But it works both ways; elders can learn a lot from those younger than them. You see this in the value of reverse mentoring, where the benefits are very much mutual.

Chip's point is well illustrated by the 2015 movie *The Intern*, in which Robert De Niro plays a widower and former business executive, Ben, who secures a position at a fashion start-up through an intern program for retirees. While Ben learns from his younger colleagues how to make use of the technology of the modern workplace, his own emotional intelligence and wisdom is valued by those he assists, and he ultimately wins the trust of his initially skeptical boss, Jules, played by Anne Hathaway. Ben enjoys the benefits of being what Chip terms a "mentern," developing his learning and curiosity, finding a purpose again in his old age, as well as a new outlet through which to express his love of life.

Not long after Chip established Joie de Vivre, when he was still in his 20s, he made a commitment to not chase profits but to focus on creating a robust and flourishing culture. At the time, he sought out a role model who was known for delighting his customers.

> Who could I learn from? The most admired company then and now for customer service was Southwest Airlines. So, I decided I would ask their CEO and co-founder Herb Kelleher to be my mentor. What I didn't know then, and what I do know now, is that I wanted him to be my Modern-Day Elder.

> His executive assistant, Colleen Barrett, answered my call. "You can't speak to Herb now, but if you write a letter to him, I bet he'll write you back," she said. So that's what I did. I wrote a single letter to him each year for ten years, containing a series of questions, and he would write back.

> Later, I discovered that Colleen had become President of Southwest Airlines. Herb saw that she excelled in creating and role modeling the culture of the company.

Chip's own experiences demonstrate that your modern elder, your muse, may be someone with whom you have an informal relationship or even someone you never meet in person. This is an increasing likelihood in these Covid times. One of the questions Chip encourages people to reflect on in relation to their work — "Beyond your boss, who in the company would you turn to, to ask for advice or wisdom?" — illuminates our interdependencies with others. "If we all did that," he suggests, "perhaps we could create heat maps of wisdom, and when we can see where wisdom resides, we can all benefit."

OUR GIFTS

"The purpose of life is to discover your gift.
The work of life is to develop it.
The meaning of life is to give your gift away."

David Viscott, *Finding Your Strength in Difficult Times*

When we move beyond the myth of separation, and reappraise our relationship with others and the natural world, one of the consequences is that we move from self-obsession to being curious about the service of others, recognizing our deep interconnection. As we have seen, the coronavirus pandemic has prompted many people to reconsider what is important to them, questioning what provides meaning in their lives. People have sought purpose, submitted themselves to callings and, in effect, opted to give their gifts away.

Richard Leider is a Modern-Day Elder and has made exploring the theme of 'calling' his life's purpose. Author of 11 books, including the *The Power of Purpose*, Richard has coached thousands of people on discovering their purpose, which he describes as "the combination of our gifts, plus our passions, plus our values." He tells a story about being invited to speak at a conference in Boston on the topic of purpose, which has gained in popularity in recent years.

It was a steamy, hot July day, and I landed at Logan Airport at 10:30 a.m. on my usual flight from Minnesota. Jumping into a taxi, I was eager to get to the conference center, as my talk was at noon. The cab driver was a typical Bostonian with a Red Sox baseball cap and a dashboard covered in religious iconography.

As they entered the Callahan Tunnel, heading towards the city, Richard could see that construction would prevent him from getting to the event on time. The cab driver could sense his anxiety and sought an alternate route. Learning that Richard was a speaker piqued his curiosity.

Driver:	What are you going to speak about?
Richard:	My talk's titled 'Whistle While You Work.'
Driver:	Mister, give me a break! I work to pay the mortgage.
Richard:	I don't want to give the talk twice, but let me ask you a few questions. On a scale of one to ten, do you love what you do?
Driver:	One. I do what I do to make a living.
Richard:	Are there parts of your job where you feel really engaged?
Driver:	Has to be a one again. Well, I do feel engaged in the evening, when I finish work and am a kids' soccer coach.
Richard:	Are there people you enjoy serving more than others?
Driver:	I love older women!
Richard:	I don't think I want to hear more about that...
Driver:	It's not what you think. I help some of the older women that live in the assisted living apartments, drop them off, and often help them to buy their groceries.
Richard:	Do they pay you more?
Driver:	No! I do it because it makes me feel happy.
Richard:	You have a calling: giving care to older women and also caring for kids by coaching them.

The driver smiled in recognition. It was such a simple thing, but it resonated with him. Richard was so touched by this incident that he ended up interviewing cab drivers all over the world. In *Work Reimagined*, every chapter begins with a cab driver's story.

In 1968, Richard spent time with psychologist Viktor Frankl, the creator of logotherapy and author of *Man's Search for Meaning*. Frankl had spent many years in a concentration camp, surviving the atrocities but bearing witness to death, brutality, despair and hopelessness. He concluded that the last of human freedoms is *choice*. Regardless of our circumstances, we can choose to make a positive difference to someone else's life. Richard elaborates, reflecting on the number of minutes in a day: "We have 1,440 purpose moments to make a difference. Being is about being there in those moments."

Amy Wrzesniewski, a psychologist at New York University, found in a study of hospital workers that even those janitors who cleaned beds and mopped up after patients experienced a sense of meaning and calling in their work. Some saw themselves as part of a team whose mission was to heal people. As such, they went above and beyond the minimum expectation of their job. Many were responsible for surprising acts of kindness that brightened up a sick patient's room, or they anticipated the needs of doctors and nurses rather than passively waiting for instruction. In doing so, they exercised their autonomy and satisfied their need to have an effect on the world. This provided both enjoyment and fulfillment in their work.

It is not always necessary to change what we do. Instead, we can change our perspective regarding the significance and meaning of our contribution. This is about being purposeful rather than finding our purpose. In an increasingly fragmented supply chain, we may never see the results of our labor, but we can develop what organizational behavior author Charles Handy refers to in *The Empty Raincoat* as "Cathedral thinking." That is, the ability to continue to work for something without immediate gratification or experiencing of the fruits of our labor, just like the stone masons and artisans who worked on the construction of medieval cathedrals but did not live long enough to see the buildings completed.

Richard's research suggests that our gifts — something more than innate talent or learned and practiced skills — are a product of both nature and nurture. Often, though, we are unaware of what our gifts are, as if we have been born with amnesia. If we are lucky, over time, through curiosity, we learn more about ourselves and what we love, and find ourselves drawn to and chosen by our calling. Our gifts, always present, have finally been unlocked. An associated sense of purpose, Richard believes, is fundamental to health, happiness and longevity.

> Purpose is not a luxury for the chosen few. When people come to me and say they don't know their purpose, I tell them that we each have a default purpose for which we are accountable. Purpose is a verb, it is behavior, but it shifts who you are.

Richard's long-term relationship with the Hadza people, a hunter-gatherer tribe living in northern Tanzania, has provided him with powerful lessons on gift sharing and purpose. Owning few possessions, the Hadza have a sharing culture: everything they have or receive is shared, including gifts from outsiders and items brought back from a hunt. In the Hadza community, there is great shame in not sharing your gifts with others, as it is recognized that society is based both on knowing your gifts and also sharing them with your community. Wisdom, too, can be a gift.

On one occasion, Richard was sitting near a fire with a Hadza elder named Kampala, who was in his 80s. As Kampala tired of responding to Richard's questions through a translator, he posed a question of his own.

Kampala: Do you know the two most important days of your life?
Richard: Birth and death.
Kampala: No. Birth is correct, as you survived and came to life. But the second most important day is when you discover *why* you were born.

We do not discover our *why* as a fixed thing outside of us. Rather, we can attend to what matters to us in each moment and respond to an evolving array of *whys* in our lives. While we may have many wants as human beings, among our fundamental needs are the need to belong and the need to matter. On our shared journey, we have learned that when we see beyond the myth of separation — when we set aside our self-concern, when we truly give ourselves away — that is precisely when we most belong, when we most matter, when we have discovered the essence of Not Being.

DO YOU KNOW THE TWO MOST IMPORTANT DAYS OF YOUR LIFE?

"I have always been fascinated by the law of reversed effort. Sometimes I call it the 'backwards law.' When you try to stay on the surface of the water, you sink; but when you try to sink, you float. When you hold your breath, you lose it — which immediately calls to mind an ancient and much neglected saying, 'Whosoever would save his soul shall lose it.'"

Alan Watts, *The Wisdom of Insecurity*

BIBLIOGRAPHY

@AdamMGrant. "The root of insecurity is craving the approval of others. It gives them the power to inflate or deflate our self-esteem. A stable sense of self-worth stems from putting identity above image: worrying less about what others think of us than what we (...)." *Twitter*, 15 Oct. 2020, 3:37 p.m., <https://twitter.com/AdamMGrant/status/1316750048022138881>.

Achebe, Chinua. *Things Fall Apart*. Penguin Books, 1994.

Ackerman, Diane. *Deep Play*. Vintage Books USA, 2000.

American Beauty. Dir. Sam Mendes. 1999.

Anderson, Monica and Jingjing Jiang. "Teens, Social Media & Technology 2018." *Pew Research Center*, 31 May 2018, <https://www.pewresearch.org/internet/2018/05/31/teens-social-media-technology-2018/>.

Andreasson, Ulf. "In the shadow of happiness." *Nordic Council of Ministers*, 2018, <http://norden.diva-portal.org/smash/get/diva2:1236906/FULLTEXT02.pdf>.

"Animal Agriculture Is to Blame for Wildfires Around the Globe." *PeTA* <https://www.peta.org/features/animal-agriculture-causes-wildfires/>.

Arendt, Hannah. *Eichmann in Jerusalem: A Report on the Banality of Evil*. Penguin Classics, 2006.

—. *The Origins of Totalitarianism*. Penguin Classics, 2017.

aTimeLogger. <http://www.atimelogger.com/>.

Atwood, Margaret. *The Blind Assassin*. Anchor, 2001.

Banks, Michael. *Gotta Kidney?!: A Journey Through Fear to Hope and Beyond*. Gottakidney, 2017.

Barber, Paul. *Becoming a Practitioner-Researcher: A Gestalt Approach to Holistic Inquiry*. Middlesex University Press, 2006.

Bauman, Zygmunt. *Liquid Modernity*. John Wiley & Sons, 2013.

Baumeister, Roy F. *Escaping the Self: Alcoholism, Spirituality, Masochism, and Other Flights from the Burden of Selfhood*. Basic Books, 1993.

Bayles, David. *Art & Fear: Observations on the Perils (and Rewards) of Artmaking*. Image Continuum Press, 2002.

Beattie, Karen. "4 Destructive Traits Of Perfectionism, From Dr. Brené Brown." *The Growth Faculty Blog*, 7 Jan. 2019, <https://www.thegrowthfaculty.com/blog/4destructivetraitsofperfectionismfromDrBrenBrown>.

Beckett, Samuel. *Waiting for Godot*. Faber & Faber, 2006.

Berger, Jennifer Garvey. "A summary of the Constructive-Developmental Theory Of Robert Kegan." (2003,2007), <https://wiki.canterbury.ac.nz/download/attachments/6358104/berger+on+kegan+narrative.doc>.

Bewick, MW and Ella Johnston. *The Orphaned Spaces: Waste ground explored*. Dunlin Press, 2018.

Blade Runner. Dir. Ridley Scott. 1982.

Brackett, Marc. *Permission to Feel*. Celadon Books, 2019.

Breeding, John. "The Dangers Of Refusing To Answer The Call Of The Hero's Journey." *Kindred*, 11 Nov. 2015, <https://www.kindredmedia.org/2015/11/the-dangers-of-refusing-to-answer-the-call-of-the-heros-journey/>.

Briers, Francis. *My Tao Te Ching - A Fool's Guide to Effing the Ineffable: Ancient spiritual wisdom translated for modern life*. Warriors of Love Publishing, 2014.

Brooks, David. *The Second Mountain: The Quest for a Moral Life*. Penguin, 2020.

Brown, Brené. "Brené Brown — Striving versus Self-Acceptance, Saving Marriages, and More." Interview by Tim Ferris, 6 Feb. 2020, <https://www.youtube.com/watch?app=desktop&v=Wh5SUF0gPWQ&ab_channel=TimFerriss>.

—. "Marc Brackett and Brené on 'Permission to Feel'." *Brene Brown*, 14 Apr. 2020, <https://brenebrown.com/transcript/marc-brackett-and-brene/#close-popup>.

Browning, Robert. *The Ring and the Book*. Yale University Press, 1981.

Buechner, Frederick. *Wishful Thinking: A Seeker's ABC*. Bravo Ltd, 1993.

Cage, John. *Silence: Lectures and Writings*. Marion Boyars Publishers Ltd, 1978.

Calhoun, Laurence G. and Richard G. Tedeschi. "Posttraumatic growth: The positive lessons of loss." *Research Gate* 2001, <https://www. researchgate.net/publication/313567748_Posttraumatic_growth_The_ positive_lessons_of_loss>.

Calvino, Italo. *If On A Winter's Night A Traveller*. Vintage Classics, 1992.

Campbell, Joseph. *The Hero with A Thousand Faces*. New World Library, 2012.

Carse, James. *Finite and Infinite Games*. Free Press, 2013.

Carver, George Washington. "Thoughts on the Business of Life." *Forbes Quotes* <https://www.forbes.com/quotes/2256/>.

Chapman, David. "Nebulosity." *Meaningness* <https://meaningness.com/ nebulosity>.

Charlton, Emma. "New Zealand has unveiled its first 'well-being' budget." *World Economic Forum*, 30 May 2019, <https://www.weforum.org/ agenda/2019/05/new-zealand-is-publishing-its-first-well-being-budget/>.

Ch'eng-en, Wu. *The Monkey King: Journey to the West*. Trans. Julia Lovell. Penguin Classics, 2021.

"Climate Change Quotes." *This Spaceship Earth*, <https://thisspaceshipearth.org/quotes/page/17/>.

Colonna, Jerry. "#373: Jerry Colonna — The Coach With the Spider Tattoo." Interview by Tim Ferriss. 14 Jun. 2019, <https://tim.blog/2019/06/14/ the-tim-ferriss-show-transcripts-jerry-colonna-373/>.

Conley, Chip. *Peak: How Great Companies Get Their Mojo from Maslow*. Wiley, 2017.

"Coronavirus: Swedish King Carl XVI Gustaf says coronavirus approach 'has failed'." *BBC News*, 17 Dec. 2020, <https://www.bbc.co.uk/news/ world-europe-55347021>.

Cozzolino, Philip J. and Laura E. R. Blackie. "I Die, Therefore I Am: The Pursuit of Meaning in the Light of Death." *Research Gate*, Jun. 2013. <https://www.researchgate.net/publication/242022474_I_Die_ Therefore_I_Am_The_Pursuit_of_Meaning_in_the_Light_of_Death>.

Crawford, Matthew. *The Case for Working with Your Hands: Or Why Office Work is Bad for Us and Fixing Things Feels Good*. Penguin, 2010.

—. *The World Beyond Your Head: How to Flourish in an Age of Distraction*. Penguin, 2016.

DeKoven, Bernie. *The Well-Played Game: A Playful Path to Wholeness.* iUniverse, 2002.

Denton, Danny. *The Earlie King & the Kid in Yellow.* Granta Books, 2019.

"Depression." *World Health Organization*, 30 Jan. 2020. <https://www.who.int/news-room/fact-sheets/detail/depression>.

Didion, Joan. *The White Album.* Fourth Estate, 2017.

"Diffusion of innovations." *Wikipedia*, <https://en.wikipedia.org/wiki/Diffusion_of_innovations>.

D'Souza, Steven and Diana Renner. *Not Doing: The art of effortless action.* LID Publishing, 2018.

—. *Not Knowing: The Art of Turning Uncertainty into Opportunity.* LID Publishing, 2014.

Dunn, Elizabeth and Michael Norton. *Happy Money: The New Science of Smarter Spending.* Oneworld Publications, 2014.

Easterbrook, Gregg. *The Progress Paradox: How Life Gets Better While People Feel Worse.* Random House, 2003.

Edelman, Marian Wright, *The Measure of Our Success: A Letter to My Children & Yours*, Beacon Press, 1992.

Eger, Edith. *The Choice: A true story of hope.* Rider, 2018.

Einstein, Charles. "Living in the Gift." *Charles Einstein*, Nov. 2018. <https://charleseisenstein.org/essays/living-in-the-gift/>.

Eliade, Mircea. *Rites and Symbols of Initiation: The Mysteries of Birth and Rebirth.* Trans. Willard R. Taske. Spring Publications, 2017.

Elkins, James. *The Object Stares Back: On the Nature of Seeing.* Thomson Learning, 1999.

Emerson, Brian and Kelly Lewis. *Navigating Polarities: Using Both/And Thinking to Lead Transformation.* Paradoxical Press, 2019.

Emerson, Ralph Waldo. "Gifts." *Emerson Central*, <https://emersoncentral.com/texts/essays-second-series/gifts/>.

—. "The Poet." *Emerson Central*, <https://emersoncentral.com/texts/essays-second-series/the-poet/>.

Enter the Dragon. Dir. Robert Clouse. 1973.

Erikson, Erik H. and Joan M. Erikson. *The Life Cycle Completed: Extended Version*. W. W. Norton & Company, 1998.

Falconar, Ted. *Creative Intelligence and Self-Liberation: Korzybski, Non-Aristotelian Thinking and Enlightenment*. Crown House Publishing, 2007.

"Family Life Coach Aspen Colorado." *Find me a good job*, Accessed Nov. 2020, <https://findmeagoodjob.jobboard.com/jobs/family-life-coach-aspen-colorado/167414427-2/>.

Fitzgerald, F. Scott. "The Crack-Up." *Esquire*, 7 Mar. 2017, <https://www.esquire.com/lifestyle/a4310/the-crack-up/>.

Fleming, Sean. "Sweden is fighting loneliness by housing older and younger generations together." *World Economic Forum*, 02 Mar. 2020, <https://www.weforum.org/agenda/2020/03/sweden-loneliness-housing-generations-elderly-youth/>.

"Former surgeon general sounds the alarm on the loneliness epidemic." *CBS News*, 19 Oct. 2017, <https://www.cbsnews.com/news/loneliness-epidemic-former-surgeon-general-dr-vivek-murthy/>.

Forster, E. M. *Howards End*. Penguin Classics, 2012.

Frankl, Viktor E. *Man's Search For Meaning: The classic tribute to hope from the Holocaust*. Rider, 2004.

Franzen, Jonathan. "Liking Is for Cowards. Go for What Hurts." *The New York Times*, 28 May 2011, <https://www.nytimes.com/2011/05/29/opinion/29franzen.html>.

—. "My Bird Problem." *The New Yorker*, 31 Jul. 2005, <https://www.newyorker.com/magazine/2005/08/08/my-bird-proble>.

Friedman, Edwin H. *Generation to Generation: Family Process in Church and Synagogue*. Guilford Press, 1985.

Friedman, Uri. "How an Ad Campaign Invented the Diamond Engagement Ring." *The Atlantic*, 13 Feb. 2015, <https://www.theatlantic.com/international/archive/2015/02/how-an-ad-campaign-invented-the-diamond-engagement-ring/385376/>.

Frosh, Stephen. *Identity Crisis: Modernity, Psychoanalysis and the Self*. Palgrave Macmillan, 1991.

Gaille, Brandon. "9 Personal Development Industry Statistics." *Brandon Gaille's Blog*, 23 May 2017, <https://brandongaille.com/personal-development-industry-statistics/#:~:text=Up%20to%20%24500%20 million%20is%20spent%20on%20personal,industry%20is%20 estimated%20to%20be%20almost%20%2411%20billion>.

Gazzaniga, Michael. *Nature's Mind*. Basic Books , 1994.

—. *Who's In Charge?* Hachette UK, 2012.

Gershon, Ilana. ""I'm not a businessman, I'm a business, man": Typing the neoliberal self into a branded existence." *HAU: Journal of Ethnographic Theory*, vol. 6, no. 3, 2016, pp. 223-246, <https://www.journals. uchicago.edu/doi/10.14318/hau6.3.017>.

Gibran, Kahlil. *The Prophet*. Ed. Paul Lafrance. IAP, 2020.

Goethe, Johann Wolfgang von. *Scientific Studies*. Princeton University Press, 1995.

—. *Theory of Colours*. Trans. Charles Lock Eastlake. John Murray, Albemarle Street, 1840. <https://www.theoryofcolor.org/tiki-index. php?page=Theory+of+Color&redirectpage=Theory%20of%20Colours>.

Goleman, Daniel. *Emotional Intelligence: Why it Can Matter More Than IQ Mass*. Bloomsbury, 1996.

Grange, Pippa. *Fear Less: How to Win at Life Without Losing Yourself*. Vermilion, 2020.

Gray, John. *Straw Dogs*. Granta Publications, 2003.

—. *The Silence of Animals: On Progress and Other Modern Myths*. Penguin, 2014.

Greenfield, Susan. *You & Me: The Neuroscience of Identity*. Notting Hill Editions, 2017.

Greer, Germaine. *The Whole Woman*. Black Swan, 2007.

Guin, Ursula K. Le. *The Language of the Night: Essays on Fantasy and Science Fiction*. Putnam, 1979.

Gunn, Robert Jingen. *Journeys into Emptiness: Dogen, Merton, Jung and the Quest for Transformation*. Paulist Press, 2000.

Haidt, Jonathan. *The Righteous Mind: Why Good People are Divided by Politics and Religion*. Penguin, 2013.

Handy, Charles. *The Empty Raincoat: Making Sense of the Future*. Random House Business, 1995.

—. *The Second Curve: Thoughts on Reinventing Society*. Random House Business, 2016.

Hanh, Thich Nhat. *Interbeing: Fourteen Guidelines for Engaged Buddhism*. Parallax Press, 1987.

Hannah Ritchie, Max Roser, Esteban Ortiz-Ospina. "Suicide." *Our World in Data*, 2015, <https://ourworldindata.org/suicide#share-of-deaths-from-suicide>.

Hari, Johann. *Lost Connections: Why You're Depressed and How to Find Hope*. Bloomsbury Publishing, 2019.

—. *This could be why you're depressed or anxious*. Jul. 2019. Video File.

Harré, Niki. Interview. Conducted by Khuyen Bui. Februrary 2021.

—. *Psychology for a Better World: Working with People to Save the Planet*. Auckland University Press, 2018.

—. *The Infinite Game: How to Live Well Together*. Auckland University Press, 2018.

Harré, Niki, et al. "The University as an Infinite Game: Revitalising Activism in the Academy." *Australian Universities' Review*, vol. 59, no. 2, 2017, pp. 5-13, <https://eric.ed.gov/?id=EJ1157040>.

Harrell, Shelly P. "Communal, Contemplative, and Empowerment Processes: Culturally Syntonic Practice for 'PEaCE' with Diverse Clients." *California Psychological Association Annual Convention*. Irvine, CA, 2016. <https://www.academia.edu/35832693/Communal_Contemplative_and_Empowerment_Processes_Culturally_Syntonic_Practice_for_PEaCE_with_Diverse_Clients>.

Hayes, S. C., K. D. Strosahl and K. G. Wilson. *Acceptance and commitment therapy: An experiential approach to behavior change*. Guilford Press, 1999.

Heffernan, Margaret. *Wilful Blindness: Why We Ignore the Obvious*. Simon & Schuster UK, 2019.

Hesse, Hermann. *Steppenwolf*. Penguin Classics, 2012.

Hogg, Michael A. "Uncertainty–Identity Theory." *Advances in Experimental Social Psychology*, vol. 39, 25 Apr. 2007, pp. 69-126, <https://www.sciencedirect.com/science/article/pii/S0065260106390028>.

Holden, Robert. "What is Destination Addiction? How to Stop Thinking about What Comes Next." *Robert Holden Blog*, <https://www.robertholden.com/blog/what-is-destination-addiction/>.

Holwerda, Tjalling Jan, et al. "Feelings of loneliness, but not social isolation, predict dementia onset: results from the Amsterdam Study of the Elderly (AMSTEL)." *Journal of Neurology, Neurosurgery & Psychiatry*, vol. 85, no. 2, Feb. 2014, pp. 135-142, <https://jnnp.bmj.com/content/85/2/135>.

Homer. *The Odyssey*. Trans. Emily Wilson. W. W. Norton & Company, 2018.

Hübl, Thomas. *Healing Collective Trauma: A Process for Integrating Our Intergenerational and Cultural Wounds*. Sounds True, 2020.

—. *"Thomas Hübl: Healing Collective Trauma."* Interview by Tami Simon, <https://resources.soundstrue.com/transcript/thomas-hubl-healing-collective-trauma/>.

Hülsheger, Ute R. and Anna F. Schewe. "On the costs and benefits of emotional labor: a meta-analysis of three decades of research." *Journal of Occupational Health Psychology*, vol. 16, no. 3, Jul. 2011, pp. 361–389, <https://pubmed.ncbi.nlm.nih.gov/21728441/>.

Hustvedt, Siri. *A Woman Looking at Men Looking at Women: Essays on Art, Sex, and the Mind*. Simon & Schuster, 2016.

—. *Living, Thinking, Looking*. Picador, 2012.

Huxley, Aldous. *Brave New World*. Vintage Classics, 2007.

Hyde, Lewis. *Trickster Makes This World: How Disruptive Imagination Creates Culture*. Canongate Canons, 2017.

"Is Depression Worse in the Western World?" *Sermo*, 16 Apr. 2018, <https://www.sermo.com/depression-worse-western-world/>.

"It's time to Be Real about body image." *YMCA*, 16 Aug. 2016, <https://www.ymca.co.uk/health-and-wellbeing/feature/its-time-be-real-about-body-image>.

Jiang, Manyu. "The reason Zoom calls drain your energy." *BBC*, 22 Apr. 2020, <https://www.bbc.com/worklife/article/20200421-why-zoom-video-chats-are-so-exhausting>.

Johnson, Barry. *Polarity Management: Identifying and Managing*. H R D Press, 2014.

Johnson, Daisy. *Sisters*. Jonathan Cape, 2020.

Johnson, Whitney. *Disrupt Yourself: Master Relentless Change and Speed Up Your Learning Curve*. Harvard Business Review Press, 2019.

Jung, C. G. *The Structure and Dynamics of the Psyche*. Routledge, 1970.

"K Foundation Burn a Million Quid." *Wikipedia*, <https://en.wikipedia.org/wiki/K_Foundation_Burn_a_Million_Quid>.

Kahneman, Daniel. *Thinking, Fast and Slow*. Penguin, 2012.

Kapuscinski, Ryszard. *The Other*. Trans. Antonia Lloyd-Jones. Verso Books, 2018.

Kasser, Tim. *"A conversation with Tim Kasser." The True Cost*, <https://truecostmovie.com/tim-kasser-interview/>.

Katie, Byron. *The Work of Byron Katie*, <https://thework.com/>.

Keats, John. "'Negative Capability' (Letter to George and Tom Keats)." *Genius*, 22 Dec. 1818, <https://genius.com/John-keats-negative-capability-letter-to-george-and-tom-keats-annotated>.

Kegan, Robert. *In Over Our Heads: The Mental Demands of Modern Life*. Harvard University Press, 1995.

Keim, Brandon. "Brain Scanners Can See Your Decisions Before You Make Them." *Wired*, 13 Apr. 2008, <https://www.wired.com/2008/04/mind-decision/>.

Keller, Evelyn. *A Feeling for the Organism: The Life and Work of Barbara McClintock*. St. Martins Press-3PL, 2000.

King, Kathleen. "Unspeakable loss." *Kathleen King*, <https://www.kathleenking.org/healing-unspeakable-loss>.

King, Stephen. *The Green Mile*. Gollancz, 2008.

Kondo, Marie. *Spark Joy: An Illustrated Guide to the Japanese Art of Tidying*. Vermilion, 2020.

Kornfield, Jack. "How to Find Peace Amidst COVID-19, How to Cultivate Calm in Chaos (#414)." Interview by Tim Ferriss, 9 May 2020, <https://tim.blog/2020/05/09/jack-kornfield-covid19-transcript/>.

Korzybski, Alfred. *Science and Sanity: An Introduction to Non-Aristotelian Systems and General Semantics*. Institute of General Semantics, 1995.

Kottler, Carlson and Keeney. *American Shaman: An Odyssey of Global Healing Traditions*. Routledge, 2004.

Krajeski, Jenna. "This is Water." *The New Yorker*, 19 Sep. 2008, <https://www.newyorker.com/books/page-turner/this-is-water>.

Kramer, Adam D. I., Jamie E. Guillory and Jeffrey T. Hancock. "Editorial Expression of Concern and Correction." *Proceedings of the National Academy of Sciences*, vol. 11, no. 29, 22 Jul. 2014, <https://www.pnas.org/content/pnas/111/24/8788.full.pdf>.

Krebs, Valdis. "About." *Orgnet*, <http://www.orgnet.com/about.html>.

Kundera, Milan. *The Unbearable Lightness of Being*. Faber & Faber, 2000.

Lachard, James J. "I dreamed I had an interview with God." *Center for Global Leadership*, 30 Jun. 2012, <https://centerforgloballeadership.wordpress.com/2012/06/30/an-interview-with-god-i-stand-corrected/>.

Laing, Olivia. *The Lonely City: Adventures in the Art of Being Alone*. Canongate Books Ltd , 2017.

Lakoff, George and Mark Johnson. *Metaphors We Live By*. University of Chicago Press, 2003.

Lama, Dalai. *How to See Yourself As You Really Are*. Rider, 2008.

Langer, Ellen J. *Counter Clockwise: Mindful Health and the Power of Possibility*. Ballantine Books, 2009.

Lau-Lavie, Amichai. "First Aid for Spiritual Seekers." Interview by Krista Tippett, 13 Jul. 2017, <https://onbeing.org/programs/amichai-lau-lavie-first-aid-for-spiritual-seekers/>.

Le Guern, Claire. "When the mermaids cry: the great plastic tide." *Coastal Care, Nov. 2019*, <https://plastic-pollution.org/#:~:text=The%20results%3A%20every%20year%2C%208,plastic%20per%20foot%20of%20coastline>.

"Leadership Philosophy: Frances Hesselbein in 10 Inspiring Quotes." *The Busy Lifestyle*, 9 Jul. 2018, <https://thebusylifestyle.com/leadership-philosophy-frances-hesselbein/>.

Leider, Richard J. and David Shapiro. *Work Reimagined: Uncover Your Calling*. EDS Publications Ltd., 2015.

Leider, Richard J. *The Power of Purpose: Find Meaning, Live Longer, Better*. EDS Publications Ltd., 2015.

Leopold, Aldo. *A Sand County Almanac: And Sketches Here and There.* Oxford University Press, 2020.

Levine, Peter. "Peter Levine: Understanding memory." Interview by Serge Prengel, Dec. 2016, <https://www.relationalimplicit.com/levine-memory/>.

—. "S2 E14: Dr. Peter Levine on Waking the Tiger." Interview by David Condos, 2020, <https://beyondtheorypodcast.com/dr-peter-levine-on-waking-the-tiger/>.

Levoy, Gregg Michael. *Callings: Finding and Following an Authentic Life.* Three Rivers Press, 1920.

Lispector, Clarice. *The Passion According to G.H.* Penguin Classics, 2014.

Liu, Wendy and Jennifer Lynn Aaker. "The Happiness of Giving: The Time-Ask Effect." *Journal of Consumer Research*, vol. 35, no. 3, Oct. 2008, pp. 543-557, <https://www.researchgate.net/publication/23547473_The_Happiness_of_Giving_The_Time-Ask_Effect>.

Llosa, Patty de. "The Neurobiology of 'We'." *Parabola*, Summer 2011, pp. 68-75 <https://www.scribd.com/document/361044108/The-Neurobiology-of-We-Patty-de-Llosa>.

Lorde, Audre. *Your Silence Will Not Protect You.* Silver Press, 2017.

Loy, David. "Buddhism and Money: The Repression of Emptiness Today." *Buddhist Ethics and Modern Society*, vol. 31, 1991, pp. 297-312, <http://enlight.lib.ntu.edu.tw/FULLTEXT/JR-ENG/loy12.htm>.

Macdonald, Helen. *H is for Hawk.* Vintage, 2015.

Macy, Joanna. "Entering the Bardo." *Emergence Magazine* (2020). <https://emergencemagazine.org/op_ed/entering-the-bardo/>.

Malik, Nesrine. "With respect: how Jacinda Ardern showed the world what a leader should be." *The Guardian*, 28 Mar. 2019, <https://www.theguardian.com/world/2019/mar/28/with-respect-how-jacinda-ardern-showed-the-world-what-a-leader-should-be>.

Manguel, Alberto. *Curiosity.* Yale University Press, 2016.

Martin, Roger L. *Opposable Mind: Winning Through Integrative Thinking: How Successful Leaders Win Through Integrative Thinking.* Harvard Business Review Press, 2009.

Maté, Gabor. "CRAZYWISE Conversations: Gabor Maté – Authenticity vs. Attachment." Interview by Phil Borges, 14 May 2019, <https://www. youtube.com/watch?v=l3bynimi8HQ&ab_channel=PhilBorges>.

Mbiti, John. *African Religions and Philosophy*. 2nd. Heinemann, 1990.

McGonigal, Jane. *Reality is Broken: Why Games Make Us Better and How They Can Change the World*. Vintage, 2012.

McRaney, David. *You Are Now Less Dumb: How to Conquer Mob Mentality, How to Buy Happiness, and All the Other Ways to Outsmart Yourself*. Avery Publishing Group, 2014.

Meade, Michael. *Fate and Destiny: The Two Agreements of the Soul*. Greenfire Pr, 2012.

Mintzberg, Henry. "Networks are not Communities." *Global Peter Drucker Forum Blog*, 5 Oct. 2015, <https://www.druckerforum.org/blog/ networks-are-not-communities-by-henry-mintzberg/>.

Monbiot, George. *Out of the Wreckage: A New Politics for an Age of Crisis*. Verso Books, 2018.

Monk, Ray. *Ludwig Wittgenstein: The Duty of Genius*. Vintage, 1991.

—. "Ludwig Wittgenstein's passion for looking, not thinking." *NewStatesman*, 15 Aug. 2012, <https://www.newstatesman.com/culture/art-and-design/2012/08/ ludwig-wittgenstein%E2%80%99s-passion-looking-not-thinking>.

"Monkey (TV series)." *Wikipedia*, <https://en.wikipedia.org/wiki/Monkey_(TV_series)>.

"Monkey King." *Wikipedia*, <https://en.wikipedia.org/wiki/Monkey_King>.

Mulkern, Anne C. "Fast-Moving California Wildfires Boosted by Climate Change." *Scientific American*, 24 Aug. 2020, <https://www.scientificamerican.com/article/fast-moving-california-wildfires-boosted-by-climate-change/#:~:text=Climate%20 connection%20scrutinized,%2C%20while%20precipitation%20 dropped%2030%25.>.

Murthy, Vivek. *Together: The Healing Power of Human Connection in a Sometimes Lonely World*. Harper Wave, 2020.

My Octopus Teacher. Dirs. James Reed and Pippa Ehrlich. 2020.

Nash, Sharon R. "My Journey into Self-Inquiry." *Organization Development Review*, Winter/Spring 2020, pp. 17-25.

Newton, Isaac. *Opticks Or, A Treatise of the Reflections, Refractions, Inflections and Colours of Light*. William and John Innys, 1721. ebook. <https://www.google.co.uk/books/edition/Opticks/P36zLuhOO7wC?hl=en&gbpv=0>.

Nietzsche, Friedrich. *Twilight of the Idols*. OUP Oxford, 1998.

Nin, Anaïs. *D. H. Lawrence: An Unprofessional Study*. Ohio University Press, 1964.

Oakley, Barbara. *Mind for Numbers: How to Excel at Math and Science (Even If You Flunked Algebra)*. Tarcher, 2014.

O'Donohue, John. *To Bless the Space Between Us: A Book of Blessings*. Convergent Books, 2008.

Oliver, Mary. *Dream Work*. Atlantic Monthly Press, 1994.

Palahniuk, Chuck. *Invisible Monsters*. Vintage, 2000.

Palmer, Parker J. *Let Your Life Speak: Listening for the Voice of Vocation*. Jossey Bass, 1999.

Palmer, Parker J., Arthur Zajonc and Megan Scribner. *The Heart of Higher Education: A Call to Renewal*. Jossey-Bass, 2010.

Pascale, Richard Tanner. *Surfing the Edge of Chaos: The Laws of Nature and the New Laws of Business*. Currency, 2001.

"Past Earth Overshoot Days." *Earth Overshoot Day*, <https://www.overshootday.org/newsroom/past-earth-overshoot-days/>.

Peck, M. Scott. *Further Along The Road Less Travelled*. Pocket Books, 1997.

Perls, Fritz. "The Process of Presence; Energetic Availability and Fluid Responsiveness." *British Gestalt Journal*, vol. 16, no. 1, 2007, pp. 9 -19

Petriglieri, Gianpiero. "Why We Pick Leaders with Deceptively Simple Answers." *Harvard Business Review*, 09 May 2016, <https://hbr.org/2016/05/why-we-pick-leaders-with-deceptively-simple-answers>.

Pirsig, Robert. *Zen And The Art Of Motorcycle Maintenance*. Vintage Classics, 1991.

Prendergast, John. *The Deep Heart: Our Portal to Presence*. Sounds True, 2019.

Pressfield, Steven. *The War of Art: Break Through the Blocks and Win Your Inner Creative Battles*. Black Irish Entertainment LLC, 2012.

Puett, Michael and Christine Gross-Loh. *The Path: A New Way to Think About Everything*. Penguin, 2017.

Radin, Paul. *The Trickster: A Study In American Indian Mythology*. Literary Licensing, LLC, 2013.

Rand, Ayn. *Faith And Force: The Destroyers Of The Modern World*. Literary Licensing, LLC, 2011.

—. *The Virtue of Selfishness: A New Concept of Egoism*. New American Library, 1964.

Rath, Samir. Interview. Conducted by Steven D'Souza. Feb. 2021.

Readfearn, Graham. "More than 14m tonnes of plastic believed to be at the bottom of the ocean." *The Guardian*, 5 Oct. 2020, <https://www.theguardian.com/environment/2020/oct/06/more-than-14m-tonnes-of-plastic-believed-to-be-at-the-bottom-of-the-ocean#:~:text=A%20previous%20study%20in%20the,floating%20on%20the%20ocean%20surface>.

Richo, David. *Human Becoming: Practical Steps to Self-Respect and Compassionate Relationships*. Human development books, 2017. e-book. <http://davericho.com/images/human_becoming.pdf>.

"Risk to Health." *Campaign to End Loneliness*, <https://www.campaigntoendloneliness.org/threat-to-health/>.

Ritchie and Roser. "CO2 emissions." *Our World in Data*, <https://ourworldindata.org/co2-emissions>.

"Rite of passage." *Wikipedia*, <https://en.wikipedia.org/wiki/Rite_of_passage>.

Robertson, Derek. "'It's like family': the Swedish housing experiment designed to cure loneliness." *The Guardian*, 15 Sep. 2020, <https://www.theguardian.com/world/2020/sep/15/its-like-family-the-swedish-housing-experiment-designed-to-cure-loneliness>.

Robertson, Robin. *Sailing the Forest*. Picador, 2014.

Robinson, Simon and Maria Robinson Moraes. *Customer Experiences with Soul: A New Era in Design*. Holonomics Publishing, 2017.

Rohr, Richard. "Five Consoling Messages." *Center for Action and Contemplation*, 5 Apr. 2020, <https://cac.org/five-consoling-messages-2020-04-05/>.

Roos, Johan. Interview. Conducted by Steven D'Souza. Dec. 2020.

Rose, Nikolas. *Inventing our Selves: Psychology, Power, and Personhood*. Cambridge University Press, 2010.

Rosling, Hans, Ola Rosling and Anna Rosling Rönnlund. *Factfulness: Ten Reasons We're Wrong About The World - And Why Things Are Better Than You Think*. Sceptre, 2018.

Roth and Loudon. *Maps to Ecstasy: The Healing Power of Movement*. New World Library, 2003.

Rumi, Jalal al-Din. *The Essential Rumi, New Expanded Edition*. Trans. Coleman Barks. HarperOne, 2004.

Rushdie, Salman. *Midnight's Children*. Vintage Classics, 2008.

Safi, Michael and agencies. "Ganges and Yamuna rivers granted same legal rights as human beings. *The Guardian*, 21 Mar. 2017, <https://www.theguardian.com/world/2017/mar/21/ganges-and-yamuna-rivers-granted-same-legal-rights-as-human-beings>.

Saint-Exupery, Antoine de. *The Little Prince*. Trans. Irene Testot-Ferry. Wordsworth Editions Ltd , 1995.

"SällBo – ett nytt sätt att bo." *Helsing Borgs Hem*, <https://www.helsingborgshem.se/nyheter/sallbo-ett-nytt-satt-att-bo>.

Sallis, James. *Eye Of The Cricket*. No Exit Press, 2012.

—. *Moth*. Oldcastle Books Ltd , 2012.

Saramago, Jose. *The Stone Raft*. Vintage Classics, 2000.

Schumpeter, Joseph A. *Capitalism, Socialism and Democracy*. Routledge, 2010.

Seth, Anil. Interview. Conducted by Steven D'Souza. 11 Nov. 2020.

—. "Your brain hallucinates your conscious reality." *YouTube*, 18 Jul. 2017, <https://www.youtube.com/watch?v=lyu7v7nWzfo&ab_channel=TED>.

"Sex av tio svenskar känner sig ensamma – Vanligast bland unga vuxna och i större städer." *WSP*, 5 Sep. 2019, <https://www.wsp.com/sv-SE/nyheter/2019/sex-av-tio-svenskar-kanner-sig-ensamma>.

Shakespeare, William. *All's Well That Ends Well*. Penguin Classics, 2015.

—. *As You Like It*. Forgotten Books, 2018.

Sheldrake, Merlin. *Entangled Life: How Fungi Make Our Worlds, Change Our Minds and Shape Our Futures*. Bodley Head, 2020.

Shiva, Vandana and Kartikey Shiva. *Oneness vs. the 1%: Shattering Illusions, Seeding Freedom*. Chelsea Green Publishing Company, 2020.

Sievers, Burkard. "The Diabolization of Death. Some thoughts on the obsolescence of mortality in organization theory and practice." *Academia* 1990. <https://www.academia.edu/33409367/Sievers_1990_The_Diabolization_of_Death_doc>.

Sinek, Simon. *Start With Why: How Great Leaders Inspire Everyone To Take Action*. Penguin, 2011.

Smith, Ali. *Summer*. Penguin Books, 2020.

Solnit, Rebecca. *The Faraway Nearby*. Viking Books, 2013.

Sontag, Susan. *Illness as Metaphor and AIDS and Its Metaphors*. Penguin Classics, 2009.

Speth, Gus, quoted in *Shared Planet: Religion and Nature*, BBC Radio 4, 1st October 2013, https://www.bbc.co.uk/sounds/play/b03bqws7

Storr, Will. *Selfie: How the West Became Self-Obsessed*. Picador, 2018.

Strenger, Carlo. *The Fear of Insignificance: Searching for Meaning in the Twenty-First Century*. Palgrave Macmillan US, 2011.

"Super People." *Questia*, Accessed Nov. 2020, <https://www.questia.com/newspaper/1G1-269940041/super-people>.

"Super people - the job recruits prepped for success." *Evening Standard*, 11 Oct. 2011, <https://www.standard.co.uk/lifestyle/super-people-the-job-recruits-prepped-for-success-6454259.html>.

Taylor, Jill Bolte. "My Stroke of Insight." *YouTube*, 13 Mar. 2008, <https://www.ted.com/talks/jill_bolte_taylor_my_stroke_of_insight>.

Tempest Williams, Terry. "The Pall Of Our Unrest." *Mountain Journal*, 19 Sep. 2020, <https://mountainjournal.org/terry-tempest-williams-says-it-time-to-rally-for-nature-and-country>.

Tempest, Kae. *On Connection*. Faber & Faber, 2020.

"The Golden Bough." *Wikipedia*, <https://en.wikipedia.org/wiki/The_Golden_Bough>.

The Intern. Dir. Nancy Meyers. 2015.

"The Psychopath Test." *Wikipedia*, <https://en.wikipedia.org/wiki/The_Psychopath_Test>.

"The Virtue of Selfishness." *Wikipedia*, <https://en.wikipedia.org/wiki/The_Virtue_of_Selfishness>.

"Theory of Colours." *Wikiwand*, <https://www.wikiwand.com/en/Theory_of_Colours#/citenote18>.

Thoreau, Henry David. *Walden*. Macmillan Collector's Library, 2016.

Tollifson, Joan. *Death: The End of Self-Improvement*. New Sarum Press, 2019.

Towler, Solala. *Tales from the Tao: The Wisdom of the Taoist Masters*. Watkins Publishing, 2017.

Tsing, Anna Lowenhaupt. *The Mushroom at the End of the World: On the Possibility of Life in Capitalist Ruins*. Princeton University Press, 2017.

Up in the Air. Dir. Jason Reitman. 2009.

Vaghela, Akash. "It's Never About The Physical." *RNT Fitness*, 29 Jul. 2018, <https://www.rntfitness.co.uk/its-never-about-the-physical/>.

Valtorta, et al. "Loneliness and social isolation as risk factors for coronary heart disease and stroke: systematic review and meta-analysis of longitudinal observational studies." *Heart*, vol. 102 no. 13, 1 Jul. 2016, pp. 1009-1016, <https://heart.bmj.com/content/102/13/1009>.

Viscott, David. *Finding Your Strength in Difficult Times*. McGraw-Hill Education, 2003.

Vizard, Tim, et al. "Coronavirus and depression in adults, Great Britain: Jun. 2020." *Office for National Statistics*, 18 Aug. 2020, <https://www.ons.gov.uk/peoplepopulationandcommunity/wellbeing/articles/coronavirusanddepressioninadultsgreatbritain/june2020>.

Vogl, Charles. *The Art of Community: Seven Principles for Belonging*. Berrett-Koehler Publishers, 2016.

Wahl, Daniel Christian. *Designing Regenerative Cultures*. Triarchy Press, 2016.

Walcott, Derek. *The Poetry of Derek Walcott 1948–2013*. Faber & Faber, 2014.

Wallace-Wells, David. *The Uninhabitable Earth: Life After Warming.* Tim Duggan Books, 2020.

Warner, Sylvia Townsend. *Letters Of Sylvia Townsend Warner.* Vintage Digital, 2013.

Watts, Alan. *The Wisdom of Insecurity.* Random House USA Inc, 1988.

Watts, Jonathan. "Earth's resources consumed in ever greater destructive volumes." *The Guardian*, 23 Jul. 2018, <https://www.theguardian.com/environment/2018/jul/23/earths-resources-consumed-in-ever-greater-destructive-volumes>.

West, Geoffrey. *Scale: The Universal Laws of Life and Death in Organisms, Cities and Companies.* W&N, 2017.

Western, Simon. "An Overview of the Leadership Discourses." Preedy, Margaret, Nigel Bennett and Christine Wise. *Educational Leadership: Context, Strategy and Collaboration.* SAGE Publications Ltd, 2012.

Whyte, David. *Consolations: The Solace, Nourishment and Underlying Meaning of Everyday Words.* Canongate Books, 2019.

—. *The House of Belonging.* Many Rivers Press, 1999.

Wigert, Ben. "Employee Burnout: The Biggest Myth." *Gallup*, 13 Mar. 2020, <https://www.gallup.com/workplace/288539/employee-burnout-biggest-myth.aspx>.

Wilkinson, Richard and Kate Pickett. *The Spirit Level: Why Equality is Better for Everyone.* Penguin, 2010.

Wilson, Sarah. "4 Ways Depression Can Physically Affect the Brain." *Healthline*, 24 Oct. 2018, <https://www.healthline.com/health/depression-physical-effects-on-the-brain#Brain-inflammation>.

Wilson, Timothy D., et al. "Just think: The challenges of the disengaged mind." *Science*, vol. 345, no. 6192, 04 Jul. 2014, pp. 75-77, <https://science.sciencemag.org/content/345/6192/75>.

Winnicott, D.W. *Home is Where We Start from: Essays by a Psychoanalyst.* Penguin, 1990.

Wittgenstein, Ludwig. *Philosophical Investigations.* Wiley-Blackwell, 2009.

—. *Tractatus Logico-Philosophicus.* Cosimo Classics, 2010.

Wrzesniewski, Amy, Paul Rozin and Gwen Bennett. "Working, playing, and eating: Making the most of most moments." *ResearchGate*, Jan. 2003, <https://www.researchgate.net/publication/232516917_Working_playing_and_eating_Making_the_most_of_most_moments>.

Yeats, William Butler. "The Second Coming." <https://www.poetryfoundation.org/poems/43290/the-second-coming>.

Yorke, John. *Into The Woods: How Stories Work and Why We Tell Them.* Penguin, 2014.

Yunkaporta, Tyson. *Sand Talk: How Indigenous Thinking Can Save the World.* Text Publishing Company, 2020.

ACKNOWLEDGEMENTS

Writing this book has been a significant journey. As writers, we have not met in person. Connecting over social media, we collaborated over a year on this book, across the time zones of London and Ho Chi Minh City. Our differences in age, writing style, cultures and professional experiences have greatly enriched this work.

We would like to thank our families, friends and loved ones. It was their patience — allowing us to be away at our computers, undertaking hours of research, interviews and writing — that gave us the space to create this book. It is as much your achievement as ours.

Thank you to:

Our polymathic editor, Richard Martin, who helped us improve our writing and encouraged us to go on when this project felt too challenging.

Our inspirational illustrator Maria Helena Toscano, for her always surprising artwork and design of the book, including the beautiful cover.

Our publisher Martin Liu, for believing in this book and agreeing to publish it, even though the title is far from conventional. We also would like to thank Aiyana Curtis, Caroline Li, Brian Doyle and the entire editorial team at LID Publishing for their guidance on the project.

We would also like to thank Chip Conley for writing the Foreword, and for generously sharing his story and connections with us. He was a true 'guide at the side' — a Modern Elder.

Thank you to all those who read the manuscript, provided feedback and contributed testimonials to support the book.

This book would not have been possible without the contribution of the many people who generously shared their insights and stories. We could not include every idea or story in the book, but we would like to sincerely thank everybody who contributed. If we have omitted anyone, the failure is totally ours, and we thank you too for your support.

We would like to thank:

Anna Chaloupka, Ryan Pereira, María García Tejon, Lynne Sedgmore, Jayaraja, Paula Lavric, Alex Schlotterbeck, Oksana Dovorecka, Nic Ellem, Anil Seth, Home Nguyen, Ilona Cuinaite, Francis Briers, Adam Bucko, Akash Vaghela, Hymie Wyse, Francis Akpata, Anna Simioni, Kathleen King, Sharon Nash, Simon Western, Rupert Callender, Ha Tran, Anushia Reddy, Steve Rowe, Daniel Beaumont, Leng Lim, Kerry Radcliffe, Johan Roos, Charles Davies, Niki Harré, Charles O'Malley, Samir Rath, Jennifer McKewen, Samantha Thomas, Michael Banks, Karin Jordan, Jude Kelly, Jolanda van den Berg, Kenny Mammarella D'Cruz, Jojo Fresnedi, Rhodora Fresnedi, Richard Leider, Agnieszka Mazur, Ben Hughes.

Finally, a heartfelt thanks to you, our reader, for engaging with our work. This book was written for you.

Steven
I would like to thank:
Diana Renner, the co-author of Not Knowing *and* Not Doing.
Without Diana's work on the first two books, there would be no trilogy to complete. I hope Not Being *is a worthy addition.*

Dominika Olszowy, for her wonderful support, showing endless patience and care, and for painstaking compilation of the bibliography.

Jochen Encke, for encouraging me to proceed, value and write Not Being *in my own voice, using poetry as an expression.*

Finally, Khuyen, for his lightheartedness, patience and ability to take feedback, as well as for being one of the most creative embodied spirits I know.

Khuyen
I would like to thank all the friends who kept asking me, 'How's the book going?' Your care made the whole journey worthwhile. Special thanks to my dear friend and former lover, Linh Trinh, for bearing with me throughout this birthing process with the joke, "It's like watching a spouse going through pregnancy." Except, in the reverse.

Thank you, Steven, for being the unwavering source of this book, showing not telling, making things happen. I have learned a beautiful lesson on commitment and action from and with you.

ABOUT THE AUTHORS

Steven D'Souza is an executive educator, coach and keynote speaker. He has authored or co-authored five books: *Made in Britain, Brilliant Networking, Not Knowing, Not Doing* and *Not Being*. Steven has been recognized by Thinkers50 on its Radar list and was included in *HR Magazine*'s 'Most Influential' list. His work has been featured in national and international media, including *Harvard Business Review, Bloomberg, The Independent, The Guardian* and *The Sunday Times*. Steven is passionate about helping leaders explore purpose and meaning in their lives, making transitions in their careers, and finding joy and fulfillment. His work blends contemplative wisdom, spirituality, psychology and philosophy with practical approaches to career, leadership and organizational development.

He can be contacted at:
stevendsouza.com

Khuyen Bui is an author, speaker and sought-after facilitator who guides individuals and organizations to uncover the goodness that is already here. Graduated *cum laude* from Tufts University, where he studied Computer Science and Philosophy, he thrives on bringing analytical rigor into his inquiries of human messiness. Khuyen enjoys writing and storytelling and has won several awards, notably the Peter Drucker Challenge Essay Award and The Moth Boston StorySLAM Award. He is currently teaching Contact Improvisation in Ho Chi Minh City, Vietnam, where he is pioneering fresh new ways of living, working and being together. Khuyen loves opening his mind, heart and body to the wonders of life.

He can be contacted at:
khuyenbui.com